# GUIDING PRINCIPLES FOR STABILIZATION AND RECONSTRUCTION

D1516164

# GUIDING PRINCIPLES FOR STABILIZATION AND RECONSTRUCTION

UNITED STATES INSTITUTE OF PEACE PRESS
WASHINGTON, D.C.

U.S. ARMY PEACEKEEPING AND STABILITY OPERATIONS INSTITUTE

The views expressed in this book do not necessarily reflect views of the United States Institute of Peace and the U.S. Army Peacekeeping and Stability Operations Institute.

United States Institute of Peace
1200 17th Street NW
Washington, DC 20036-3011
www.usip.org

First published 2009

To request permission to photocopy or reprint materials for course use, contact the Copyright Clearance Center at www.copyright.com. For print, electronic media, and all other subsidiary rights e-mail permissions@usip.org.

Printed in the United States of America

The paper used in this publication meets the minimum requirements of American National Standards for Information Science—Permanence of Paper for Printed Library Materials, ANSI Z39.48-1984.

**Library of Congress Cataloging-in-Publication Data**

Guiding principles for stabilization and reconstruction / United States Institute of Peace and U.S. Army Peacekeeping and Stability Operations Institute (PKSOI).
   p. cm.
  ISBN 978-1-60127-033-7 (pbk.)
  1. Peace-building, American--Developing countries. I. United States Institute of Peace. II. Peacekeeping and Stability Operations Institute.
  JZ5584.D4G85 2009
  341.5'84--dc22
                   2009032300

# CONTENTS

## Project Director
Beth Cole

## Lead Writers
Beth Cole

Emily Hsu

## Contributing Writers
Elena Brineman

Christina Caan

Megan Chabalowski

William Flavin

Vivienne O'Connor

Courtney Rusin

## Research Support
Stephanie Blair

Sarah Kreps

Catherine Morris

Jemma McPherson

## Acknowledgments
The *Guiding Principles for Stabilization and Reconstruction* would not have been possible without the generous time and support of many individuals and organizations. Chief among them was Daniel P. Serwer, who provided constant support. Our deepest gratitude goes to Lt. Gen. William B. Caldwell, Amb. John Herbst, Amb. Richard H. Solomon, and Sir Richard Teuten for their inspirational encouragement throughout this effort. We would also like to thank Col. John Agoglia for launching this effort with us, along with Elena Brineman, Col. Tom Cosentino, Janine Davidson, William Flavin, Lt. Col. Steve Leonard, Ugo Solinas, and Necla Tsigiri for their incredible vision and invaluable input in shaping the project design. Special acknowledgment also goes to those individuals who put forth valuable time and effort to help refine the manual: Scott Carlson, Phyllis Dininio, Mike Dziedzic, Michael Esper, Raymond Gilpin, Jeff Helsing, Col. John Kardos, Richard Ponzio, and Leonard Rubenstein. Finally, we would like to extend our enduring appreciation to the hundreds of others who provided input on the manual along its path to completion. The many institutions that helped vet this manual are listed in Appendix B.

# Section 1

# Introduction

# 1.0 Context

Terrorists, transnational organized crime syndicates, local warring factions, warlords, and petty thieves have all found common cause in states and regions in conflict. This nexus of interests has grown in sophistication over the past decade, aided by money and technology and fueled by greed and fanaticism. Civilians have increasingly become the victims of violence fostered by this nexus. The required response is a comprehensive[1] one that brings together specialized organizations to stabilize extremely dangerous and hostile environments while laying the foundations for a sustainable peace. This journey is a continuum that nests stabilization[2] within conflict-sensitive development. Stabilization aims to prevent the renewal of violent conflict; conflict-sensitive development seeks to enable a long-lasting peace.

While some progress has been made over the years, the U.S. capability and those of its partners to leverage and coordinate adequate civilian and military assets for this journey still lags behind the current adaptive abilities of the enemies of peace. To address the capacity challenge in the United States, the Clinton administration issued Presidential Decision Directive 56 (PDD/NSC-56) in 1997, the first U.S. directive to provide for whole-of-government planning and execution.[3] Eight years later, the Bush administration issued National Security Presidential Directive 44 (NSPD-44), another executive decision to bolster a whole-of-government response.[4]

Against this backdrop, thousands of U.S. government personnel from more than a dozen civilian agencies have deployed to more than a dozen stabilization and reconstruction (S&R) missions during the past two decades.[5] But the U.S. government does not engage in this business alone. It is but one player in a complex maze of peacebuilders working in increasingly harsh places like Afghanistan, the Congo, Somalia, Sudan, and Haiti. Indeed, sixty operations have been conducted under the auspices of the United Nations since 1948.[6] UN-led operations in 2009 have surged once again to an all-time high. Another signal is the doubling of operations mounted by regional organizations in the past decade.[7]

As global trends indicate, instability is likely to pose greater, and perhaps more numerous, challenges in the years to come.

> Statistical modeling shows that economic crises increase the risk of regime-threatening instability if they persist over a one- to two-year period. Besides increased economic nationalism, the most likely political fallout for US interests will involve

---

1. See Appendix E, Acronyms and Glossary of Selected Key Terms.
2. Ibid.
3. United States President, "United States Presidential Decision Directive 56, Managing Complex Contingency Operations," 1997.
4. United States President, "United States National Security Presidential Directive 44, Management of Interagency Efforts Concerning Reconstruction and Stabilization," 2005.
5. This includes, but is not limited to, the U.S. Departments of State, Labor, Treasury, Justice, Homeland Security, Agriculture, Energy, Commerce, Health and Human Services, Housing and Urban Development and Transportation; and agencies including the U.S. Agency for International Development, the Central Intelligence Agency, and the Administrative Office of the U.S. Courts.
6. United Nations Department of Peacekeeping Operations and Department of Field Support, *Peacekeeping Operations Principles and Guidelines,* 2008. Hereafter: UNDPKO, *Principles and Guidelines,* 2008.
7. International Forum for the Challenges of Peace Operations, *A Comparative Study on Doctrine and Principles for Multinational Peace Operations: A Case for Harmonization and Enhanced Interoperability,* 2007.

allies and friends not being able to fully meet their defense and humanitarian obligations.[8]

Dennis C. Blair
Director of National Intelligence
February 12, 2009

Learning how to succeed in these missions is one of the greatest challenges of the century.

## 1.1 Purpose

For the sake of comparison, the U.S. military is equipped with doctrine that guides its decisions and actions. This guidance is the basis for decision-making, planning, education, training, and implementation on the ground. Yet more than a decade after U.S. troops crossed the River Sava to help build peace in Bosnia and years after entering Afghanistan, *civilian* agencies of the U.S. government still lack any comprehensive strategic guidance. No guidance exists to inform decision makers, planners, or practitioners who deploy from civilian agencies to understand exactly *what* these missions are all about. In cloakrooms and conference rooms, in forward operating bases and humanitarian compounds, those who are engaged in these operations ask: *what* are we trying to achieve? The *Guiding Principles for Stabilization and Reconstruction* is an attempt to fill this gap.

Each S&R mission is quite unique depending on the local context. There are, however, general "rules of the road" or "principles" that have emerged from decades of experience in these missions. These principles serve as a handrail for decision makers, planners and practitioners as they attempt to navigate through these challenging environments. For the first time, the *Guiding Principles* manual seeks to present strategic principles for all major activities in S&R missions in one place. It seeks to provide a foundation for decision makers, planners, and practitioners—both international and host nation—to construct priorities for specific missions.

## 1.2 Caveats

- The *Guiding Principles* manual bears no government stamp, nor has the U.S. government adopted it officially. It is offered as a strategic tool.
- The manual is not intended to replace any single agency's "doctrine," strategic guidance, or mission statements. It is intended to incorporate the major principles embedded in them.
- This document should be treated as a living document and should be revised as new lessons emerge, learning advances, new strategies are tested, and the multiple gaps are filled.
- The manual is not intended to prescribe priorities, but rather a comprehensive view of complex S&R missions.
- The *Guiding Principles* is not a panacea for the extreme political complexities and financial constraints of these missions. These constraints may force difficult trade-offs in implementation.

---

8. Dennis C. Blair, "Annual Threat Assessment of the Intelligence Community for the Senate Select Committee on Intelligence" (Washington, D.C.: U.S. Office of the Director of National Intelligence, 2009).

## 1.3 Methodology

The manual rests on a comprehensive review of major strategic policy documents from state ministries of defense, foreign affairs, and development, along with major intergovernmental and nongovernmental organizations (NGO) that toil in war-shattered landscapes around the globe. The collection of documents[9] was built through consultations with dozens of major institutions and reviewed by a team of researchers over the course of a year and a half. It is extensive, but not exhaustive.

Many U.S. agencies, UN organizations, regional institutions and major foreign state partners and their respective agencies involved in these operations have had an opportunity to vet this manual.[10] It has been reviewed by a number of NGOs that are present before most missions deploy, during the mission, and after the peace is largely in the hands of the host nation.

## 1.4 Scope

The manual focuses on host nation outcomes, not programmatic inputs or outputs. It is focused primarily on what the host nation and international actors are trying to achieve, not how they are trying to achieve it at the tactical level. It is not about how to conduct an election or disarm warring parties—it is about the outcomes that these activities support. Excellent "how-to" guides already exist across the U.S. government and partner institutions. These should be accessed regularly and used diligently in the conduct of these missions.

### 1.4.1 Audience

The primary audience for the manual is U.S. government agencies engaged in S&R missions—principally their decision makers, planners, and practitioners. At the time of this writing, these agencies' contributions are coordinated under the leadership of the Office of the Coordinator for Reconstruction and Stabilization at the U.S. Department of State (S/CRS).[11] Though not written specifically for U.S. partners and others who labor in these difficult environments, the manual may be of value to them as well since it is based in part on their good work. In the final analysis, it is intended to help host nations and victims of conflict rebuild shattered societies.

### 1.4.2 Boundaries

• *Type of Mission.* This manual deals with missions that involve helping a country move from violent conflict to peace. It is a mission requiring the presence of peacekeeping and peace enforcement forces and other peacebuilding institutions. The mission will have some international leadership governing the institutions deployed.[12] Finally, the mission should be guided by a mandate, preferably from the United Nations.

• *Temporal Dimension.* Many institutions align their objectives according to particular phases or time spans of a mission. For the purposes of this manual, the principles apply from the moment the need for an intervention is first recog-

---

9.  See Appendix A, Resource List.
10. See Appendix B, Participants in Review Process.
11. United States Department of State, "Office of the Coordinator for Reconstruction and Stabilization," www.state.gov/s/crs/.
12. The international leadership could be the United Nations, a lead nation, a coalition of nations, a regional organization, or some hybrid of these institutions.

nized through the time when the host nation can sustainably provide security and basic services to its population. Local conditions in the host country will determine the type and length of international engagement. Based on the last few decades of experience, it takes at least ten years to achieve this. A stroke of good fortune and diligent action can deliver the result in less time.

- **Focus.** Due to these deliberate boundaries, the manual does not attempt to address the development challenges that take generations to overcome. The focus here is on that unique, perilous stage where everything must be viewed through the lens of conflict. A focus on short-term objectives is essential to help the host nation get off life support and on a sustainable path to recovery. But to ensure coherence, these objectives must be nested within longer-term development goals.

## 1.5 Comprehensive Review of Frameworks: A Snapshot

In seeking to offer a common set of guidelines, the writers performed a canvas of major institutional frameworks for this document.[13] This comprehensive review hopes to act as a Rosetta stone for S&R missions by extracting and building upon what is common and highlighting, for the future, areas of divergence.

One area of divergence worth mentioning is the fine separation—both cultural and intellectual—between guidance focused on stabilization and peacekeeping and that written for long-term development. Ironically, the vetting process reveals that stabilizers need to understand principles for sustainable development, while the development community needs to understand how to apply conflict-sensitive approaches to S&R environments. The literature in both communities of practice is now slowly reflecting these imperatives. Another area of divergence involves terminology and definitions. The multiple institutions working side by side in S&R missions do not share either of these.

Perhaps the strongest point of convergence involves the major components of these missions, or what the U.S. government calls "technical sectors."[14] Almost all frameworks address security, political, economic, social and justice dimensions. That important agreement is the starting point for this document.[15]

To elevate this shared construct to the level of strategic guidance, the *Guiding Principles* manual translates these shared components into purpose-based end states:[16] a safe and secure environment, the rule of law, stable governance, a sustainable economy, and social well-being. End states represent the ultimate goals of a society emerging from conflict.[17] These conform to the technical sectors currently used by the U.S. government: security, justice and reconciliation, governance and participation, economic stabilization and infrastructure, and humanitarian assistance and social well-being.

---

13. See Appendix C, Summary of Strategic Frameworks Surveyed.

14. United States Department of State, Office of the Coordinator for Reconstruction and Stabilization, *Post-Conflict Reconstruction Essential Tasks*, 2005.

15. See Appendix D, Snapshot of Components From Overarching Resources.

16. United States Army, *Field Manual 3-07: Stability Operations* (Washington, D.C.: Department of the U.S. Army, 2008). Hereafter: U.S. Army, *FM 3-07, 2008*.

17. Daniel P. Serwer and Patricia Thomson, "A Framework for Success: International Intervention in Societies Emerging from Conflict," in *Leashing the Dogs of War* (Washington, D.C.: U.S. Institute of Peace, 2008).

| Guiding Principles End States | U.S. Government Technical Sectors |
|---|---|
| Safe and Secure Environment | Security |
| Rule of Law | Justice and Reconciliation |
| Stable Governance | Governance and Participation |
| Sustainable Economy | Economic Stabilization and Infrastructure |
| Social Well-Being | Humanitarian Assistance and Social Well-Being |

## 1.6 A Note to Readers

This is a relatively short document to describe a massive challenge. A comprehensive understanding of what the mission is trying to achieve is required for success. In order to appreciate the interdependence and linkages among all actors and all actions—host nation and international—this manual should be read in its entirety. It represents a step toward professionalization for those engaged in the complex art of stabilization and reconstruction.

# Section 2

# Strategic Framework for Stabilization and Reconstruction

## 2.0 The Strategic Framework for Stabilization and Reconstruction

The Strategic Framework for Stabilization and Reconstruction offers a comprehensive look at the complexity of these missions. Based on a comprehensive review of guidance, it provides a foundation from which to determine priorities with and based on the needs of the host nation. The framework below depicts the major *end states*, as well as the *necessary conditions* that should be established to achieve those end states. The framework also elevates a set of *cross-cutting principles* that applies to each and every actor and impacts each end state. This framework recognizes that the end states and their associated conditions cannot be pursued independently of one another. The overlapping circles underscore this interdependence.[18]

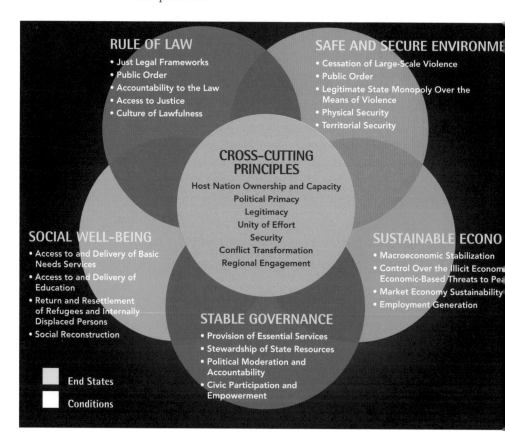

18. The development of this framework occurred over a two-step process. The U.S. Institute of Peace developed the "Framework for Success for Societies Emerging From Conflict" in 2006. In developing this manual, the objectives and sub-objectives were translated into conditions necessary to reach the core end states. This new construct is based on a review of hundreds of core strategic documents and a nine-month vetting process.

## 2.1 End States[19]

Below is a summary description of each end state, framed according to the perception of the host nation population, as they will be the final arbiters of whether peace has been achieved.

- **Safe and Secure Environment**
  *Ability of the people to conduct their daily lives without fear of systematic or large-scale violence.*

- **Rule of Law**
  *Ability of the people to have equal access to just laws and a trusted system of justice that holds all persons accountable, protects their human rights and ensures their safety and security.*

- **Stable Governance**
  *Ability of the people to share, access or compete for power through nonviolent political processes and to enjoy the collective benefits and services of the state.*

- **Sustainable Economy**
  *Ability of the people to pursue opportunities for livelihoods within a system of economic governance bound by law.*

- **Social Well-Being**
  *Ability of the people to be free from want of basic needs and to coexist peacefully in communities with opportunities for advancement.*

## 2.2 Cross-Cutting Principles

The following are high-level principles that should be applied by every person and to every activity that is conducted in support of the S&R mission. The division of labor into five core end states helps to focus and standardize actions based on decades of experience. But this division also neglects the big picture—the overarching guidance that cuts across every end state and affects every action of every individual:

- **Host Nation Ownership and Capacity**
- **Political Primacy**
- **Legitimacy**
- **Unity of Effort**
- **Security**
- **Conflict Transformation**
- **Regional Engagement**

---

19. See Appendix D, Snapshot of Components From Overarching Resources.

## 2.3 Structure of the Manual

The manual is structured according to the framework. Cross-cutting principles are presented in Section 3. Each end state corresponds with a dedicated section in the body of this manual. Each section includes descriptions for the necessary conditions, and the major approaches that have been used to establish those conditions based on decades of experience. Relevant trade-offs, gaps, and challenges[20] are also addressed at the end of each section.

---

20. See Appendix E.

# SECTION 3
# CROSS-CUTTING PRINCIPLES

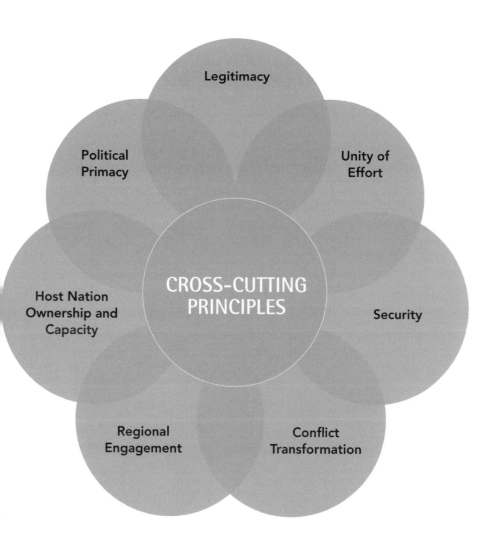

## 3.0 What are cross-cutting principles?

Cross-cutting principles apply to every actor across every end state—no matter who you are, international or local; where you are, in the UN Security Council or in a host nation municipality; or what you are doing, running a school or creating a new banking system. The principles are focused, according to the purpose of this manual, on outcomes. Legitimacy, for example, is an outcome of an untold number of actions. It is a cross-cutting principle that should guide all actions. Maintaining legitimacy is the responsibility of all actors in an S&R mission. The cross-cutting principles included here are discussed throughout the manual.

## 3.1 What are the key cross-cutting principles in an S&R environment?

- *Host nation ownership and capacity* means that the affected country must drive its own development needs and priorities even if transitional authority is in the hands of outsiders.[21] Ownership requires capacity, which often needs tremendous strengthening in S&R environments.

- *Political primacy* means that a political settlement is the cornerstone of a sustainable peace. Every decision and every action has an impact on the possibility of forging political agreement.

- *Legitimacy* has three facets: the degree to which the host nation population accepts the mission and its mandate or the government and its actions; the degree to which the government is accountable to its people; and the degree to which regional neighbors and the broader international community accept the mission mandate and the host nation government.

- *Unity of effort* begins with a shared understanding of the environment. It refers to cooperation toward common objectives over the short and long term, even when the participants come from many different organizations with diverse operating cultures.[22]

- *Security* is a cross-cutting prerequisite for peace. The lack of security is what prompts an S&R mission to begin with. Security creates the enabling environment for development.

- *Conflict transformation* guides the strategy to transform resolution of conflict from violent to peaceful means. It requires reducing drivers of conflict and strengthening mitigators across political, security, rule of law, economic, and social spheres, while building host nation capacity to manage political and economic competition through peaceful means.[23]

- *Regional engagement* entails encouraging the host nation, its neighboring countries, and other key states in the region to partner in promoting both the host nation's and the region's security and economic and political development. It has three components: comprehensive regional diplomacy, a shared regional vision, and cooperation.

---

21. United States Agency for International Development, "Nine Principles of Development and Reconstruction," 2005. http://www.usaid.gov/policy/2005_nineprinciples.html, accessed July 2009.
22. U.S. Army, *FM 3-07*, 2008.
23. United States Department of State and United States Joint Forces Command, *United States Government Draft Planning Framework for Stabilization, Reconstruction and Conflict Transformation*, 2005.

## 3.2 Why is it necessary to fulfill these cross-cutting principles?

S&R missions are messy and complex endeavors involving thousands, if not millions, of moving parts. The same principles that guide one individual charged with implementing a political settlement must guide another who is responsible for operating a transitional prison system to achieve peace.

## 3.3 Host Nation Ownership and Capacity

### 3.3.1 What is host nation ownership and capacity?

If the end game is a locally led, sustainable peace, then host nation ownership must be developed at all times by all actors. This means that the affected country must drive its own long-term development needs and priorities.[24] Ownership requires capacity, and in these environments, capacity may need strengthening. Emphasize the building of capacity for public and private, national and local, and formal and informal institutions to mitigate and manage drivers of conflict.[25]

### 3.3.2 Locally led peace

The international community can impose stability, but only the host nation population can create sustainable peace. A situation requiring the intervention of military forces to enforce peace is always deeply complex and can only be resolved through local settlements and institutions.[26]

### 3.3.3 Host nation ownership and capacity depend on:

* *Understanding the local context*
  Every region, every state and every village has unique economic, cultural, religious, political, and historical characteristics. In assessing the local context, always carefully consider all of these characteristics.

* *Fostering ownership*
  The ultimate responsibility for the stabilization and reconstruction process belongs to the host nation. This means assisting the host nation government and civil society to lead and participate in both planning and implementation.[27] Utilization of host nation processes and structures, both formal and informal, builds ownership. For example, using the central budget of the host nation government, with appropriate safeguards, allows host nation actors to shape priorities and meet the needs of the population.

* *Inclusivity*
  Partnerships with host nation actors should be guided by impartiality, inclusiveness, and gender considerations based on a solid understanding of the local context (to include civil society; private sector actors; and all ethnic, religious,

---

24. USAID, "Nine Principles," 2005.

25. United States Department of State, Office of the Coordinator for Reconstruction and Stabilization, *Principles of the USG Planning Framework for Reconstruction, Stabilization and Conflict Transformation*, 2008. Hereafter: S/CRS, *Principles*, 2008.

26. United Kingdom Stabilisation Unit, *The United Kingdom Approach to Stabilisation—A Stabilisation Guidance Note*, 2008. Hereafter: UK Stabilisation Unit, *UK Approach to Stabilisation*, 2008.

27. S/CRS, *Principles*, 2008.

and minority groups). Seek to include those who have demonstrated support for the peace process and made efforts to end the violence.

- *Capacity*
Capacity building involves transferring technical knowledge and skills to the host nation, individuals, and institutions to help them develop effective policies and administer public services across the economic, social, political, and security realms.[28] This requires adequate resources for a basic level of civil service capacity and perseverance to mentor and assist in building that capacity. Experience has shown that it is still preferable to deliver services "with" rather than "for" the host nation government, despite weak capacity.[29]

- *Formal and informal systems*
Building on and reforming existing structures and systems is more fiscally sustainable and often more palatable to the host nation population than starting from scratch, as long as the institution has not been one of the principal drivers of conflict. Local customs and structures that are legitimate are better than transplanted models that are unfamiliar. Often, the population's contact with formal state institutions—including those responsible for justice and security—is negligible or very negative. On the other hand, contact with informal systems, such as customary justice, may have been frequent and positive. Understanding the role of formal vs. informal systems is a prerequisite for action.

- *Early resources*
Early resources tend to be used for projects that produce quick and visible results—often known as "quick impact"—to demonstrate that things are different in the country. Some examples include rehabilitating infrastructure or cleaning the streets. Early resources may be important, but only if they contribute to increasing host nation ownership over development, supporting the peace process, and building capacity over the long term. Be vigilant about monitoring and accounting for resources by establishing mechanisms to track money flows and progress.

- *The role of women*
The engagement of women is necessary to ensure sustainable peace, economic recovery, and social well-being.[30] Include women at the peace table, in the recovery process, in the host nation government, and in local public and private sector institutions. Protect them at all times so they can make their unique contribution to peace. Train them and give them the capacity to lead and participate. Women improve the chances for legitimacy when they are involved in mobilizing constituencies for peace and helping to design core programs such as security sector reform (SSR).[31]

28. USAID, *Nine Principles*, 2005.
29. UK Stabilisation Unit, *UK Approach to Stabilisation*, 2008.
30. United Nations Development Group and World Bank, "DRAFT Joint Guidance Note on Integrated Recovery Planning Using Post Conflict Needs Assessments and Transitional Results Frameworks," 2007. Hereafter: UNDG/WB, "DRAFT Joint Guidance Note," 2007. United Nations Security Council, "United Nations Security Council Resolution 1325," www.peacewomen.org/un/sc/res1325.pdf (accessed June 17, 2009).
31. Camille Pampell Conaway, *The Role of Women in Stabilization and Reconstruction* (Washington, D.C.: U.S. Institute of Peace, 2006).

- *Effective transitions from international to host nation*
  In these environments, international actors may help manage crucial state functions until there are leaders who are committed to peace and institutions with the capacity to run a legitimate government. Effective transitions to full host nation ownership looms as a large gap in knowledge and practice across end states for all institutions.

# 3.4 Political Primacy

## 3.4.1 What is political primacy?

Political primacy refers to the basic premise that everything is political. Violent conflict occurs when nonviolent political processes break down and when authority structures are no longer viewed as legitimate by some or all of the population. Political settlements may seek to end this violence, but the motives for conflict may not have been extinguished. Each action in the recovery phase must be carefully weighed against its impact on the politics of the conflict. Additionally, the politics between donors, within governments, and in and among international organizations and regional institutions, impact prospects for a political settlement.

## 3.4.2 Political primacy requires:

- *Using a conflict lens.*
  The perceptions of the population about rewards and punishment, and winners and losers are ultimately what count. A unique assessment and understanding of the political, social and economic "rules of the game" is necessary.

- *Fostering and sustaining a political process.*
  Fostering and sustaining a political process is essential. Negotiating a political settlement can be an intricate and volatile process. How the agreement is written can shape the kinds of challenges that arise in implementing the agreement. Key considerations to remember when negotiating settlements include

  - Relationships among conflicting parties are often unequal.
  - Support those who support the political process and oppose those who oppose it.
  - There is a need to address the unresolved issues that underlie the conflict and other interrelated conflicts.
  - There is often a perceived or real bias of international players.
  - Disagreements over implementation can undermine peace (usually regarding politically sensitive processes such as SSR; disarmament, demobilization, and reintegration [DDR]; power sharing; or resource distribution.
  - Agreement on measurable goals to enhance accountability of the parties.
  - Unrealistic goals and timetables can create challenges in implementation.
  - Host nation leadership is critical for the political process and its implementation.

- *Inclusivity of warring parties and marginalized groups.*
  Political processes are more sustainable when they include all parties that have the power to obstruct the process in violent ways if they do not have a substan-

tial stake in it. Equally important is the inclusion of marginalized groups, such as women and minorities, who may have been victimized or excluded in the past.[32] This can ensure that their needs are reflected and their rights are protected.

- *Effective strategic communications.*[33]
  Political processes should not take place exclusively in the "official" arena. The involvement of the population through public dialogue and civil society underpins the success of any political settlement. Effective strategic communications should aim to

  - Deliver credible messages about the objectives of the peace process.
  - Ensure these messages are articulated in a way that is understandable by the population.
  - Manage expectations by painting a realistic picture of the situation and the capacity of the host nation government and international community to implement agreements.

## 3.5 Legitimacy

### 3.5.1 What is legitimacy?
Every actor and every action can contribute to legitimacy. This term has several meanings:

- The degree to which the local population accepts and supports the mission, its mandate and its behavior over time.

- The degree to which the local population accepts and supports the host nation government (which can include informal governance structures as well), and the manner in which the government attains power.

- The extent to which regional neighbors and the international community accept the mission's mandate and its actions and the host nation government and its actions.

### 3.5.2 Legitimacy derives from:
- *A bargain between citizens and the government*
  The generally accepted concept of state legitimacy is based on a bargain between state and citizenry. Legitimacy here is what citizens grant to the state in exchange for security.[34] In this century, however, more is required. In addition to the provision of security, legitimacy is also derived from the ability of the state to perform critical functions in the economic, political, and social spheres in an accountable manner.[35] Legitimacy also requires the state to observe international law and protect human rights. The bargain today may exist between citizens and subnational entities, both formal and informal.

---

32. John Darby, *The Effects of Violence on Peace Processes* (Washington, D.C.: U.S. Institute of Peace, 2001). United Kingdom Stabilisation Unit, *Quick Guide to Stabilisation Planning*, 2007.

33. U.S. Army, *FM 3-07*, 2008.

34. United Nations Development Programme and United States Agency for International Development, *First Steps in Post-Conflict State-Building: a UNDP-USAID Study*, 2007. Hereafter: UNDP/USAID, "First Steps," 2007.

35. Ashraf Ghani and Clare Lockhart, *Fixing Failed States: A Framework for Rebuilding a Fractured World* (Oxford: Oxford University Press, 2008). Hereafter: Ghani/Lockhart, Fixing Failed States, 2008.

- *Mandate and authorities*
To establish mission and host nation legitimacy, a UN Security Council Resolution and mandate is the preferred route. The mandate or peace agreement should provide clear rules for how the host nation will be managed after war in terms of executive, legislative, and judicial structure and functions; participation (citizens' rights, civil liberties); and accountability (especially elections).[36] Specifying the short-term stability requirements along with provisions for transferring all long-term responsibilities to the host nation helps to ensure ownership and facilitate transition.[37] Developing this mandate with all key stakeholders of the peace process aids legitimacy.

- *Matching resources to goals and delivering a timely peace dividend*
The goals of a mandate are only achievable when the resources provided are adequate and rapidly distributed to affirm credibility and legitimacy. The early establishment of a credible presence can help to deter spoilers and other threats and diminish the likelihood that force will be needed to implement the mandate.[38] Mobilize a minimum of assets to provide immediate security and restore essential services with funded plans for mandated activities such as DDR and the training or retraining of indigenous police that typically accompany DDR.[39] Short-term efforts to establish legitimacy can be sustained by fully resourcing longer-term initiatives.

- *Leadership*
There are two levels of leadership: (1) that of an international mission typically authorized by the UN and (2) that of the host nation. Those charged with the responsibilities in a mandate should have the authorities to make decisions and implement them. Sometimes, leaders will have to work with a mandate, which may be ambiguous. Navigating this ambiguity and maximizing flexibility is a job for political leaders, not technocrats, and informs what kind of leadership is required for the mission and host nation. A sustainable peace depends on how adeptly the custodian of the peace process can guide the transformation of conflict among warring factions.[40]

- *Accountability and transparency*
Basic systems for accountability—both for the international mission and the host nation—are critical factors for legitimacy. Accountability requires transparency. This means making government transparent to the population through media, civil society, and other reporting mechanisms. Together, these are the basic building blocks for any approach to limit the de-legitimizing corruption that often pervades war-torn environments—both in host nation institutions and those of international actors.

---

36. Ibid.
37. UK Stabilisation Unit, "UK Approach to Stabilisation," 2008.
38. UNDPKO, *Principles and Guidelines,* 2008.
39. James Dobbins, Seth G. Jones, Keith Crane, and Beth Cole DeGrasse, *The Beginner's Guide to Nation-Building* (Santa Monica, Calif.: RAND Corporation, 2007). Hereafter: Dobbins/Jones/Crane/Cole DeGrasse, *Beginner's Guide,* 2007.
40. Jack Covey, Michael J. Dziedzic, and Leonard R. Hawley, eds., *The Quest for Viable Peace: International Intervention and Strategies for Conflict Transformation* (Washington, D.C.: U.S. Institute of Peace, 2005). Hereafter: Covey/Dziedzic/Hawley, *Quest for a Viable Peace,* 2005.

- *Management of expectations and communication*
  Constant and clear communication helps manage expectations about the realities of donor and state resources and progress of reconstruction. It also dispels rumors and counters spoiler narratives that undermine peace. Local voices and traditional forms of communication deliver messages more effectively and can help sustain support. Communication requires dedicated resources throughout the life of a mission.

- *Constituencies for peace*
  A peace process will only be successful if the local population is engaged in and committed to peace.[41] In the literature, this is often referred to as "buy-in" or "consent," but the essential ingredient remains the same: Prospects for a durable political settlement rest on active constituencies for peace that must be brought in to the political process. To maintain credibility and to prevent supporters from becoming fence sitters or spoilers, confront those who oppose the political process. Building constituencies for peace requires concerted efforts to tap into capacities across the wider society, including those offered by women, ethnic minorities, youth, and local leaders.[42]

- *Engagement of the international community*
  Legitimacy falters when the international community is not engaged. It is not enough to pass a Security Council resolution. Engagement should begin with a UN mandate and continue through the active participation of donors putting qualified personnel and resources to assist the host nation make the transition from violent conflict to peace. Managing this engagement may include mission-specific consultative mechanisms or host nation advisory structures to coordinate efforts and confront challenges.

## 3.6 Unity of Effort

### 3.6.1 What is unity of effort?

Unity of effort is the outcome of coordination and cooperation among all actors, even when the participants come from many different organizations with diverse operating cultures.[43] This applies to efforts among agencies of the U.S. government, between the U.S. government and the international community, and between the host nation government and the international community. Unity of effort is an important cross-cutting principle because the U.S. government will always find itself to be just one player among numerous local and international actors.

### 3.6.2 Unity of effort is based on:

- *A shared understanding of the situation*
  Unity of effort begins with a shared understanding of the situation that is derived from an assessment. Within the U.S. government, that shared understanding is based on a whole-of-government assessment of the dynamics driving and

---

41. International Forum for the *Challenges of Peace Operations, Meeting the Challenges of Peace Operations: Cooperation and Coordination, Challenges Project Phase II Concluding Report*, 2003–2005, 2006.

42. UNDG/WB, "DRAFT Joint Guidance Note," 2007.

43. U.S. Army, *FM 3-07*, 2008.

mitigating violent conflict within a country.[44] The United Nations and agencies of other nations employ similar assessment frameworks. Creating a common picture from these disparate assessments is a challenge confronted frequently in developing UN mandates and shaping country-specific strategies.

- *A shared strategic goal*
  Based on a shared understanding, an overarching goal is determined to unify the efforts of U.S. agencies behind a strategic plan. This should ideally be linked with the goals of other international and host nation actors.

- *Integration*
  Integration means that capabilities across the U.S. government will be brought together in a coherent manner to achieve unity of effort. This process of integration is also occurring outside of the U.S. government, within the UN, within other states and among nongovernmental humanitarian organizations. Linking these integrated systems is a challenge that has yet to be met.

- *Cooperation and coherence*
  Full integration may be achievable within individual states or organizations, but may be very difficult to attain across disparate systems. Cooperation, however, may be a realistic goal to strive for and arrived at through tight or loose forms of coordination.[45] Cooperation exists when information is shared and activities are deconflicted as much as possible among independent institutions so as not to undermine a shared strategic goal. The outcome of cooperation should be a coherent effort by multiple actors to establish sustainable peace.

- *Civil-military cooperation*
  Civil-military cooperation needs to be understood in three ways: cooperation between civilian and military actors of official government and inter-governmental institutions, between the military and NGOs (among international actors), and between the military and host nation government and its population. The size and strength of the military, with its own command and control structure, creates a unique impact that requires specific forms of cooperation. In environments where military forces are engaged in combat and S&R missions simultaneously, consider specific guidelines for relations between the U.S. military and U.S. NGOs.[46]

- *Recognition of humanitarian space*
  There are actors who remain outside of the unity of effort campaign for good reason. Maintain clear separation between politically motivated actions to end violent conflict and movement toward development, and apolitical humanitarian assistance based exclusively on impartial response to assessed need.[47]

---

44. United States Department of State, Office of the Coordinator for Reconstruction and Stabilization, *Interagency Conflict Assessment Framework*, 2008. Hereafter: S/CRS, *Interagency Conflict Assessment Framework*, 2008.
45. See Section 5, Fundamentals of a Comprehensive Approach.
46. Interaction, U.S. Department of Defense, U.S. Institute of Peace, "Guidelines for Relations Between U.S. Armed Forces and Nongovernmental Humanitarian Organizations in Hostile or Potentially Hostile Environments," 2006.
47. UNDPKO, *Principles and Guidelines*, 2008.

# 3.7 Security

### 3.7.1 What is security?

The importance of security jumps off every page of every major institutional framework. It is one of the few preconditions for enduring peace. In its broadest sense, security is an "all encompassing condition" that takes freedom, safety, governance, human rights, public health, and access to resources into account.[48] This is commonly known as "human security."[49] For the purposes of cross-cutting principles presented here, security is defined as the physical security that permits the freedom necessary to pursue a permanent peace

### 3.7.2 Security is the platform for development.

It is a prerequisite for a safe and secure environment, the rule of law, stable governance, a sustainable economy, and social well-being. The human security imperative is addressed in all sections of this manual, but the physical aspect is covered in Section 6. It cannot be delegated only to peacekeepers or military intervention forces or begin and end with a successful DDR program. Many aspects are cross-cutting and are highlighted here.

### 3.7.3 Security rests on:

- *Information*
  Sharing timely information about threats and potential threats to the peace process or the population is vital to security. This information may address a potential threat to women foraging for firewood outside the perimeter of a refugee camp, an assassination threat to a government minister, or illicit power structures engaged in arms trafficking. Having access to this kind of information requires deep links with the population. The sharing of information should not jeopardize the work of impartial NGOs or the neutrality of the International Committee of the Red Cross.

- *Management of spoilers*
  Spoilers are individuals or parties who believe that the peace process threatens their power and interests and will therefore work to undermine it.[50] Understand what gives power brokers power, including their financing, their roles in the previous regime and their standing in the community.[51] Recognize that they exist in the economic, political, and security arenas, at both the local and national level. They may have fed off the conflict or emerged in the wake of defeat as new spoilers. If reconcilable, spoilers should be encouraged to change their behavior over time. Depending on their motives and capacity at state and local levels, spoilers may need to be dealt with militarily or through political or economic negotiations.

- *Reform of the security sector*
  Control of the security apparatus is the basic source of state power and its use

---

48. Japan International Cooperation Agency, *Handbook for Transition Assistance*, 2006. Hereafter: JICA, *Handbook for Transition Assistance*, 2006.
49. See Appendix E, Acronyms and Glossary of Selected Key Terms.
50. UNDG/WB, "DRAFT Joint Guidance Note," 2007.
51. Karen Guttieri and Jessica Piombo, eds. *Interim Governments: Institutional Bridges to Peace and Democracy?* (Washington, D.C.: U.S. Institute of Peace, 2007). Hereafter: Guttieri/Piombo, *Interim Governments*, 2007.

will likely have been one of the major drivers of conflict. Its reform therefore is a priority.[52] Security sector reform touches every aspect of an S&R mission: actors directly involved in protecting civilians and the state from violence (e.g., police and military forces and internal intelligence agencies), institutions that govern these actors and manage their funding (e.g., ministries of interior, defense, and justice, and national security councils), and oversight bodies (legislative and nongovernmental).[53] Reform aims to create a professional security sector that is legitimate, impartial, and accountable to the population.[54]

- *Protection of human rights*[55]
  A human rights-based approach, where all actions uphold human rights, is required to establish the necessary conditions for each end state. This involves a mandate to protect and promote human rights and ensure that the host nation has the will and capacity to do so on its own.[56] Rights protected under international law include life, liberty, and security of person; the highest attainable standard of health; a fair trial; just and favorable working conditions; adequate food, housing, and social security; education; equal protection of the law; and a nationality. These also include freedom from arbitrary interference with privacy, family, home, or correspondence; arbitrary arrest or detention; torture and cruel, inhuman, or degrading treatment or punishment; slavery; and freedom of association, expression, assembly, and movement.[57]

# 3.8 Conflict Transformation

### 3.8.1 What is conflict transformation?[58]
Conflict will always persist in these environments and affect security, governance, and economic development in ways that threaten peace and undermine legitimacy. The goal of conflict transformation is to reach the point where the host nation is on a "sustainable positive trajectory," where it can independently manage the dynamics causing violent conflict. Conflict transformation requires reducing the drivers of conflict while supporting those that mitigate conflict across security, economic, and political spheres. For the long term, transformation rests on the ability of the host nation to sustain stability and create conditions for long-term development.

---

52. UK Stabilisation Unit, "UK Approach to Stabilisation," 2008.

53. United States Department of State, United States Department of Defense, and United States Agency for International Development, *Security Sector Reform*, 2008.

54. Sean McFate, *Securing the Future: A Primer on Security Sector Reform in Conflict Countries* (Washington, D.C.: U.S. Institute of Peace, 2008).

55. Rights are cross-cutting and are enshrined in law, including the "Universal Declaration of Human Rights," the "International Covenant on Civil and Political Rights," the "International Covenant on Economic, Social and Cultural Rights," the "Convention of the Rights of the Child," the "Convention Against Torture and Other Cruel, Inhuman or Degrading Treatment or Punishment," and the "Convention on the Elimination of All Forms of Discrimination Against Women."

56. UNDPKO, *Principles and Guidelines*, 2008.

57. United Nations Office of the High Commissioner for Human Rights, *Frequently Asked Questions on a Human Rights-Based Approach to Development Cooperation*, 2006.

58. S/CRS, *Principles*, 2008. Covey/Dziedzic/Hawley, *Quest for a Viable Peace*, 2005.

### 3.8.2 Conflict transformation focuses on:
- *Understanding drivers and mitigators of conflict*
Identify key groups that may threaten the peace process, if they do not perceive the benefits of peace, and regions and localities at risk, where visible reconstruction is important.[59] Identify sources of institutional resilience and other mitigating factors critical for peace. Understand how upcoming events (elections, transitional justice processes, events in neighboring countries) may have an impact on both drivers and mitigators. Understand what motivates opponents to peace, why they resort to violence, where they derive their support, how they make decisions and what might convince them to support peace and renounce violence.

- *Reducing drivers of conflict and strengthening mitigators*
No matter how inclusive the emerging political settlement, powerful groups that want to continue the violence need to be reckoned with either through mediation and co-option or military defeat. Contain spoilers by constraining or removing them, disrupting their flow of resources and channeling the competition for power from bullets to ballots. Enhance the capability for dispute resolution and support institutional and social resilience to transform conflict.

- *Building host nation capacity to manage the drivers of conflict through nonviolent means and support long-term development*
This is the end game. It cycles back to the strategic framework and five end states that underpin this manual: a safe and secure environment that enables development; the rule of law that allows grievances to be addressed through a system of justice and confronts impunity; stable governance that permits contestation for power to take place peacefully; a sustainable economy that provides the framework for licit economic competition; and social well-being that affords equal access to basic human needs and the opportunity to live in communities that have mechanisms for peaceful resolution of conflict.

## 3.9 Regional Engagement

### 3.9.1 What is regional engagement?
Neighboring countries play a major role—at times positive and negative—in the host nation's stabilization and reconstruction. Regional interests, issues, and unresolved conflicts can continue to influence and affect the host nation throughout an S&R mission. The host nation may be at risk from its neighbors' domestic instabilities and foreign policies.[60] And conflict within the host nation may have bled across borders through refugee flow and arms trafficking. A long-term solution for the host nation must include a consideration of the effects of both its conflict on the region and the region on its conflict.[61] Regional engagement entails encouraging the host nation,

---

59. S/CRS, "Interagency Conflict Assessment Framework," 2008. UNDG/WB, "DRAFT Joint Guidance Note," 2007.

60. Marvin G. Weinbaum, *Afghanistan and Its Neighbors: An Ever Dangerous Neighborhood* (Washington, D.C.: U.S. Institute of Peace, 2006).

61. Chester A. Crocker, Fen Osler Hampson, Pamela Aall, *Leashing the Dogs of War: Conflict Management in a Divided World* (Washington, D.C.: U.S. Institute of Peace Press, 2007).

its neighboring countries, and other key states in the region to partner in promoting both the host nation's and the region's security and economic and political development.

### 3.9.2 Regional engagement is based on:

- *Comprehensive regional diplomacy*
  While the host nation's neighbors should not, at a minimum, sabotage stabilization and reconstruction, their active engagement and cooperation is advantageous. Conduct a comprehensive diplomatic offensive that aims to halt any destabilizing actions by the host nation's neighbors. Elicit their support for a stable and peaceful host nation and region, and the security of the host nation's borders. Obtain their cooperation in providing economic and military assistance, giving political support and engaging in trade and commerce.[62] The region should continue or restore diplomatic relations with the host nation, where appropriate.

- *A shared regional vision*
  Left to their own devices, neighbors may act according to their own strategic interests, which could be destabilizing for the host nation and the region. Instead, the neighbors—typically with encouragement and assistance from the international community—should collaborate to develop a shared vision for the region. Be sure to recognize and consider the neighbors' concerns and interests during this process.[63]

- *Cooperation*
  Ensure the neighbors' ongoing active participation by forming or supporting regionwide structures—necessary in today's globalized world—that promote the region's security, economic growth, and social and political development.[64] These structures should encourage and solidify mutually beneficial cooperation in fields such as transportation, trade, science and technology, health, natural resources, energy, culture, education, and politics; strengthen goodwill between the states; collaborate to maintain the region's peace and security by reducing mutual perceptions of threat; and develop common political values and systems.[65] For the state emerging from violent conflict, the structures should help the host nation in ways that support its legitimacy and sovereignty, determined with the consent of the host nation.[66]

---

62. Iraq Study Group, *The Iraq Study Group Report: The Way Forward—A New Approach* (New York: Vintage Books, 2006). Hereafter: Iraq Study Group Report, 2006.
63. Ibid.
64. Ghani/Lockhart, *Fixing Failed States*, 2008.
65. Southern African Development Community, "SADC Profile," www.sadc.int/ (accessed June 18, 2009). Shanghai Cooperation Organization, "Shanghai Cooperation Organization," www.fmprc.gov.cn/eng/topics/sco/t57970.html (accessed June 18, 2009); Economic Community of West African States, "ECOWAS in brief," www.comm.ecowas.int/sec/index.php?id=about_a&lang=en (accessed June 18, 2009).
66. *Iraq Study Group Report*, 2006.

# HIGH-LEVEL TRADE-OFFS, GAPS, AND CHALLENGES

# 4.0 High-Level Trade-offs

Many decisions in S&R missions involve difficult trade-offs. Trade-offs refer to the inherent conflicts that exist between objectives. They involve making concessions between those objectives and understanding the impact on stability. For example, bringing a warlord into government can undermine legitimacy of the government, but it may be the only way to end violence in a particular part of the country. Banning a group of people from government can signal an end to impunity for some, while also fueling an insurgency. Understanding these trade-offs can help guide strategy and mitigate possible negative consequences. Trade-offs are highlighted throughout this manual and embedded in specific discussions of the five end states. The following high-level trade-offs are overarching:

**4.1** *Stability vs. host nation legitimacy* refers to the trade-off between the urgent need for international actors to secure the peace and the possibility that these actions are not seen by the host nation population as connected to their local leaders or government and do not build the legitimacy or capacity of the host nation.

**4.2** *Expediency vs. sustainability* refers to short-term actions that show a peace dividend and signal that violent conflict is over but are not sustainable by the host nation over time. Inherent conflicts between short- and long-term objectives can include maintaining employment vs. cutting jobs in order to restructure the economy.[67] Large infrastructure projects, oversized armies, and expensive national elections are other examples related to this trade-off.

**4.3** *Meeting needs vs. building capacity* refers to the quandary faced by international actors—governmental and nongovernmental—when it is easier to fulfill needs directly than to build host nation capacity to deliver critical assistance.

# 4.4 High-Level Gaps and Challenges

Gaps refer to weaknesses that exist in knowledge and that recur from mission to mission. Challenges refer to shortfalls in practice, even when best practices have already been identified. Both gaps and challenges are addressed throughout the manual.[68]

**4.5** *Lack of an agreed overall vision or "storyline"* that sets the strategic direction for stabilization and reconstruction. See Sections 3.4, Political Primacy and 3.6, Unity of Effort.

**4.6** *Insufficient realism in the timelines for key recovery outcomes,* resulting in unreasonable expectations on the part of the host nation population and leadership and international partners. See Section 3.5, Legitimacy.

**4.7** *Inadequate links between priorities* across the security, rule of law, governance, economic and social arenas. See Section 3.6, Unity of Effort.

---

67. United States Agency for International Development, *Guide to Economic Growth in Post-Conflict Countries,* 2009.

68. UN Development Group, UN Development Programme, World Bank, *Practical Guide to Multilateral Needs Assessments,* 2004. United Kingdom Department for International Development, *Review of the United Kingdom Government Approach to Peacebuilding and Synthesis of Lessons Learned from United Kingdom Government Funded Peacebuilding Projects, 1997–2001,* 2003. Joint Utstein Study of Peacebuilding, *Towards a Strategic Framework for Peacebuilding: Getting Their Act Together,* 2004. UK Stabilisation Unit, "UK Approach to Stabilisation," 2008.

**4.8** *Loss of momentum after the key transition event,* such as a peace agreement or election. See Section 3.3, Host Nation Ownership and Capacity.

**4.9** *Ineffective transitions from international to local control* to sustain peace and prevent a relapse into conflict. See Section 3.3, Host Nation Ownership and Capacity.

**4.10** *Insufficient understanding of host nation context and needs.* See Section 3.3, Host Nation Ownership and Capacity.

# Section 5
# Fundamentals of a Comprehensive Approach

## 5.0 What are the fundamentals of a comprehensive approach?

An understanding of the Strategic Framework for S&R is necessary. Just as important is an understanding of the fundamentals of a comprehensive approach. These fundamentals come from almost every official guidance document that has been written on these missions and appear to be widely shared.

## 5.1 Interdependence

- *"Everything is connected to everything else,"* as General Anthony Zinni (retired U.S. Marine Corps) wrote in the aftermath of the 1990s missions in Somalia.[69] The end states and conditions described in this manual are part of an interlocking system of systems: Security requires the rule of law, essential services require governance, the rule of law is dependent on security, sustainable economies are dependent on the rule of law, ownership requires capacity, and meeting basic human needs requires all of the above. It is a spider web of interdependence that requires as much integration as possible.

- *Interdependence requires that all actors break out of their stovepipes.* Actors in the political, security, economic, and social realms are not independent. Failing to achieve success in one realm jeopardizes success in all the others. Understand one's role and connection to others in the big picture.[70]

## 5.2 Cooperation[71]

- *A shared strategic vision enables different actors to work cooperatively toward the same goal.* This vision is the "storyline" that must be communicated through mandates, by leadership, and with full participation by the host nation population.[72]

- *Understanding organizational cultures and interests is necessary for cooperation.* A basic knowledge of different organizational principles and cultures of actors is required.[73] Understanding must be followed by a high degree of sensitivity to their interests and operating cultures or what motivates them and directs them to operate in a certain manner.

- *Cooperation requires constant communication, dialogue, and negotiation among all actors—international, host nation, government, and nongovernment.* Communication involves mechanisms for sharing and reporting information about goals and activities. Active dialogue entails open exchanges between actors to facilitate a mutual understanding that may lead to better cooperation. When differences impede cooperation, negotiation may be required.

---

69. Lt. Gen. Anthony Zinni, "Lt. Gen. Zinni's Twenty Lessons Learned for Humanitarian Assistance and Peace Operations," presented at the Center for Naval Analysis Annual Conference Proceedings: Military Support to Complex Humanitarian Emergencies, 1995.

70. Organisation for Economic Co-operation and Development, *Whole of Government Approaches to Fragile Societies*, 2006.

71. Cooperation is also addressed in Section 3.6 Unity of Effort in Cross-Cutting Principles.

72. UNDG/WB, "DRAFT Joint Guidance Note," 2007.

73. Robert Perito, ed. *Guide for Participants in Peace, Stability and Relief Operations* (Washington, D.C.: U.S. Institute of Peace, 2007).

## 5.3 Prioritization

- *Priorities are necessary but must be flexible.* Experience reveals that there are fundamental priorities in most societies emerging from conflict.[74] Prioritization is required because multiple competing demands on the ground cannot be met with the available time and resources.

- *Focus priorities on:*

  - Sources of conflict and stability[75]
  - Implementation of a political settlement[76]
  - Provision of services that meet basic human needs.

## 5.4 Nesting

- *Short-term objectives should be nested in the longer-term goals.* An S&R mission restores peace to enable development. The millennium development goals embraced by member states of the United Nations *are* the longer-term goals.[77] This requires a conscious nesting of the short-term stabilization imperative within the longer-term development objective. For example, the short-term need to establish order may require the involvement of international police. This should be nested in longer-term objectives to have routine law enforcement conducted by local, not international, police.[78]

- *Focus on rapid results, while understanding the impact on longer-term goals.* Speedy commencement of assistance and the ability to deliver quick, observable, high-impact results establishes credibility.[79] This still requires understanding the impact of urgent actions on the long-term.

- *Do not neglect the medium term.* The rapid pace of S&R missions often gives way to a slower, more sluggish, middle-age period, where interest and resources decline. This widespread phenomenon risks a return to violent conflict. Focus on the importance of a medium-term framework for distributing international resources.[80]

## 5.5 Flexibility of Sequencing and Timing

- *Sequencing and timing or phasing are dependent on context.* Any plan based on sequenced or timed and phased actions is a notional understanding of how events might proceed. In reality, local conditions are likely to change during the duration of each phase. They may even cause progress to revert from one phase to the other or to jump across phases:

---

74. Dobbins/Jones/Crane/Cole DeGrasse, Beginner's Guide, 2007.
75. S/CRS, "Principles," 2008.
76. UNDP/USAID, "First Steps," 2007. UK Stabilisation Unit, "UK Approach to Stabilisation," 2008.
77. United Nations Development Programme, "Millennium Development Goals," 2000, www.undp.org/mdg/basics.shtml (accessed June 18, 2009).
78. United Nations Department of Economic and Social Affairs, *Conflict Prevention, Peace Building and Development*, 2004.
79. Japan International Cooperation Agency, *Handbook for Transition Assistance*, 2006. S/CRS, *Principles*, 2008. United States Agency for International Development, Fragile States Strategy, 2005.
80. Ghani/Lockhart, *Fixing Failed States*, 2008.

Post-conflict environments are characterized by high volatility. Needs may change (new population displacements, for example); priorities may change (subsequent realization that a marginalized region or population segment poses a risk for peace building if their needs are not addressed); national counterparts may change, with implications for their views on recovery priorities; reforms or capacity building may prove to be more difficult than originally envisaged, necessitating changes in timing; the composition of the donor or international support group may change; and costs of reconstruction may change, due to security conditions or changes in possible sources of supply of materials or services.

Source: UNDP/WB, "DRAFT Joint Guidance Note on Integrated Recovery Planning." 2007.

- *Locally led input on sequencing and timing actions is essential for success.* Legitimate national and local representatives of the host nation should participate fully in shaping sequencing and timing of actions. The UN Peacebuilding Commission and its Peacebuilding Support Office have pioneered this consultative path with groundbreaking work in Burundi and Sierra Leone.[81] Knowing if or when to strengthen substate, suprastate, or nonstate institutions; avoiding an often inappropriate replication of Western institutional models; and avoiding recreating institutions that caused conflict in the first place requires local input and deep consultation.[82]

- *The opening days and months of an S&R mission provide an opening to seize the initiative.* The arrival of peacekeepers provides an opportunity to maximize initial efforts and solidify a fragile peace. Relief among the local population tends to be widespread and resistance among spoilers is often unorganized.[83]

- *Learn and adapt.* The successful transition from conflict to sustainable peace involves managing change through constant learning and calibration of strategies to particular country circumstances that are always in flux.[84]

- *Forget linearity.* Planned or logical sequencing will almost always be disrupted by the unpredictability of activities on the ground. Asynchronicity is the rule, not the exception.[85] Since S&R missions do not unfold with any linear logical process, the need for a strategic vision and direction towards that vision is crucial.[86]

## 5.6 Measurements of Progress

- *A system of metrics translates lofty goals into measurable outcomes.* The best goals can be undermined by inadequate initial analysis that does not identify the drivers and mitigators of conflict.[87] A system of metrics should not measure success against inputs, but rather outcomes. For example, rather than measuring progress

81. Burundi and the United Nations, *Strategic Framework for Peacebuilding in Burundi*, 2007.
82. Charles Call, *Institutionalizing Peace: A Review of Post-Conflict Peacebuilding, Concepts and Issues for DPA* (New York: United Nations, 2005).
83. Dobbins/Jones/Crane/Cole DeGrasse, *Beginner's Guide*, 2007.
84. S/CRS, *Principles*, 2008.
85. Guttieri/Piombo, *Interim Governments*, 2007.
86. UK Stabilisation Unit, "UK Approach to Stabilisation," 2008.
87. Craig Cohen, *Measuring Progress in Stabilization and Reconstruction* (Washington, D.C.: U.S. Institute of Peace, 2006).

by the number of police trained, the system should assess whether there has been a reduction in crime.

- *Measuring progress allows continuous adjustments to strategy and implementation to improve success.* Ongoing measurements should contribute to adjusting the goals, plans, and activities of all actors. Measuring Progress in Conflict Environments[88] (MPICE) is a tool that is organized according to the five end states presented in this manual and offers a means to assess whether conflict drivers have been diminished and whether host nation institutions can maintain stability without significant international assistance.

---

88. Michael Dziedzic, Barbara Sotirin, and John Agoglia, eds., *Measuring Progress in Conflict Environments (MPICE)—A Metrics Framework for Assessing Conflict Transformation and Stabilization,* Defense Technical Information Catalog, 2008.

# END STATES

## SAFE AND SECURE ENVIRONMENT
## RULE OF LAW
## STABLE GOVERNANCE
## SUSTAINABLE ECONOMY
## SOCIAL WELL-BEING

# Section 6

# Safe and Secure Environment

## Cessation of Large-Scale Violence
- Separation of Warring Parties
- Enduring Cease-fire/Peace Agreement
- Management of Spoilers
- Intelligence

## Public Order
- A Comprehensive System
- Interim Law Enforcement
- Interim Judiciary
- Humane Detention and Imprisonment

## SAFE AND SECURE ENVIRONMENT
Ability of the people to conduct their daily lives without fear of systematic or large-scale violence.

## Territorial Security
- Freedom of Movement
- Border Security

## Legitimate State Monopoly Over the Means of Violence
- Disarmament and Demobilization
- Reintegration of Ex-Combatants
- Security Sector Reform

## Physical Security
- Security of Vulnerable Populations
- Protection of Infrastructure
- Protection of War Crimes Evidence

# Safe and Secure Environment
*Ability of the people to conduct their daily lives without fear of systematic or large-scale violence.*

## 6.0 What is a safe and secure environment?

A safe and secure environment is one in which the population has the freedom to pursue daily activities without fear of politically motivated, persistent, or large-scale violence. Such an environment is characterized by an end to large-scale fighting; an adequate level of public order; the subordination of accountable security forces to legitimate state authority; the protection of key individuals, communities, sites, and infrastructure; and the freedom for people and goods to move about the country and across borders without fear of undue harm to life and limb.

## 6.1 What are the key security challenges in societies emerging from conflict?

The most immediate concern is personal physical safety from violence. Even after the bulk of fighting is over, physical insecurity is often pervasive throughout society from politically motivated violence, rampant gunfire, retaliation by former enemies, gender-based violence, landmines, and emerging armed criminal elements. State authority and security institutions, meanwhile, are likely to be politicized, part of the problem, and severely impaired or nonexistent, creating a security vacuum that insurgents, terrorists, extremists, or criminals will seek to fill. The security threats in transitional environments call for a dual capability to subdue large-scale threats to the peace process while also maintaining public order.

## 6.2 Why is a safe and secure environment a necessary end state?

A country's recovery from violent conflict depends first and foremost on the establishment of security.[89] Without security, parties to the conflict will not lay down their arms, and a country will never progress beyond a state of siege and will remain stagnant in its economic, political, and social development. People will refrain from resuming normal activities that are fundamental to a healthy and vibrant society, like sending their children to school, opening shops for business, or traveling to the market. Civilian agencies will be unable to begin laying the critical foundation for promoting the rule of law, good governance, economic growth, and healthy social development.

## 6.3 What are the necessary conditions to achieve a safe and secure environment?

- *Cessation of Large-Scale Violence* is a condition in which large-scale armed conflict has come to a halt, warring parties are separated and monitored, a peace agreement or cease-fire has been implemented, and violent spoilers are managed.

---

89. In this section, the term "security" is used within the context of S&R missions in a society that is just emerging from conflict. It refers primarily to physical safety, although broader definitions of security exist within the development community for "human security." See Appendix E.

- *Public Order* is a condition in which laws are enforced equitably; the lives, property, freedoms, and rights of individuals are protected; criminal and politically motivated violence has been reduced to a minimum; and criminal elements (from looters and rioters to leaders of organized crime networks) are pursued, arrested, and detained.
- *Legitimate State Monopoly Over the Means of Violence* is a condition in which major illegal armed groups have been identified, disarmed and demobilized; the defense and police forces have been vetted and retrained; and national security forces operate lawfully under a legitimate governing authority.
- *Physical Security* is a condition in which political leaders, ex-combatants, and the general population are free of fear from grave threats to physical safety; refugees and internally displaced persons can return home without fear of retributive violence; women and children are protected from undue violence; and key historical or cultural sites and critical infrastructure are protected from attack.
- *Territorial Security* is a condition in which people and goods can freely move throughout the country and across borders without fear of harm to life and limb; the country is protected from invasion; and borders are reasonably well-secured from infiltration by insurgent or terrorist elements and illicit trafficking of arms, narcotics, and humans.

## 6.4 General Guidance for a Safe and Secure Environment

*6.4.1 Build host nation ownership and capacity.* While international actors may have to do the bulk of heavy lifting in the initial phases, the importance of using host nation resources, whenever possible and appropriate, is twofold: (1) to build host nation capacity and (2) to promote state legitimacy through programs that are internally promulgated rather than externally imposed.[90] This is difficult in countries emerging from violent conflict and may only be possible after essential reforms have been implemented. Local forces are often poorly trained, notorious for human rights abuses or are linked to criminal enterprises.

*6.4.2 Act only with an understanding of the local context.* Societies emerging from conflict are bewilderingly complex and can differ vastly from one another. Understanding the unique forces at play helps create an effective security strategy. These include, but are not limited to, the following:

- Who are the primary actors in the conflict and what drives them?
- To what extent will their interests be satisfied or undermined by a successful peace process?
- What are their interests, relationships, capabilities, resources, agendas, incentives, and resources?
- What are the motives driving the conflict (economic, cultural, political, ethnic, religious, institutional)?
- What capacity do host nation institutions and actors have in performing critical security functions, restoring basic services, and implementing other emergency phase activities?
- What role do host nation institutions and actors play in managing or exacerbating conflict?

---

90. UK Stabilisation Unit, *UK Approach to Stabilisation*, 2008.

- What are host nation perceptions of security? How do host nation actors measure security?[91] Is the military or police a symbol of corruption and abuse?

**6.4.3 Prioritize to stabilize.**[92] The fundamental goal of a stabilization and reconstruction mission is to prevent a relapse of large-scale armed conflict. While interim decisions may not necessarily be ideal or most efficient, it is important to aim for what is "good enough" to maintain a fragile peace. Security priorities include promoting a political settlement, neutralizing hostile groups, providing basic protection for vulnerable populations and individuals, and securing critical sites and evidence of mass atrocities.[93] Maintaining realistic expectations is essential for success.

**6.4.4 Use a conflict lens.** S&R missions should not be development as usual. All actions must be weighed against their impact on the political situation. Many actions have the potential to affect the balance of power among rival groups and become politically explosive, such as investigating war crimes and human rights violations, choosing where to locate an army base, releasing political prisoners, naming interim officials, deciding which mosque or site to protect, or helping refugees and internally displaced persons (IDPs) return to minority areas.[94] Always be sure to assess and understand political ramifications of every action.

**6.4.5 Recognize interdependence.** Security is often considered a precondition for long-term development because without it, reconstruction activities cannot begin or be sustained and people cannot resume their daily activities. Conversely, progress made in the social, economic, and governance arenas also boosts security by giving people a stake in the peace process and providing them a viable alternative to violence. All of these pieces are interdependent. One cannot happen without the other.

# 6.5 Necessary Condition: Cessation of Large-Scale Violence

### 6.5.1 What is the cessation of large-scale violence? Why is it a necessary condition?
The cessation of politically motivated and large-scale violence is a condition in which major hostilities among warring parties have come to a halt. Armed groups responsible for the conflict have for the most part been defeated[95] or physically separated from one another, while faction leaders and extremists are separated from their forces and supporters. In some cases, a cease-fire agreement temporarily sets the terms for a halt in violence. Ending the fighting is the first step in creating lasting peace. Without this, civilians cannot begin their work to restore institutions and services, nor can the host nation population resume normal life. Stopping the violence creates the necessary time

---

91. United Kingdom Stabilisation Unit, "Helping Countries Recover," 2008. Hereafter: UK Stabilisation Unit, "Helping Countries Recover," 2008.

92. Ibid.

93. UK Stabilisation Unit, *UK Approach to Stabilisation*, 2008.

94. Jack Covey, Michael J. Dziedzic and Leonard Hawley, eds., *The Quest for Viable Peace: International Intervention and Strategies for Conflict Transformation* (Washington, D.C.: United States Institute of Peace Press, 2005). Hereafter: Covey/Dziedzic/Hawley, *Quest for Viable Peace*, 2005.

95. Michael Dziedzic, Barbara Sotirin, and John Agoglia, eds. *Measuring Progress in Conflict Environments (MPICE)—A Metrics Framework for Assessing Conflict Transformation and Stabilization*, Defense Technical Information Catalog, 2008. Hereafter: Dziedzic/Sotirin/Agoglia, *Measuring Progress in Conflict Environments*, 2008.

and space for a peace agreement to be reached and/or implemented, allowing the warring parties to continue their competitive pursuits in nonviolent ways and within a framework of rules.

## 6.5.2 Guidance for the Cessation of Large-Scale Violence

### 6.5.3 Approach: Separation of Warring Parties
Separating warring parties involves establishing distinct areas of control that keeps factions apart from one another and allows peacekeeping forces to monitor their actions. This limits further suffering among civilians, asserts control over fighting forces, and builds confidence nationwide in the prospects for peace. The separation of combatants must be followed up with observation and monitoring of a cease-fire.

**6.5.4 Move quickly to separate warring parties and stop the violence.** In the early moments of an intervention, the population will likely be shocked and relieved at the sight of peacekeeping troops, while resistance from armed groups will be weak.[96] Establishing control at this stage and bringing large-scale fighting to a halt demonstrates authority and assertiveness of the mission.[97] The role of international forces in ensuring stability is vital early on until local forces have become effective and accountable enough to provide security.

**6.5.5 Separate forces to create time and space for the peace process.** Separation of forces can tamp down tensions so that negotiations and implementation of a peace process can proceed. The nature of the conflict will determine how the forces are separated. In interstate conflicts, separation typically involves interpositioning of peacekeepers to create a buffer zone between the two sides. In internal conflicts where combatants and civilians are intermingled, areas or zones of separation are established on the territory as a neutral space or no-man's land between the parties. Civilians in this neutral space may need to be protected.[98] Zone boundaries and entry points must be agreed upon by all parties, clearly marked, and physically identifiable on a map or formal record provided to all parties.[99]

**6.5.6 Apply principles of restraint, impartiality, and consent when dealing with parties to the conflict.**[100] Because peace is fragile at this stage, be sure to carefully assess the impact of all actions on reigniting conflict. Exercising principles of restraint, impartiality and consent is key.

- *Restraint.* Exercising restraint in the use of force against any host nation actor or group of actors is especially important early on when public scrutiny and skepticism are high. A single incident of excessive force could undermine legitimacy by alienating certain groups or enabling spoilers to rally the population against the intervention. Having decisive lethal capacities in these

---

96. U.S. Army, *FM 3-07*, 2008.
97. UK Stabilisation Unit, "UK Approach to Stabilisation," 2008.
98. JICA, *Handbook for Transition Assistance*, 2006.
99. United Kingdom Ministry of Defence, *Joint Warfighting Publication 3-50: The Military Contribution to Peace Support Operations*, 2006. Hereafter: UK MOD, *JWP 3-50*, 2006.
100. United Nations Department of Peacekeeping Operations, *Handbook on United Nations Multidimensional Peacekeeping Operations*, 2003. Hereafter: UNDPKO, Handbook on UN Peacekeeping Operations, 2003. UNDPKO, *Principles and Guidelines*, 2008.

environments is a must, but it is equally important that they be combined with non-lethal capabilities for responding to civil disturbances and managing spoilers.[101]

- *Impartiality.* In dealing with warring parties, avoid actions that could be construed as being partial to an ethnic or religious group. Be sure to communicate the reasons behind certain actions and enforce compliance between groups with consistency against the standards of the peace agreement.

- *Consent.* There are various dimensions of consent for the presence of the mission, including consent of the host nation population, the host nation government, neighboring countries, and broader international community. While political complexities will likely make it impossible to achieve full consent on all levels, maximizing the consent of all parties is critical for the legitimacy of the intervention. On the other hand, failure to deal effectively with politically motivated violence will erode consent among those suffering from such violence.

### 6.5.7 Approach: Enduring Cease-fire/Peace Agreement
The peace agreement is a contract among warring parties that symbolizes the willingness to end violence and paves the way for a longer-term political settlement. At times, this process includes or follows a cease-fire agreement that temporarily halts fighting for the purpose of negotiating the settlement. The ultimate goal is to transform the competitive pursuit of political and economic power from violent to peaceful means.[102] All actions in these operations must be tailored to support or advance the peace process.

### 6.5.8 Understand that stopping armed conflict requires political, not military, solutions.
Imposed stability from an international force may be enough to stop the fighting, but it does not ensure that peace will last. A robust political settlement is the cornerstone for sustainable peace that enables warring parties to share power within an agreed framework and resolve their political differences in peaceful ways.[103] Whereas traditional UN peacekeeping deployments were almost entirely military in nature, mission mandates today often include a direct role for a force commander to help facilitate a political solution to the conflict, by providing good offices or promoting dialogue and reconciliation. Additional aspects of the political process are discussed in Section 3.4.

### 6.5.9 Transform the conflict.
Reaching a viable political settlement requires convincing faction leaders that their interests are better served through peaceful rather than violent means. Conflict transformation involves a strategy of "diminishing the means and motivations"[104] for violence while creating ways for pursuing political and economic goals in nonviolent ways. Engineering such an outcome requires thoroughly understanding the conflict players and their motivations and confronting the forces that prosper from the use of violence. Develop strategies to persuade combatants that there are prospects for a better life and incentives for moving forward with a political settlement, rather than fixating themselves on the bitter grudges of the past.[105] There

---

101. U.S. Army, *FM 3-07,* 2008.
102. UK Stabilisation Unit, *UK Approach to Stabilisation,* 2008.
103. UK Stabilisation Unit, "Helping Countries Recover," 2008.
104. Covey/Dziedzic/Hawley, *Quest for a Viable Peace,* 2005.
105. Ibid.

are a number of approaches for doing this, including transforming armed movements into political parties that contend for seats in a national parliament or for executive powers.[106] Conflict transformation is also addressed in Section 3.8.

### 6.5.10 Approach: Management of Spoilers

A peace agreement rarely satisfies the interests of all parties. They often involve political concessions, ambiguous treatment of core issues in the dispute, an exchange of promises that may not be kept, or a loss of control for those whom the conflict has served well. As a result, there often remain powerful incentives for spoilers—paramilitaries, warlords, and extremists—to continue conflict-era activities, feed lawlessness, and maintain illicit or parallel power structures.[107] Spoilers perceive the peace process as contradicting their own interests and try to undermine it through violence and intimidation.[108] Spoilers are difficult to categorize but are generally defined by their motivations, capability and activities. They can include organized groups, loose confederations of people with related goals, or individuals working alone.[109] Spoilers are also addressed in Sections 7.6.5, 7.6.7, 8.7, and 9.6.

***6.5.11 Anticipate obstructionists and understand their motivations.*** Understanding the characteristics of spoilers can shape the strategies used to influence them, whether it's bringing them into the process or marginalizing them from it. Ask the following questions to better understand the nature of the spoilers:[110]

- Is the group willing to compromise and share power?
- Can the group be considered a "total" spoiler, unwilling to consider limitations on its power?
- Is the group greedy—does the group's demands grow with the prospect of appeasement?
- Does the group enjoy the support of a neighboring state or have access to resources?
- Which individuals or communities, if any, have influence over the spoilers?

***6.5.12 Create a plan for managing the spoilers.*** There are two primary approaches for dealing with spoilers in the peace process:

- *Inclusion*—Inclusion involves persuading spoilers that their aims can be met peacefully through compromise and the peace process. This approach may be the best option for "limited spoilers," those whose pursuits are limited and who are willing to accept political compromise. Other methods of inclusion are the reintegration of ex-combatants into society and transforming armed groups into political parties.[111]

---

106. JICA, *Handbook for Transition Assistance*, 2006.

107. Covey/Dziedzic/Hawley, *Quest for a Viable Peace*, 2005.

108. Stephen Stedman, "Spoiler Problems in Peace Processes," *International Security*, vol. 22, no. 2 (Fall 1997). Hereafter: Stedman, "Spoiler Problems," 1997.

109. North Atlantic Treaty Organization, *Allied Joint Publication 3.4.1: Allied Joint Doctrine for Peace Support Operations*, 2007. Hereafter: NATO, *AJP 3.4.1*, 2007.

110. UK Stabilisation Unit, "UK Approach to Stabilisation," 2008.

111. JICA, *Handbook for Transition Assistance*, 2006.

- *Exclusion*—Exclusion entails arresting spoilers, shutting them out of the peace process or marginalizing them to limit their influence on the peace process. This can be done in many ways, including by military force or the transitional justice process. Exclusion is appropriate for "total" spoilers—those see the world in all-or-nothing terms, refuse to renounce violence and are unlikely to compromise in achieving their goals. Total spoilers are often motivated by religious or political idealism. The costs of excluding spoilers include greater potential for retaliation and violence, but it may be necessary for zealots whose aims cannot be met through compromise. Exclusion must be used with caution to avoid inciting tensions.[112]

These approaches, however, are increasingly difficult to apply in complex conflict environments, as many actors may change their positions and demands from one day to the next. Strategies will have to be highly adaptive and dynamic and seek to transform spoilers, through subordination to legitimate government authority, marginalization, defeat, or reintegration.

**6.5.13 Maintain the primacy of the peace process.** The "primacy of the peace process" means the mission should support those who support the peace process while actively opposing spoilers who obstruct it.[113] This forces people to focus on supporting political processes, not personalities or factions.[114] All actions, particularly responses to incidents, should be balanced against the requirements of the political process.[115] Using the peace process as a standard by which all parties are dealt with allows peacekeepers to respond impartially across the board in a legitimate way. Aspects of the political process are also addressed in Section 3.4.

**6.5.14 Adopt an "assertive position" with regard to peace agreement enforcement.** Threats to the peace process can exist in many forms: illicit power structures, organized crime networks, rogue intelligence organizations, warlords, militants, fanatical religious groups, or terrorists. Many of these groups have no regard for international laws of war. To assert control over these threats, peacekeeping forces should have the mandated authority to use "all necessary means" to enforce the peace process and show spoilers their aims cannot be achieved outside of that process.[116] They must be prepared to investigate violations of the peace agreement and observe refugee movements and potential points of tension. If a breach is witnessed, authorities should swiftly secure evidence, question witnesses before they are coached on what to say, and deal with perpetrators within the legal constraints of the mission. This often involves arrest and detainment of violators to be handed over to civil legal authority. When dealing with members of warring parties, actions should seek to contain rather than exacerbate tensions. Ultimately, peacekeepers must be impartial in dealing with the parties, but not neutral in responding to behavior that obstructs the peace process. *See Trade-off: Section 6.10.3, Applying force vs. maintaining mission legitimacy.*

---

112. UK Stabilisation Unit, "Helping Countries Recover," 2008; Stedman, "Spoiler Problems," 1997; NATO, "AJP 3.4.1," 2007.
113. Covey/Dziedzic/Hawley, *Quest for a Viable Peace,* 2005.
114. UK Stabilisation Unit, "UK Approach to Stabilisation," 2008.
115. UK Stabilisation Unit, "Helping Countries Recover," 2008.
116. Covey/Dziedzic/Hawley, *Quest for a Viable Peace,* 2005.

### 6.5.15 Approach: Intelligence

Intelligence is not a dirty word. It is essential for security. Police need actionable information on politically motivated violence, crimes, and civil disturbances, which requires aggressive and continuous reconnaissance and surveillance. Knowledge allows the police to identify potential hot spots within communities before they ignite and gather information on hostile groups or individuals, terrain, weather, and even the performance of other local police officers. The gathering of intelligence must conform with human rights standards. *See Gap/Challenge: Section 6.11.2, Intelligence.*

**6.5.16 Remember that the population is the best resource for information.** Hiring professional and knowledgeable host nation counterparts, who can speak the language and discern cultural nuances, may be key to gathering necessary information. Other ways are to commission detailed studies on the local political economy and power structures or to build local intelligence institutions or information coordination mechanisms. Overall, a greater investment must be made upfront to acquire adequate knowledge about the country.[117] Police also gather intelligence by being present in the communities, building trust, and talking to people. Many humanitarian agencies also have deep knowledge of the situations because they often precede the arrival of peacekeeping forces. Reports, Web sites, and databases created by these organizations can provide rich insight into local situations.[118]

**6.5.17 Local intelligence is a must, but be very aware of sensitivities.** Mounting an effective operation against insurgents, militants, spoilers, and other threats requires accurate local intelligence. Intelligence collection should cover the geopolitical situation in the country; historical and cultural influences on the host nation population; and updated assessments on the attitudes, capabilities, intentions, and likely reactions of all relevant actors in a society. While open sources and strategic sources are critical, the richest source of information will be humans on the ground. Intelligence activities, however, can rouse extreme political sensitivities and jeopardize the safety of NGOs, intelligence sources, third-party individuals, international aid workers, commercial enterprises, and foreign governments supporting the operation. Specifically, intelligence-gathering activities must not hamper the neutrality of the International Committee of the Red Cross and its mandate to entertain contacts with non-state actors. Humanitarian principles are further addressed in Section 6.8.4.

**6.5.18 Given the sensitivities, be creative in acquiring critical information.** Innovative and safe ways to acquire information include public reports routinely published by human rights monitors or NGOs, cease-fire observers, patrol units, and other actors who interact with the host nation population.[119] Acquiring critical information can also be improved by providing the population with security, especially in situations involving active insurgencies. In these cases, populations often sit on the fence and are more likely to provide tips on insurgent bases or weapons caches if they feel safe enough to do so.

---

117. UK Stabilisation Unit, "Helping Countries Recover," 2008; Seth G. Jones, Jeremy M. Wilson, Andrew Rathmell, and K. Jack Riley, *Establishing Law and Order After Conflict* (Santa Monica, Calif.: RAND Corporation, 2005).

118. Dobbins/Jones/Crane/Cole DeGrasse, *Beginner's Guide,* 2007.

119. UK MOD, *JWP 3-50,* 2006.

*6.5.19 Coordinate military-police intelligence sharing.*[120] Police forces, as does the U.S. military, stand up centers to lawfully collect information and develop it into actionable intelligence. Whenever possible in S&R missions, these police and military intelligence centers should be colocated to maximize both efficiency and effectiveness of collection and analysis and to quickly share information.

*6.5.20 Develop the capacity to conduct intelligence-led operations against spoilers.* Intelligence-led operations target those who seek to oppose the peace process through violent and criminal means. Military and international police resources should be focused on collecting actionable information about the identity of the individuals responsible for extremist violence, their networks, and their vulnerabilities. An intelligence-led operation must contribute to the overall peace process and promote public confidence in the mission. There must be a proactive information campaign to achieve this as part of the overall plan for any such operation. The purposes of intelligence-led operations include the following:[121]

- *Disruption*: The operation may be triggered through the receipt of intelligence that indicates a specific activity has been planned. Thus the operation seeks to interdict the planned event.
- *Dislocation*: The operation may be designed to separate a particular individual from extremist or criminal activity by attacking links. It may also seek to undermine popular support for extremist or criminal groups. Deterrence may follow dislocation.
- *Decisive Action*: The desired result is a successful criminal prosecution and thus sufficient evidence must be gained from the operation to achieve conviction.

## 6.6 Necessary Condition: Public Order

Public order is a necessary condition of both Safe and Secure Environment and Rule of Law. It is described fully in Section 7.6 Necessary Condition: Public Order.

## 6.7 Necessary Condition: Legitimate State Monopoly Over The Means of Violence

### 6.7.1 What is legitimate state monopoly over the means of violence? Why is it a necessary condition?

The legitimate state monopoly over the means of violence is a condition in which a state's security forces operate lawfully under a legitimate civilian authority, where actors conduct themselves in accordance with democratic norms and principles of good governance.[122] This condition exists when armed groups from the conflict are disarmed, demobilized, and reintegrated into society, and a military and police force is vetted, retrained, and monitored on human rights principles. Realizing this condition usually entails two major processes: disarming, demobilizing, and reintegrating armed groups

---

120. Dobbins/Jones/Crane/Cole DeGrasse, *Beginner's Guide,* 2007.
121. Col. Hugh Boscawen, Col. Mike Redmond, and Bertram Welsing, "Intelligence to Evidence Operations," presented at the UNDPKO Command Development Seminar, Center of Excellence for Stability Police Units (COESPU), 2006.
122. Geneva Centre for the Democratic Control of Armed Forces, *Shaping a Security Governance Agenda in Post Conflict Peacebuilding,* 2005.

(known as DDR), and reforming the security sector (known as SSR)—the system of actors and institutions that provide for the security of the state and the host nation population. Both processes are extremely time- and resource-intensive ones that are always challenging and politically volatile. In war-torn countries where security and security oversight institutions are weak, citizens become vulnerable to intimidation; arbitrary arrest; serious criminal activity; and general fear of violence, oppression, and injustice. These threats disproportionately affect vulnerable and marginalized populations, including women and children. A core responsibility of the state to its citizens is protection against external and internal threats.[123] Accountable and effective state security institutions are necessary for these functions.

### 6.7.2 Guidance for the Legitimate Monopoly Over the Means of Violence

### 6.7.3 Approach: Disarmament and Demobilization (DD)
Dealing with combatants is a first-order step in moving to peace. Disarming and demobilizing ex-combatants is a highly visible process that can increase public confidence in the peace process. Disarmament involves collecting and destroying weapons; demobilization involves dismantling military units and transitioning combatants to civilian life through orientation programs and transportation to their communities. Demobilization involves registering individuals and monitoring them in assembly camps while they await reintegration. Reintegration is typically grouped together with disarmament and demobilization and benefits from similar guidance points, but it is separated here to emphasize the unique challenges of successfully reinserting ex-combatants into society.

### 6.7.4 Start DD planning early. Strategic planning for disarmament and demobilization should commence before a peace process begins or at least while negotiations are still ongoing.[124] This ensures that details of the DD program are entrenched in the peace agreement. Be careful not to rush the start of disarmament until sufficient peacekeeping troops are in place for security. The strategic planning period should address the role of the host nation government vice international agencies; define roles for implementing and monitoring the disarmament and demobilization program; identify rebel groups, government forces, and their weapons; determine eligibility for the DD program; and build confidence, buy-in, and host nation ownership. The role of women in DD programs has proven to be critical to their success, so be sure they are included.[125] Build in flexible and realistic timetables to account for implementation delays and to build public confidence.

### 6.7.5 Tailor the DD strategy to local conditions.[126] A great deal of information is needed to properly tailor a disarmament and demobilization program to the situation on the ground. Assess the nature of the conflict, the set of targeted clients, and the overall

23. UNDP/USAID, "First Steps," 2007.

24. Deutsche Gesellschaft für Technische Zusammenarbeit GmbH (GTZ), *DDR: A Practical Field and Classroom Guide*, 2004. Hereafter: GTZ, *Practical Guide*, 2004. European Union, *EU Concept for Support to Disarmament, Demobilisation and Reintegration*, 2006. Hereafter: EU, *Concept for DDR*, 2006.

25. Camille Pampell Conaway, *The Role of Women in Stabilization and Reconstruction* (Washington, D.C.: U.S. Institute of Peace, 2006). Hereafter: Conaway, *The Role of Women*, 2006.

26. United States Department of State, Office of the Coordinator for Reconstruction and Stabilization, *Lessons-Learned: Demobilization, Disarmament, and Reintegration (DDR) in Stabilization and Reconstruction Operations*, 2006.

power balance among warring parties. For the disarmament phase, peacekeepers should collect information on the number, types, and locations of weapons used during the conflict, along with storage depot sites and stockpiles that exist throughout the country. In devising a demobilization program, be sure to profile combatant demographics, paying special attention to vulnerable groups, such as women and children.

*6.7.6 Include details of disarmament and demobilization in the peace agreement.* Details of the program must be entrenched within the peace agreement[127] and broader peace-building strategies to minimize inconsistency in the implementation of disarmament and demobilization and the training of forces carrying out disarmament. In particular, the peace agreement should specify details where possible, such as when a cease-fire is to come into effect; flexible target dates and benchmarks for progress; the types of weapons and ammunition being collected and modes of their disposal; and the institutions that will implement the DDR and SSR programs. Participants in the process can include formal national security forces, paramilitary units, intelligence operatives, private militias, or other armed groups, as well as non-combatants who supported those groups.

*6.7.7 Provide credible security guarantees to build confidence in disarmament.*[128] The provision of credible security guarantees helps ensure that disarmament and demobilization participants have the confidence to give up their weapons. The peacekeeping force must have the capacity to provide this security at all phases of the program, particularly at demobilization camps where many ex-combatants gather while waiting to be reintegrated into society. This also means paying close attention to the balance of power among factions throughout the process. International support can lend credibility to these efforts, by overseeing disarmament and demobilization implementation or participating in a national oversight commission to ensure that disarmament rates among rivals are comparable.[129] This support should also ensure that disarmament violations are investigated, confronted, and corrected.

*6.7.8 Maximize host nation ownership in the disarmament and demobilization strategy.* Ownership requires not just the buy-in of the host nation government, but the participation of the community and civil society, and the political will of the parties.[130] Ownership may be difficult to achieve in the immediate aftermath of a conflict because capacity is low. In the transition, a robust partnership between host nation and international actors is essential, where host nation actors provide the drive and international actors provide the necessary technical capacity. International actors should maintain active consultation with host nation actors to maximize ownership.

*6.7.9 Inform the population to build popular support.* A strong public information and education campaign that boosts transparency and accountability is essential to a successful disarmament and demobilization campaign.[131] Sensitizing the population to the objectives of the program will build confidence for the effort and demonstrate the

---

127. EU, *Concept for DDR*, 2006.
128. United Nations DDR Resource Centre, *Integrated Disarmament, Demobilization and Reintegration Standard*, 2006. Hereafter: UN DDR, *Integrated DDR*, 2006. Covey/Dziedzic/Hawley, *Quest for a Viable Peace*, 2005.
129. Dobbins/Jones/Crane/Cole DeGrasse, *Beginner's Guide*, 2007.
130. GTZ, *Practical Guide*, 2004; UN, *Integrated DDR*, 2006.
131. UN, *Integrated DDR*, 2006.

importance of accepting ex-combatants into communities to give them a chance at an alternative life. The information campaign should also inform combatants of their rights and obligations in the process, details on disarmament and cantonment sites, as well as the benefits of participation.

*6.7.10 Aim for inclusivity of all warring parties.* Disarmament and demobilization programs are most successful when *all* parties to the conflict demonstrate a desire to abide by the terms of and participate in the broader peace process. In turn, the program must include and treat all warring parties equitably, regardless of gender, race, class, or political positions.[132] The rate of disarmament among different warring parties should be comparable to avoid a sudden change in the balance of military power.

*6.7.11 Include affected nontraditional combatants.* The disarmament and demobilization program must carefully consider vulnerable groups within the ex-combatant community, such as female and child soldiers, disabled and chronically ill individuals, as well as the families of combatants whose livelihoods may have been derived from militias.[133] Many of these individuals may not have carried guns but were involved in the logistics of the conflict. Programs should also be "gender-aware" (both male and female), which includes having a clear understanding of gender relations in the country, an understanding of masculinities and patterns of male violence, as well as female-specific interventions to ensure women have the same access to disarmament and demobilization benefits as do men.

*6.7.12 Ensure accountability to human rights standards through identification.*[134] Registration and identification of ex-combatants can ensure that the bad guys are not inadvertently reintegrated into state security forces and are prevented from sabotaging or subverting the peace process. Identification can also encourage participation in representative government, aid in resolving property disputes, and be used to validate professional credentials. Creating an identification program can involve securing documents on personal information, including identification cards, land titles, court records, professional certificates, voter registration, birth certificates, and driving licenses.

*6.7.13 Ensure that DD is civilian-led, with technical input and operational support from international forces.* Disarmament and demobilization is largely a civilian effort, though the military has a critical role in the methodology for disarmament and ensuring security during this process. Overall, DD requires high levels of coordination between civilians and the military. The military has a big role in disarmament; military and civilians assist in demobilization, while civilians are primarily involved in the reintegration phase of the conventional DDR program.[135]

*6.7.14 Approach: Reintegration of Ex-Combatants*
Reintegration is a social and economic process in which ex-combatants return to community life and engage in alternative livelihoods to violence.[136] Integrating ex-combatants into civilian life gives ex-combatants a stake in the peace and reduces the likelihood that they

---

132. Ibid.
133. EU, *Concept for DDR*, 2006. GTZ, *Practical Guide*, 2004. UN, *Integrated DDR*, 2006.
134. GTZ, *Practical Guide*, 2004. UN, *Integrated DDR*, 2006.
135. JICA, "Handbook for Transition Assistance," 2006.
136. United Nations Secretary-General, "Note to the General Assembly," A/C.5/59/31, 2005.

will turn to criminal activity or join insurgent groups to support themselves if they cannot find gainful employment. Reintegration activities include creating microenterprises, providing education and training, and preparing communities to receive ex-combatants.[137] Reintegration is attached to the DDR process, but in reality it requires the attention, resources, and expertise of a very specific set of social and economic actors. It is a big gap for peacebuilders. Economic aspects of reintegration are further discussed in Section 9.6.17. Education for demobilized soldiers is addressed in Section 10.6.12.

**6.7.15 Prepare for reintegration to be the most sensitive and difficult phase of DDR.** The reintegration of former combatants is the most politically sensitive element of the conventional DDR program and thus presents a more complex challenge than either disarmament or demobilization. While DD processes are time-bound and quantifiable, reintegration is much less discrete, making it harder to implement, monitor, and measure for success. Successful reintegration requires deep understanding of the social and economic needs of the combatants, as wielding weapons may have become a major part of their identity or livelihood. Reintegration also requires careful treatment of psychosocial impacts for child soldiers or women and girls who were abused during violent conflict.[138] Another reintegration challenge involves preparing and convincing host communities to accept ex-combatants into their neighborhoods. In particular, consider the risk of displacing women who may have assumed head-of-household responsibilities during the conflict.[139]
*See Gap/Challenge: Section 6.11.5, Reintegration of ex-combatants.*

**6.7.16 Avoid making ex-combatants a privileged class by integrating them into broader recovery strategies aimed at all conflict-affected populations.** While ex-combatants may need special attention to prevent them from destabilizing the peace, paying exclusive attention to them risks generating resentment from the broader population. Other groups also requiring substantial social and economic support include refugees, IDPs, women, and children who were victims of the conflict. Security should be balanced with equity. As much as possible, integrate strategies for ex-combatants with broader strategies addressing resettlement and rehabilitation for displaced populations, reconciliation efforts, rule of law, and governance.[140] Doing so will also help to prevent ex-combatants from becoming stigmatized or isolated from the rest of the community.

**6.7.17 Sustain international support for the reintegration process.**[141] International actors often show great enthusiasm for disarmament and demobilization, and they fund these programs based on peacekeeping assessments in UN missions. But their commitment to reintegration programs may be less certain. Inadequacy of resources has frequently hampered reintegration efforts in the past.[142] Successful reintegration requires a prompt and sustained commitment of international financial and technical assistance for many years.

---

137. UN, "Integrated DDR," 2006.
138. UNDP/USAID, "First Steps," 2007.
139. Conaway, "The Role of Women," 2006.
140. UN, "Integrated DDR," 2006.
141. EU, "Concept for DDR," 2006.
142. Organisation for Economic Co-Operation and Development, *Economic Reconstruction in Post-Conflict Transitions: Lessons for the Democratic Republic of Congo,* 2003.

**6.7.18 Approach: Security Sector Reform**
Security sector reform is the set of policies, plans, programs, and activities that a government undertakes to improve the way it provides safety, security and justice.[143] Developing an integrated system of actors, institutions and oversight bodies is the only mechanism through which the government can provide security. All security forces must always be subordinate to and act at the direction of a legitimate civilian authority. This is challenging in societies emerging from conflict where the population may retain a deeply ingrained perception of security institutions as self-serving and dangerous as opposed to existing for the protection of the public.[144]
*See Gap/Challenge: Section 6.11.1, Security sector reform.*

**6.7.19 Ensure that reforms reflect the security needs of the host nation population.**[145] Reforms cannot be imposed from the outside and should reflect the needs and priorities of the population. The success of SSR principles, policies, laws, and structures depends heavily on consideration of unique local history, culture, legal framework, and institutions. Transform the culture of insecurity by supporting new institutions and forces that operate in accordance with democratic principles, the rule of law, and respect for human rights. Promote the participation of women in new ministries and security forces.[146] Building a police force should also be prioritized over the military, as internal threats are more likely to pose a greater threat to security than external threats.[147] Police are better equipped and trained to handle common threats to public order, such as arms trafficking and transnational organized crime.

**6.7.20 Strengthening security forces is not enough; promote good governance and legitimate civilian oversight to ensure long-term accountability.**[148] The focus for SSR has been skewed toward building new military and police forces. While important, more attention must be paid to strengthening civilian oversight mechanisms for accountability of those forces over the long term. Oversight should come from across the government, as well as civil society and the media. Legislative committees, for example, can call ministers and other military/intelligence leaders before them to account for proper use of public funds. When building training platforms and providing material assistance to security forces, also provide infrastructure, personnel, and administrative support for civilian oversight institutions. Good governance over the security sector is also discussed in Section 8.6.13.

**6.7.21 Prevent infiltration of security forces through robust vetting.** Police forces may comprise individuals who have committed human rights violations or who are corrupt. Lustration or vetting may be necessary. Vetting requires a great deal of time and resources. It typically begins with identification. For example, in the police, there are

143. U.S. Department of State, U.S. Department of Defense, and U.S. Agency for International Development, *Security Sector Reform*, 2008.
144. Geneva Centre for the Democratic Control of Armed Forces, *The Post-Conflict Security Sector*, 2006.
145. Organisation for Economic Co-Operation and Development, *Economic Reconstruction in Post-Conflict Transitions: Lessons for the Democratic Republic of Congo*, 2003.
146. Conaway, "The Role of Women," 2006.
147. OECD DAC, *SSR Handbook*, 2007. UNDP/USAID, "First Steps," 2007. Oakley/Dziedzic/Goldberg, *Policing the New World Disorder*, 2002.
148. Geneva Centre for the Democratic Control of Armed Forces, *Border Control Services and Security Sector Reform*, 2002; JICA, "Handbook for Transition Assistance," 2006; and U.S. Army, *FM 3-07*, 2008.

often no records to confirm whether someone was indeed on the police roster. Set up stringent recruiting criteria to eliminate incompetent or corrupt individuals. Develop effective monitoring and auditing mechanisms to maintain those standards.[149] Also keep in mind that widespread vetting and lustration early on can pose risks by eliminating the majority of human capital from the police forces. Balance this risk against the harm that may ensue if human rights violators are allowed to remain in the force and contravene rule of law standards. Recruit only individuals, not groups, to avoid allowing groups to consolidate control in a force that is still weak. Ensure that the force is representative of the population in terms of gender, ethnicity, religion, and language.[150] For a discussion of vetting the judiciary, see Section 7.6.18.

**6.7.22 Focus on public service ethos and competence when training security forces.** Instilling concepts of human rights and accountability will restore confidence in the security forces over the long term. Communicating these concepts to the population can also help build support for the security forces. Focus on competence through imparting technical knowledge and skills, including those for management, investigation, intelligence, search and seizure, and forensics. Also work closely with senior-level police, whose buy-in and political support will be critical to the success of reform and bringing about cultural change in the whole organization. Provide gender-sensitive training for forces with specific attention to the need to prevent and treat gender-based violence.[151]

**6.7.23 Support the improvement of police-community relations and police responsiveness.** Historic mistrust and lack of respect for the police makes people turn to other forms of justice. For the police to be seen as a force for good, community-police relations need to be improved. Relations can be fostered through community policing committees or consultative fora where the community has an opportunity to share their concerns with the police. Information gathered from the public about general public order problems or specific incidents can both have a preventative effect and aid police investigations. Consultations also help enhance the responsiveness of the police.[152] Other ways to enhance police responsiveness are to ensure there are more officers on foot or bicycle patrol, making them more accessible to the public, and to train police to courteously explain the reasons for their actions.

**6.7.24 Ensure coherence of strategy and effort among major actors.**[153] SSR is highly cooperative in nature and should involve the military, intergovernmental organizations, NGOs, multinational partners, civil society, media, and the host nation. The security sector comprises all actors who collectively provide security:[154]

- Core actors directly involved in protecting civilians and the state from violent harm (e.g., police and military forces and internal intelligence agencies)

---

149. UK Foreign & Commonwealth Office, *Peace Support Operations: Information and Guidance for UK Police Personnel,* 2007. Hereafter: UK FCO, *Police Personnel,* 2007.

150. David H. Bayley, *Changing the Guard: Developing Democratic Police Abroad* (Oxford: University Press Oxford, 2006). Hereafter: Bayley, *Changing the Guard,* 2006.

151. Conaway, "The Role of Women," 2006.

152. Bayley, *Changing the Guard,* 2006.

153. U.S. Army, *FM 3-07,* 2008.

154. Sean McFate, *Securing the Future: A Primer on Security Sector Reform in Conflict Countries* (Washington, D.C.: U.S. Institute of Peace, 2008).

- Institutions that govern these actors (e.g., ministries of interior, defense, and justice, and national security councils)
- Oversight bodies.

Reform of any of these elements must be conducted in tandem with other reform activities in the security sector. A weak justice system, for example, can undermine any benefits of policing by enabling organized crime, corruption, extrajudicial killings, and petty crime.[155] It can also lead to a militarized security or the use of forces outside of the appropriate human rights and justice frameworks.

*6.7.25 Promote the civil authority of the state; long-term stability depends on it.*[156] S&R missions are no longer dominated by traditional military tasks (e.g., interpositioning, supervising ceasefires, verifying peace agreement compliance). While the military is still crucial for containing hardcore militants, pursuing insurgents, interdicting arms supply chains, or confronting obstructionists to the peace process,[157] it should always act at the direction of the civilian authority to ensure support for the broader political strategy.

## 6.8 Necessary Condition: Physical Security

### 6.8.1 What is physical security? Why is it a necessary condition?

A safe and secure environment requires the physical security of civilians (host nation and international), critical infrastructure, public forums, and key historical or cultural sites. Under this condition, civilians are largely free from persistent fear of grave threats to physical safety, including national and host nation leaders, international aid workers, returnees, women, and children. Protecting people and critical places is vital to preventing a renewal in violence and keeping the peace process and delivery of services on track. Attacks on certain groups of civilians or assassinations of key leaders can invite retributive attacks from opposing parties, leading to escalation of large-scale hostilities. Similarly, attacks against key cultural or religious symbols can quickly reignite violent conflict. Violence against critical infrastructure can disrupt delivery of vital services and sow panic.

### 6.8.2 Guidance for Physical Security

*6.8.3 Approach: Security of Vulnerable Populations*

Vulnerable populations can include any individual or community of people that is particularly subject to imminent and persistent physical attack. This often includes disenfranchised groups, women, children, minorities, displaced people, elderly, people living with HIV/AIDS, as well as host nation leaders, judges, and aid workers, who may be targets of political violence. Protecting these groups is vital for preventing suffering and ensuring human rights while also strengthening confidence in peace in the eyes of the people, neighboring countries and the global community.[158]

---

155. Dobbins/Jones/Crane/Cole DeGrasse, *Beginner's Guide*, 2007.
156. UK Stabilisation Unit, "UK Approach to Stabilisation," 2008.
157. Ibid. UNDPKO "Principles and Guidelines," 2008. Covey/Dziedzic/Hawley, *Quest for a Viable Peace*, 2005.
158. U.S. Army, *FM 3-07*, 2008.

*6.8.4 Respect the boundaries of humanitarian space and understand humanitarian principles of independence, humanity, impartiality, and neutrality.*[159] Humanitarian organizations will operate with these core principles in mind, some more strictly than others. Those providing physical security must facilitate rapid and unimpeded passage of all relief consignments, equipment and personnel from impartial humanitarian agencies, including the International Committee of the Red Cross (ICRC). Recognizing the impartial domain of humanitarian assistance providers helps ensure the safety of those delivering the services and the effectiveness of that delivery. *Humanity* refers to the goal of alleviating human suffering in all circumstances, protecting life and health, and ensuring respect for the individual.[160] *Impartiality* refers to the principle that humanitarian assistance must be based on need alone, without regard to nationality, race, religion, class, or politics.[161] While the concept of *neutrality* is more widely disputed, many humanitarian organizations, including the ICRC, use it to mean it will not take sides in hostilities or engage in controversies involving politics, race, religion, or ideology.[162] *Independence* refers to the autonomy of humanitarian actors from the actions or policies of any government, so that they are able to adhere to these principles.[163] *See Gap/Challenge: Section 10.10.1, Protection of humanitarian space.*

*6.8.5 Ensure that the UN mandate includes the obligation to protect civilians under imminent threat of physical violence.* The protection of civilians from physical violence, including genocide, ethnic cleansing, war crimes, and crimes against humanity, is a vital function of S&R missions. Civilians and international workers are increasingly the direct targets in armed conflict and make up the bulk of casualties.[164] Require the protection of civilians under immediate threat of physical violence in the UN mandate,[165] along with wounded or sick combatants who no longer partake in the armed conflict. The most vulnerable groups are often refugees, IDPs, women, and children. When deciding to return to minority areas, refugees and IDPs care first and foremost about their personal security. Women also require unique attention, having often borne a disproportionate share of the consequences of violent conflict.[166]

*6.8.6 Protect vulnerable public officials.* Many public officials become targets for assassination by those who oppose the peace process. These include local political leaders,

---

159. Interaction, U.S. Department of Defense, U.S. Institute of Peace, *Guidelines for Relations Between U.S. Armed Forces and Nongovernmental Humanitarian Organizations in Hostile or Potentially Hostile Environments,* 2007. In some instances, international forces may be tasked to provide security for designated NGOs delivering humanitarian assistance. International military forces must never disguise themselves as NGO personnel nor their equipment as NGO equipment.

160. International Committee of the Red Cross, "The Fundamental Principles of the Red Cross," 1979, available at: http://www.icrc.org/Web/eng/siteeng0.nsf/html/EA08067453343B76C1256D2600383BC4?OpenDocument&Style=Custo_Final.3&View=defaultBody3 (accessed June 18, 2009). Hereafter: ICRC, "Fundamental Principles," 1979.

161. Ibid..

162. Ibid.

163. Ibid.

164. Report of the International Commission on Intervention and Sovereignty, *The Responsibility to Protect,* 2001. The "responsibility to protect" is "the idea that sovereign states have a responsibility to protect their own citizens from avoidable catastrophe—from mass murder and rape, from starvation—but that when they are unwilling or unable to do so, that responsibility must be borne by the broader community of states."

165. UNDPKO, "Principles and Guidelines," 2008.

166. UNDPKO, "Handbook on UN Peacekeeping Operations," 2003.

judges, prosecutors, defense counsels, or any individual who is willing to take risks for peace or has a role in ending impunity or implementing unwanted reforms. Establishing close protection programs for these individuals may be necessary to ensure their safety, including special convoy arrangements for travel, bodyguards, and other security measures.

***6.8.7 Address all aspects of landmines.*** The presence of landmines wreaks havoc on civilian populations long after warfare has ceased. These weapons exist in the form of unexploded ordnance (UXO), antipersonnel mines (APM), and antitank mines. Some APMs are designed to injure rather than kill their victims, which creates an increased burden on society, prolongs memories of conflict, and impedes healing and reconciliation processes. Wider effects include restricting the freedom of movement and hindering international trade. Protecting the population will require emergency de-mining and UXO removal, marking mined areas that have yet to be cleared and mapping minefields to provide a baseline for clearance operations.[167] Other means of enhancing civilian protection from these threats include the following:[168]

- Educating people on the risks of mines to prevent casualties through mass media campaigns, posters, television spots, and radio messages
- Assisting victims by providing aid, relief, comfort, and support to reduce physical and psychological trauma
- Destroying stockpiles of APMs.

Clearing minefields also has critical impacts on international troops that need access to all parts of the mission area when carrying out their tasks, including maintaining critical supply lines.[169] The sharing of landmine master maps with key actors is critical.

***6.8.8 Coordinate across military, law enforcement, and civilian actors to provide security.*** Military, police, and civilian actors in a mission all play a role in protecting civilians. Concerted and coordinated action must therefore be mainstreamed into all planning and execution. Coordination should include UN humanitarian agencies and NGO partners, which also play a major role in civilian protection.[170] All interactions among these actors should be conducted transparently to protect humanitarian boundaries.[171]

### 6.8.9 Approach: Protection of Infrastructure

Infrastructure protection is an essential and wide-reaching responsibility that includes securing structures and sites that are vulnerable to attack: critical public infrastructure such as roads, port facilities, and telecommunications systems; historical, cultural, or community institutions like churches, schools, graveyards, mosques, and museums; markets and other public places; and international military installations or relief agency headquarters. Protect these structures to ensure that attacks do not inflame wartime tensions and that the population has access to assistance.

---

167. U.S. Army, FM 3-07, 2008.
168. UNDPKO, "Handbook on UN Peacekeeping Operations," 2003.
169. Ibid.
170. UNDPKO, "Principles and Guidelines," 2008.
171. U.S. Army, *FM 3-07,* 2008.

**6.8.10 Protect and promote safety of cultural and historical sites to mitigate conflict.**[172] Protection of cultural sites and resources can prevent renewal of fighting and build the trust of the population. Many groups take immense pride in their cultural institutions, such as museums and libraries that house collections of ancient objects, archives, books, and art. Other sites of significance can include religious structures, graveyards, or natural resources. By protecting these entities, the mission and/or host nation demonstrates respect for the people, who are more likely to reciprocate with trust. Be prepared to provide protection from attacks, while also ensuring that no damage is done to archaeological sites when constructing infrastructure such as building roads, digging canals, or putting up cellphone towers.

**6.8.11 Protect high-value infrastructure targets to prevent disruption to peace.**[173] Critical economic infrastructure vulnerable to sabotage by spoilers is a prime object of attack in S&R environments. To enable humanitarian assistance and economic recovery efforts, protection is essential for key government installations and for transportation, telecommunications, and other essential infrastructure. Additionally, securing courthouses involving high-profile legal cases is a recurring requirement. Infrastructure development is addressed in Section 9.7.3.

**6.8.12 Approach: Protection of War Crimes Evidence**
The protection of war crimes evidence is an immediate priority to ensure that evidence will be admissible for use in war crimes prosecutions. Evidence can include mass graves, buildings used as interrogation facilities, or testimony from people. Documenting evidence is an enormous task requiring significant investment of resources in personnel to conduct fieldwork.

**6.8.13 Prioritize witness protection programs to ensure willingness of people to testify.** People who witness crimes become victims of threats and intimidation to themselves and their families. Protecting these individuals is key to giving witnesses confidence to come forward to testify against criminals so that justice can be served.[174] Protection can include physical security of individuals and their families, including relocation and psychosocial support.

**6.8.14 Move quickly to secure crime sites to avoid tampering or sabotage by spoilers.** Wartime perpetrators seeking to protect themselves will try to sabotage evidence in any way they can. Sometimes the host nation population will tamper with evidence inadvertently in an effort to memorialize loss. Because the military is often first on the scene, soldiers must be prepared to identify, secure, and preserve evidence of war crimes effectively so it can be used in courts or tribunals for war crimes. This process may include creating an atrocity reporting system; documenting evidence; protecting witnesses; and assisting in the investigation, arrest, and transfer of suspected criminals.[175] Technologies may also play an important role in identifying the location of bodies and graves or photographing crime scenes. For more on transitional justice, see Section 7.7.3.

---

172. U.S. State Department, Office of the Coordinator for Reconstruction and Stabilization, "Sectoral Practices and Experiences in Coordination (SPEC) on Cultural Resources," 2007.

173. U.S. Army, FM 3-07, 2008.

174. Colette Rausch, ed., *Combating Serious Crimes in Post-Conflict Societies: A Handbook for Policymakers and Practitioners* (Washington, D.C.: U.S. Institute of Peace Press, 2006).

175. U.S. Army, *FM 3-07, 2008.*

# 6.9 Necessary Condition: Territorial Security

### 6.9.1 What is territorial security? Why is it a necessary condition?

Territorial security is a necessary condition in which ordinary citizens and legitimate goods are able to move in relative freedom within the country and across its borders, while illicit commodities and individuals that present threats to security are denied free passage. Establishing this condition has been extremely challenging in war-torn countries—many are peppered with landmines, roadside bombs, and roadblocks; suffer from porous borders with daunting terrain; and have air, land, and seaports controlled by spoilers and criminals. Freedom of movement allows children to travel to school without fear of attack and farmers to take their goods to market. The ability to move about also promotes social integration of communities that might otherwise remain isolated. Controlling state borders is necessary to track what enters and exits the country or to prevent threats to security and legal commerce. Many destabilizing elements come from outside state borders in the form of transnational organized crime, hostile neighbors, arms proliferation, and international terrorism. Improving customs and export processes at the border can also benefit international trade and economic development in the long term.

### 6.9.2 Guidance on Territorial Security

*6.9.3 Approach: Freedom of Movement*
Freedom of movement refers to the free flow of people and goods throughout the country without fear of physical harm or disruption, while spoilers, illicit commodities, and other sources of instability are restricted in movement. Enabling freedom of movement has wide-reaching benefits, promoting economic growth and social normalization among communities.

*6.9.4 Facilitate movement for people and goods.* Establish rules on where to enable, limit, or deny access. Enabling access can be done by removing roadblocks that impede movement of people or vehicles, removing landmines from fields, creating safety corridors to help refugees and IDPs move freely without harassment, and ensuring roadways are free of explosives.[176] Ensure the safety of movement by registering identities at checkpoints and establishing checkpoints to monitor who or what is able to travel through certain territories.

*6.9.5 Deny movement to opponents of the peace.* Restricting the movement of criminals and spoilers may require guarding ships at sea, establishing maritime or air exclusion zones, or creating vehicle checkpoints. Establishing such rules allows security personnel to identify individuals who may be wanted for war crimes or other offenses that contribute to instability and restricts the movement of weapons and protects installations and population centers. It also enables members of former warring parties to travel more safely in areas controlled by their rivals.[177]

*6.9.6 Be aware of cultural sensitivities when conducting checkpoint, cordon and search, and convoy operations.* At the tactical level, personnel at checkpoints represent the face

---

176. UK MOD, "JWP 3-50," 2006.
177. Dziedzic/Sotirin/Agoglia, "Measuring Progress in Conflict Environments," 2008; U.S. Army, *FM 3-07,* 2008; and UK MOD, "JWP 3-50," 2006.

of the S&R mission. Because they interface with the people, it is vital that duties are performed with full awareness of local customs, particularly in dealing with women, children, and the elderly. Clear communication of the rules of the checkpoint is key. Define rules for the "escalation of force"[178] to reduce avoidable civilian casualties. The escalation of force involves a sequence of actions that include both nonlethal (e.g., flags, spotlights, lasers) and lethal means (e.g., warning, disabling, or deadly shots to protect the force). It may be appropriate to use local forces in these scenarios because they have more familiarity with the context.

### 6.9.7 Approach: Border Security
Border security involves managing the movement of people and goods across state borders (including air and seaports) to ensure that these elements do not destabilize the country. There are two distinct but related aspects of border security: (1) Physical border security, which involves monitoring interstate border areas for crime, refugee flows and the movement of irregular forces, and (2) Customs and export control, which regulates the flow of people, animals, and goods into and out of the country.[179]

**6.9.8 Pay attention to border issues; they are oft overlooked at the peril of the mission.** Borders are particularly problematic in countries where insurgent recruits flow across borders and illicit trades provide funding to prolong conflict. Transnational organized crime has also become a top source of border insecurity, helping to fund conflict and sustain illicit economic and political power structures that undermine the peace process.[180] Specific cross-border threats include the smuggling of people, arms, natural resources, and other commodities that contribute to instability.

**6.9.9 Address border security in the mandate, cease-fire, and peace agreements.** The mission mandate should explicitly address border security to ensure it is recognized as a critical security imperative. Cease-fire and peace agreements and other political documents should also underscore the importance of securing borders.[181] Because border security connotes sovereign authority, it has historically been a very politically sensitive issue. The UN has unequivocally stated that it does not do border security, preferring the terms "border control" or "monitoring," which includes traditional activities like monitoring ceasefires, refugees, and IDPs; humanitarian activities; and illicit trafficking and trade.[182] The UN typically places the burden on member states to protect their borders and prevent terrorists or weapons of mass destruction from crossing their territories.[183] Political sensitivities, however, do not negate the fact that border security is essential to short- and long-term stability.

**6.9.10 Be prepared to perform border security functions for an indeterminate period.** In spite of political and practical difficulties, international actors should be prepared to

178. United States Army, *Escalation of Force Handbook*, 2007.

179. U.S. Army, *FM 3-07*, 2008.

180. Katherine Andrews, Brandon Hunt, and William Durch, *Post-Conflict Borders and UN Peace Operations* (Washington, D.C.: The Henry L. Stimson Center, 2007). Hereafter: Andrews/Hunt/Durch, *Post-Conflict Borders*, 2007.

181. Andrews/Hunt/Durch, "Post-Conflict Borders," 2007.

182. Ibid.

183. United Nations Security Council, "UN Security Council Resolution 1373, Threats to International Peace and Security Caused by Terrorist Acts," 2001. United Nations Security Council, "UN Security Council Resolution 1540, Non-proliferation of Weapons of Mass Destruction."

perform border security functions to help the country manage its land border areas, airspace, coastal and territorial waters, and, when necessary, exclusive economic zones. Specific border security activities include the following:[184]

- Establishing border stations to efficiently regulate movement of goods and people.
- Establishing information-sharing protocols to help detect and prevent illegal trafficking, organized crime, irregular force movements, terrorism, and other activities that threaten the security of border areas.
- Training local forces on patrolling and monitoring individuals and goods crossing the border, and eventually developing a sustainable civil border service.

***6.9.11 Build host nation capacity for border security as a first-order priority.*** Local forces must be trained and equipped to perform border security tasks. Training conducted in country is usually the most successful. Train the trainers is a best practice approach. More host nation participation is better because they have more familiarity with context. Colocating international and local forces for mentoring and monitoring will likely be required for some time. Effective border security also relies on solid intelligence about wanted individuals seeking to enter or exit the country. Build cooperative relationships between border security forces and intelligence agencies to ensure critical data are shared.

***6.9.12 Use existing models for regional cooperative trade programs.*** After the September 11, 2001, terrorist attacks, many new border security programs were implemented at airports, seaports, and other border crossings. These initiatives targeted terrorists, weapons proliferation, human and narcotics trafficking, illegal immigration, and money laundering. Many regional and global cooperative programs of this nature have been effective in these objectives and should be looked at as a model for improving cooperative efforts for border control and nonproliferation.[185] For more on regional engagement, see Section 3.9.

***6.9.13 Manage border relations with neighbors.*** Many conflict countries share extensive state borders with adjacent countries from which a number of destabilizing threats originate. Garnering the political support of adjoining states and establishing cross-border protocols early can reduce further instability and prove beneficial for the security of adjoining states. For more on regional engagement, see Section 3.9.

# 6.10 Trade-offs

***6.10.1 Prioritizing short-term stability vs. confronting impunity.*** Dealing with groups or individuals who prosecuted the conflict may be necessary early on to bring certain factions into the fold or to mitigate tensions. But turning a blind eye to continued use of political violence against rivals or exploitation of criminal networks to generate illicit revenue will enshrine a culture of impunity that threatens sustainable peace.

***6.10.2 Using local security forces to enhance legitimacy vs. using international security***

---

184. U.S. Army, *FM 3-07*, 2008.
185. Andrews/Hunt/Durch, "Post-Conflict Borders," 2007.

*forces to ensure effectiveness.* While international security forces may be more effective in performing security functions, having local security forces assume these responsibilities would enhance legitimacy. But local forces often lack the capacity to perform effectively and may have a reputation for corruption and grave human rights abuses. Balancing this trade-off involves training and mentoring local forces and gradually transitioning responsibilities from international actors.

*6.10.3 Applying force vs. maintaining mission legitimacy.* Public order operations may require the use of force, especially where spoilers and a culture of impunity are widespread. Assertive action ensures credibility, but excessive force can also jeopardize the legitimacy of the mission, especially early on when a mission is under public scrutiny. Finding a way to balance this trade-off is essential and should involve international stability police who are proficient in the use of nonlethal force.[186]

*6.10.4 Public order functions performed by the military vs. the police.*[187] Achieving public order in these environments often presents a difficult dilemma as to which institution—military or police—should perform public order functions. While the military has training and experience in the use of force against violent spoilers, they lack the requisite skills in investigations, forensics, and other critical law enforcement functions. Traditional police units, on the other hand, are trained in nuanced use of force and nonlethal means. Meshing the capabilities of both these organizations is critical to meet public order needs.

*6.10.5 Short-term security imperatives vs. investments in broader security reform.* With limited resources to work with, it may be difficult to balance short- and long-term requirements. The need for immediate security (i.e., protection for elections) may divert donor resources and energy from long-term SSR efforts. Demonstrating quick wins can build credibility, but may jeopardize the development of a foundation for deeper reform of the security sector.[188] A proper balance must be struck.

# 6.11 Gaps and Challenges

*6.11.1 Security sector reform.* Local security institutions are often viewed as corrupt, abusive, and lacking in public service ethos. Reshaping this perception among the population, building the capacity of security institutions, creating civilian oversight structures to ensure accountability, and developing sound security policies are all elements of SSR that have proven to be very difficult. It is a major gap that must be filled.

*6.11.2 Intelligence.* Establishing a safe and secure environment in a society emerging from conflict requires actionable intelligence about potential threats that may arise. But intelligence is not a formal or acknowledged part of S&R missions. Doctrinal guidance and cooperation on this function is sorely needed to ensure that critical information is collected and appropriately shared.

---

186. Robert Oakley, Michael Dziedic, and Eliot M. Goldberg, eds., *Policing the New World Disorder* (Honolulu: University Press of the Pacific, 2002.) Hereafter: Oakley/Dziedzic/Goldberg, *Policing the New World Disorder,* 2002.

187. Ibid.

188. United Nations Department of Peacekeeping Operations, *Security Sector Reform and Peace Operations: "Improvisation and Confusion" from the Field,* 2006.

*6.11.3 Corrections.* Corrections systems are critical elements of public order, providing a place to house convicted criminals or spoilers. While both the UN and ICRC have published principles on the treatment of individuals in detention, very little guidance exists on the effective development of corrections institutions to complement the development of police forces, court systems, and other important aspects of public order.

*6.11.4 The role of private security firms.* The employment of private security firms—both external and within the host nation—is ubiquitous in S&R missions. The lack of oversight of these entities has proven to be detrimental to peace and legitimacy of the mission. More guidance and accountability is needed to mitigate their destructive effects.

*6.11.5 Reintegration of ex-combatants.* Successful reintegration has proven extremely challenging because it requires immense sustained support to ensure that ex-combatants, once disarmed and demobilized, do not return to a life of violence. Reintegration should be addressed during peace negotiations and followed up with a robust strategy that includes thorough planning and sustained international support.

*6.11.6 Civilian oversight of the security forces.* SSR strategies have focused overwhelmingly on developing the security forces, while giving short shrift to improving civilian oversight over those forces. Building the forces is important, but keeping them accountable over the long run requires deeper reforms of the institutions that govern the security sector.

*6.11.7 Border security.* Border security is not given adequate attention in S&R missions, in spite of the fact that many sources of insecurity originate outside the border, including the illegal arms trade and foreign terrorist groups. Border security is not mentioned in any landmark reports on UN peacekeeping.

*6.11.8 Holistic security strategy.* Security sector reform is carried out in an ad hoc and piecemeal manner. Rarely has there been an overarching strategic framework that ensures integration of all the efforts, from intelligence to incarceration.

# Section 7
# Rule of Law

**Just Legal Frameworks**
- Legal Framework Assessment
- Short-Term Law Reform
- Law Reform Process
- Content of New Laws

**Public Order**
- A Comprehensive System
- Interim Law Enforcement
- Interim Judiciary
- Humane Detention and Imprisonment

## RULE OF LAW
Ability of the people to have equal access to a self-sustaining justice system that is consistent with international human rights standards and is equally applied.

**Culture of Lawfulness**
- Participation and Communication
- Education and Culture

**Accountability to the Law**
- Transitional Justice
- Horizontal and Vertical Accountability

**Access to Justice**
- Equal Access
- Remedies for Grievances
- Fairness

# Rule of Law

*Ability of the people to have equal access to just laws and a trusted system of justice that holds all persons accountable, protects their human rights, and ensures their safety and security.*

## 7.0 What is the rule of law?[189]

Rule of law refers to an end state in which all individuals and institutions, public and private, and the state itself are held accountable to the law, which is supreme. Laws must be consistent with international human rights norms and standards, legally certain, legally transparent, drafted with procedural transparency, and publicly promulgated.[190] This end state requires equal enforcement and equality before the law, independent adjudication of the law, fairness in the application of the law, and avoidance of arbitrariness. Access to justice—the ability of people to seek and obtain a remedy through informal or formal institutions of justice—is a mutually reinforcing component of rule of law. The rule of law requires the separation of powers and participation in decision-making. Rule of law is the ideal that states strive for; stabilization requires urgent focus toward this end.

## 7.1 What are the key rule of law challenges in societies emerging from conflict?

Historically, the justice system may have been repressive and discriminatory, particularly against marginalized populations, and may have been used only as a tool of powerful elites or criminal power structures. Impunity for those in power constitutes another common barrier to reform. Compounding this challenge is the likelihood that conflict has paid handsomely—through illicit means—leading to criminalization of state institutions, including the justice system. Public trust may be very low. The population may prefer to access justice through non-state, localized systems of justice or vigilante groups to solve grievances instead. The justice system may be severely debilitated or may have collapsed. Its infrastructure (e.g., court houses, public buildings, prisons, police stations, and ministries) may be destroyed, looted or dilapidated and in need of repair. Basic material resources may also be lacking. There may be a shortage of qualified rule of law actors (e.g., judges, court staff, police, prosecutors, prison officials, lawyers).

## 7.2 Why is the rule of law a necessary end state?

Without rule of law, criminal and politically motivated violence will perpetuate the threat that warring parties posed during violent conflict. A poorly functioning justice system will allow petty crime, violent crime, politically and ethnically motivated crime, sexual and domestic violence, and organized criminal activities to flourish. Crime may be perpetrated or tacitly supported by those in power, where government structures have become criminalized, and by former warring parties that have transformed into organized crime gangs.

---

189. United Nations Secretary-General, *Report of the Secretary-General on the Rule of Law and Transitional Justice in Conflict and Post-conflict States (UN Doc S/2004/616)*, 2004. Hereafter: *UN Sec-Gen, Secretary-General's Report*, 2004.

190. Procedural transparency means that the public can easily see the process by which a law is drafted, including what body is drafting new laws and any process by which the public can make comments on proposed laws.

Unless groups that have been involved in violent conflict regard the justice system as a more attractive alternative to violence for resolving disputes, peace will not be sustainable. For the population, rule of law is necessary to ensure safety and security for individuals, families, property, and businesses and to allow freedom of movement to access public services such as education and health. Rule of law is the foundation for economic and political recovery[191] and prosperity.[192]

## 7.3 What are the necessary conditions to achieve the rule of law?

- *Just Legal Frameworks* is a condition in which laws are consistent with international human rights norms and standards; are legally certain and transparent; are drafted with procedural transparency; are equitable, and are responsive to the entire population, not just powerful elites.

- *Public Order* is a condition in which laws are enforced equitably; the lives, property, freedoms, and rights of individuals are protected; criminal and politically motivated violence has been reduced to a minimum; and criminal elements (from looters and rioters to leaders of organized crime networks) are pursued, arrested, and detained.

- *Accountability to the Law* is a condition in which the population, public officials, and perpetrators of past conflict-related crimes are held legally accountable for their actions; the judiciary is independent and free from political influence; and horizontal and vertical accountability mechanisms exist to prevent the abuse of power.

- *Access to Justice* is a condition in which people are able to seek and obtain a remedy for grievances through formal or informal institutions of justice that conform with international human rights standards, and a system exists to ensure equal and effective application of the law, procedural fairness, and transparency.

- *Culture of Lawfulness* is a condition in which the general population follows the law and seeks to access the justice system to address its grievances.

## 7.4 General Guidance for the Rule of Law

*7.4.1 Build host nation ownership and capacity.* Partnership rather than substitution is an appropriate paradigm for host nation ownership. Host nation actors who are committed to making the peace process work should be involved from the beginning. Promoting ownership takes time and commitment and has two components: capacity and willingness. Capacity can be developed through helping the host nation articulate needs,[193] engage in strategic planning, manage reforms, and build rule of law knowledge. Strengthen willingness by demonstrating that violent opponents of the peace process will be confronted and that those who take risks for peace will be supported. Willingness may be fostered through dialogue with justice institutions, and among justice institutions, civil society, and the population.[194] Where there is little political will at

---

191. United Kingdom Stabilisation Unit, *Stabilisation Issues Notes: Rule of Law and Stabilisation.* 2008. Hereafter: UK Stabilisation Unit, *Rule of Law and Stabilisation,* 2006.

192. United Nations Secretary-General, *In Larger Freedom: Towards Development, Security and Human Rights for All* (UN Doc A/59/2005), 2005.

193. United Kingdom Justice Assistance Network, *Principles of Engagement,* 2005. Hereafter: UK JAN, *Principles of Engagement.* 2005.

194. Organisation of Economic Co-operation and Development, Development Assistance Committee, *Hand-*

the top, a push from the bottom, namely civil society and the general population, may stimulate reform, although this will be a long-term process.

***7.4.2 Act only with an understanding of the local context.***[195] A proper rule of law assessment is vital because assistance should be designed in relation to the context rather than universal templates. A multidisciplinary team comprising both host nation and international actors, that covers both urban and rural areas, is optimal. Consult the users of the system as well as justice institutions. Key questions for assessment include the following:

- What does the formal justice system look like on paper and in practice? Can it perform basic rule of law functions?
- What are the informal rules, traditions, and culture that underlie the system and its capacity[196] and needs?
- What subsystems of justice are used by the population, including non-state justice and policing?
- What are the broader conflict-related factors, including regional influences, the security/crime situation, how human rights are being protected, the socioeconomic and political context, the cultural context, and the treatment of marginalized groups?
- What was the role of the justice system in the conflict? Was it part of the problem or part of the solution?
- What are the key drivers and mitigators of conflict that are affecting or could affect rule of law?

*See Gap/Challenge: Section 7.11.1, Comprehensive, coordinated rule of law assessments.*

***7.4.3 Prioritize to stabilize.*** Immediately after violent conflict, a window of opportunity exists to improve the rule of law. Rather than attempting to fix everything at once, the international community and host nation counterparts should adopt a human rights–based approach to rule of law;[197] pay special attention to marginalized groups, and focus on urgent problems including major crimes, human rights violations, and politically motivated violence.[198] See also Section 9.5.27. Providing legitimate state monopoly over the means of violence and providing legal authority that extends to all people in all parts of the country are priorities.[199] Generally no rule of law strategy

---

*book on Security Sector Reform* (Paris, France: OECD Publishing, 2007). Hereafter: OECD DAC, SSR Handbook, 2007.

195. United Nations Office on Drugs and Crime, *Criminal Justice Assessment Toolkit*, 2006. United Nations Office of the High Commissioner for Human Rights, *Rule-of-Law Tools for Post-Conflict States: Mapping the Justice Sector*, 2006. Hereafter: UNHCHR, *Rule of Law Tools: Mapping the Justice Sector*, 2006.

196. See United Nations Development Programme, *Access to Justice Practice Note*, 2004. Hereafter: UNDP, *Access to Justice*, 2004.

197. This means that human rights principles (e.g., universality, nondiscrimination, equality) should guide activities, and activities should enhance the ability of "duty bearers" to meet their obligations and the ability of "rights bearers" (i.e., the population) to claim their rights. (United Nations Secretary-General, *Guidance Note of the Secretary-General: UN Approach to Rule of Law Assistance*, 2008. Hereafter: UN Sec-Gen, *UN Approach to Rule of Law Assistance*, 2008).

198. UN Sec-Gen, "UN Approach to Rule of Law Assistance," 2008. United Nations Development Group, *The Human Rights Based Approach to Development Cooperation: Towards a Common Understanding Among UN Agencies*, 2003.

199. United States Agency for International Development, *Guide to Rule of Law Country Analysis: The Rule of Law Strategic Framework*, 2008. Hereafter: USAID, *Guide to ROL*, 2008.

exists and the groundwork for one should be laid very early on. A strategy must go beyond establishing institutional capacity and shape the local context by disrupting, dislodging, and dismantling spoiler networks that are bent on subverting the rule of law. The entire legal spectrum, from intelligence to incarceration, will need to be capable of transforming systemic threats to the rule of law. Developing effective strategies for overcoming deficits in the willingness and ability of the host nation legal system to confront systemic threats, including impunity of war criminals and warlords, will be the primary determinant of whether rule of law emerges.

*See Trade-off: Section 7.10.2, Security vs. human rights.*
*See Trade-off: Section 7.10.4, Quick fixes vs. a strategic approach.*
*See Gap/Challenge: Section 7.11.3, Prioritization and sequencing.*

***7.4.4 Use a conflict lens.*** Rule of law reform involves asking political as well as technical questions,[200] which can be extremely sensitive following violent conflict. Pay special attention to the political aspects of rule of law reforms.[201] For example, reforming a police force is inherently political as it involves shifting of power and influence. The political buy-in of senior-level government officials is essential for funding and supporting new laws that may need to be adopted.[202] Understand that officials who derive their power from violence, intimidation, and illicit sources of revenue will likely resist reforms and may use political power to influence adjudication of cases. Be aware of the need to foster political will of informal leaders who hold de facto power in society, such as religious leaders, tribal elders, and village chiefs. In the allocation of power, everything has the possibility to create conflict or be perceived as rewarding one party or another. Examples include the appointment of judges and police chiefs and the location of courts and prisons. Take this into account when assigning authority to groups or individuals or locating rule of law facilities.

***7.4.5 Recognize interdependence.*** Rule of law requires more than an exclusive focus on formal justice institutions. It is an interdependent system of many parts involving institutions that manage justice (e.g., ministries), law enforcement agencies, courts, prisons, oversight bodies, law reform agencies, and legal education institutions. The justice system also depends on interaction with non-state justice systems, non-state actors (e.g., civil society), and the general population. Progress in security, governance, economic development and social well-being are all dependent on a functioning rule of law system.

## 7.5 Necessary Condition: Just Legal Frameworks

### 7.5.1 What are just legal frameworks? Why are they a necessary condition?
Just legal frameworks refer to the body of domestic or international laws[203] that apply in a particular country, that give structure to the relationship between the state and the population, and define the parameters for legal conduct. Under this condition, laws are consistent with international human rights norms, legally certain, drafted in a

---

200. UN Sec-Gen, "Secretary-General's Report," 2004.
201. UN Sec-Gen, "UN Approach to Rule of Law Assistance," 2008.
202. UK JAN, "Principles of Engagement," 2005.
203. This includes the constitution, legal codes, acts, decrees, binding regulations, bylaws, standard operating procedures, case law, peace agreements, Status of Forces Agreements, and Security Council resolutions.

transparent way, publicly promulgated, and ensure the separation of powers, including judicial independence. Just laws will vindicate the rights of persons and punish wrongs committed.[204] Just laws are also fair, equitable, responsive to the needs and realities of the host nation[205] and benefit the entire population, not just powerful elites. This condition is necessary for stabilization and reconstruction as just laws define the role of justice sector institutions and actors; form the basis for social, economic, and political order; help a society overcome the legacy of official abuse of power; and protect the rights of vulnerable and marginalized groups.

### 7.5.2 Guidance for Just Legal Frameworks

#### 7.5.3 Approach: Legal Framework Assessment
Understand the existing legal framework as the first step in working toward a just one. Laws may be chaotic, meaning it is difficult to answer the question of what law applies. They may also be deficient, meaning they contain provisions that are inconsistent with human rights or are antiquated and fail to address common S&R challenges, such as property rights, human trafficking, and organized crime. In most war-torn states, the legal framework frequently exhibits signs of neglect and political manipulation, contains elements of discrimination and seldom meets the requirements of international human rights and criminal law standards.[206] Legal framework assessment involves a comprehensive mapping of all laws and decrees—formal and informal—followed by an analysis that identifies areas that require urgent attention or longer-term treatment.

*7.5.4 Gather, catalogue, and distribute the applicable laws first.* Reach out to legal practitioners, ministries, the courts, the police, the prison services, law schools, academics, NGOs, and legal diaspora to collect applicable laws. This will involve multiple sources of law. Identify and collect core documents including the constitution, criminal code, civil code, commercial code, civil procedure code, administrative law, citizenship law, and property law.[207] Also, look for regulations, acts, bylaws, internal procedures (e.g., police procedures), and laws and decrees regulating the customary justice system or parallel justice systems (e.g., rebel laws). Catalogue the laws gathered and translate and share them among host nation and international colleagues.

*7.5.5 Conduct a comprehensive analysis of the applicable law.* The laws gathered need to be analyzed to ascertain compliance with international human rights law, criminal law, civil law, and commercial law (e.g., treaties on organized crime; drug trafficking; the International Covenant on Civil and Political Rights; International Covenant on Economic, Social and Cultural Rights; Convention on the Rights of the Child); to assess how religion impacts the law; and to understand what problems are not addressed in the laws. One body or organization should coordinate this analysis. Have a mixed team of academics and practitioners, legal and nonlegal, who can contextualize the law as it relates to the host nation. The analysis should be carried out by both host nation and international actors, and the team should consult widely within and outside the justice system. Start the assessment early; a full assessment can take up to one or two years.

---

204. UN Sec-Gen, "Secretary-General's Report," 2004.
205. Ibid.
206. Ibid.
207. Hereafter: Dobbins/Jones/Crane/Cole DeGrasse, *Beginner's Guide*, 2007.

*7.5.6 Realize the inherent constraints of new laws if they are not enforced.* New laws are essential in these environments, but law reform can be a fatal attraction for those wishing to bring about changes in war-torn states. New laws will remain paper tigers if they do not result in changes in patterns and behavior and if they allow continuation of impunity for prominent spoilers or criminalization of the state and legal system.

### 7.5.7 Approach: Short-Term Law Reform

Consider whether short-term law reform is necessary. Short-term measures may be necessary to address deficiencies in the law that will impact stability and to address laws that are inconsistent with human rights conventions and standards. While criminal justice laws usually receive the most attention, the majority of disputes and procedural issues that arise—and directly affect the population—initially involve nonviolent offenses that may escalate into violence if victims have no legal recourse. Short-term reform should also address gaps in civil and commercial code and procedure. In this context, short term refers to the first two years after the cessation of hostilities.

*See Gap/Challenge: Section 7.11.4, Non-criminal justice assistance.*

*7.5.8 Consider the need for legal restatement in the aftermath of conflict.* Where there is no agreement on what laws should apply, legal restatement that designates what body of law applies should be considered by competent legislative authorities. Legal restatement aims to ensure legal certainty and may have been addressed in a peace agreement. But designating a particular body of law, typically mandated to be compliant with human rights, has proven challenging in practice. Lawyers end up applying provisions that meet international human rights law, disregarding those that do not, and substituting others—in effect rewriting the law. Understand the complexity of this undertaking and try to ensure that the designated law is clear. The designated law should also be politically acceptable to the legal establishment and the host nation population or it will risk being ignored.[208]

*7.5.9 Undertake discreet legal reform in the short-term if necessary.* Whether law reform should be conducted in the short term will depend on the context. Reforms may be deferred because changes to the law may make little difference. New laws that have been drafted in haste may not have been researched sufficiently, or political will for reform may be lacking. In either case, work with what is there and find creative legal solutions to filling gaps in the law or addressing deficient provisions of law (e.g., where there is no criminal offense for trafficking, use tax evasion provisions). Short-term reforms should involve discreet changes to existing laws rather than a long-term overhaul. Address urgent problems such as laws that grossly undermine human rights or inadequate laws for pretrial detention. In the economic arena, providing for predictable contract enforcement, including oral and informal contracts, is critical.[209] Dealing with real and personal property claims, developing mechanisms to resolve property (especially land, livestock, and commercial) disputes, and determining inheritance rights will always be

---

208. Mark Baskin, *Lessons Learned on UNMIK Judiciary* (Ottawa: Government of Canada, Department of Foreign Affairs and International Trade, 2001).

209. United Nations Department of Peacekeeping Operations, *Primer for Justice Components*, 2006. Hereafter: UNDPKO, *Primer for Justice Components*, 2006. UNHCHR, "Rule of Law Tools: Mapping the Justice Sector," 2006. Dobbins/Jones/Crane/Cole DeGrasse, *Beginner's Guide*, 2007. UNDP/USAID, "First Steps," 2007.

an urgent need.[210] Be aware of the impact that new laws or legal provisions will have on other laws and justice institutions.

### 7.5.10 Approach: Law Reform Process

The process by which laws are drafted is as important as the content of the new laws. In fact, experience shows that the process of making and reforming laws determines effectiveness, not content.[211] The process should be transparent and participatory and involve the adoption of a reform strategy, designation of a coordinating body, and the establishment of a sound program for promulgating and publicizing laws.

*7.5.11 Support and engage in a transparent and participatory process.* The law reform process must be procedurally transparent and participatory. Procedural transparency should prevent laws from being drafted behind closed doors. Declare who is responsible for the drafting of new laws and describe publicly any formal process for public comment. Participation is recognized as a human right[212] and is defined as the process through which people with a legitimate interest (stakeholders) influence and share control over initiatives and the decisions and resources that affect them.[213] Participation makes the population more invested in new laws, bringing the laws increased acceptability and public legitimacy. This buy-in is vital to effective enforcement of the laws. Involve a broad spectrum of society (justice actors, civil society, marginalized groups and the general population) in settings that are not overly formal or intimidating. Depending on the context, engage in public consultation using a system of written comments or open meetings. Use local media, television and radio to raise awareness of draft laws and invite comments. This consultation process may need to be preceded by a public education and awareness campaign to apprise the public of the law reform process and what potential reforms are being discussed.[214] For more on civic participation and empowerment, see Section 8.8.

*7.5.12 Decide upon a reform strategy and establish a coordinating body.* Law reform should be part of a broader justice sector reform strategy, but it needs its own strategic plan. Without a strategy, an uncoordinated, *ad hoc* approach can lead to the promulgation of overlapping or conflicting laws. Ensure the strategy is locally led and created in a transparent, coordinated manner with international partners. It should also take into account other reform measures (e.g., the drafting of a new constitution), reforms that are pending, and how the planned reform will affect other areas of law. The strategy should:

- State the vision and desired outcomes.

210. Kirsti Samuels, *Rule of Law Reform in Post-conflict Countries: Operational Initiatives and Lessons Learnt*, (Washington, D.C.: World Bank, 2006). Hereafter: Samuels, *Rule of Law Reform*, 2006. UNHCHR, "Rule-of-Law Tools: Mapping the Justice Sector," 2006. Agnes Hurwitz and Kaysie Studdard, *Rule of Law Programs in Peace Operations* (New York: International Peace Academy, 2005). Hereafter: Hurwitz/Studdard, *Rule of Law Programs*, 2005.

211. David Berkowitz, Katharina Pistor, and Jean-Francois Richard, *The Transplant Effect* (Cambridge, Mass.: Harvard University, Center for International Development, 2000).

212. See United Nations Committee on Human Rights, *International Standards of Elections: The Right to Participate in Public Affairs, Voting Rights and the Right of Equal Access to Public Service*, 1996.

213. Inter-American Development Bank, *Resource Book on Participation*, www.iadb.org/aboutus/VI/resource_book/table_of_contents.cfm?language=english (accessed July 8, 2009).

214. Lani Blackman, "Products of Law Reform Agencies," in *The Promise of Law Reform* (Sydney: The Federation Press, 2005).

- Designate a body responsible for implementing the strategy and coordinating the drafting of new laws.
- Determine the personnel and other resources available to draft new laws.
- Define how the coordinating body will work with stakeholders within and outside the justice system.
- Determine a participation strategy with a timetable for consulting on, drafting, and vetting the new laws.
- Decide how the process will be reviewed, monitored, and evaluated.

The coordinating body may be a working group, a division of a line ministry or a law reform commission. A coordinating body will require a secretariat to support its work, along with essentials like office space, supplies, research tools and research support.

***7.5.13 Set realistic time frames.*** In these settings, unrealistic time frames often govern law reform processes and overlook the importance of assessment, participation, and consultation. Laws drafted in haste are often replete with mistakes or omit key issues. Remember that a law reform timeline is between two and seven years.[215] Inevitably, there is a tension between the need to reform bad laws and the need to ensure a comprehensive law reform process. However, there is no way to accelerate the law reform process.

***7.5.14 Use outside experts wisely.*** Foreign experts have led many law reform processes in societies emerging from conflict, and solutions to legal problems are often externally conceived.[216] In some instances, international actors draft laws or transplant laws without consultation. A coordinated, supportive, partnership-approach to law reform, with international actors providing support, should be established. International actors can bring rich experiences from other countries and act as resource persons or providers of comparative knowledge and information. Facilitate exchanges between those who have been involved in law reform in similar environments and those currently engaging in reform efforts.

***7.5.15 Engage multidisciplinary, multi-skilled teams.*** The idea that law reform is too important to be left to the lawyers is well accepted. Cultivate a broad community of practitioners and legal and academic experts. Engage generalists (meaning they have a general knowledge of the whole areas of law, e.g., criminal law) and specialists (they have knowledge of a specific area, e.g., addressing organized crime).

***7.5.16 Conduct an impact assessment of new draft laws, and factor training into the strategy.*** Countless laws have been passed in war-torn states that are never implemented or enforced. An impact assessment can look at the costs, consequences, and side effects of new laws.[217] It can determine whether new provisions are financially or systemically viable. For example, if the criminal code requires juveniles to be detained in a non-prison environment such as a juvenile detention center, do such centers exist? If not, how much will it cost to build and to sustain them? Impact assessments look at whether new provisions will necessitate other reforms (e.g., a new law on money laundering will require certain banking laws) or secondary legislation (e.g., standard operating procedures, judges

215. Ibid.
216. UN Sec-Gen, "Secretary-General's Report," 2004.
217. SIGMA (A Joint Initiative of the OECD and the European Union), *Improving Policy Instruments Through Impact Assessment*, Sigma Paper no. 31, 2001.

"bench books," administrative protocols). Moreover, an impact assessment will also evaluate human resource implications from new legal provisions and the level of training required for new or existing justice actors.

**7.5.17 Ensure a sound promulgation and publicization process.** New laws should be publicly promulgated. This means that they should be officially proclaimed, published, and generally publicized so that the population at large is aware. The official proclamation is usually done by an official act of the government or legislature. Once promulgated, publish new laws so they are available to justice actors and the population. Conduct public awareness campaigns to ensure the population is aware of new laws. New laws should not come into effect immediately but be followed by a period of time between the promulgation of a new law and its enforcement. This allows training and publication to occur. Understand the strong implications of new laws on the curricula of any national academic institutions or training centers, such as universities, police academies, or magistrates' schools.

### 7.5.18 Approach: Content of New Laws

The legitimacy of laws is based on societal consensus.[218] The determination of content involves thinking about the principles, values and approaches that will underlie new laws based on dialogue with the host nation population. Old laws may have been repressive or may have violated human rights and only benefited the rich. In drafting new laws, there is an opportunity to redefine key principles and take a rule-of-law and human–rights-based approach to lawmaking.[219]

**7.5.19 Think about the details of drafting early on in the process.** Technical drafting of codes is integral to creating laws that are understandable and workable. Consider who is drafting new laws. The process should be led by a single, trained legal drafter, rather than a drafting committee, to ensure a consistent style of drafting. Another consideration is a new "plain English" style, which seeks to move away from lengthy and complicated sentences and archaic legal expressions that are inaccessible to the ordinary person.[220] This style can support legal certainty and transparency. In war-torn states, many novice justice actors may apply the law to ensure that the new laws are sufficiently detailed. Leaving provisions open to interpretation or relying on forthcoming secondary legislation for detail that may take years to draft may not be wise.

**7.5.20 Use international standards as the normative framework for law reform.**[221] The assessment of the preexisting legal framework discussed in Section 7.5.3 will reveal where the existing laws are consistent with international standards and what standards are binding on the state. It is easy to remove provisions from the preexisting law; it

218. USAID, "Guide to ROL," 2008.
219. Vivienne O'Connor and Colette Rausch, eds., *Model Codes for Post-Conflict Criminal Justice: Model Criminal Code (Volume I)* (Washington, D.C.: U.S. Institute of Peace Press, 2007). Hereafter: O'Connor/Rausch, *Model Codes: Volume I,* 2007. Vivienne O'Connor & Colette Rausch, eds., *Model Codes for Post-Conflict Criminal Justice: Model Code of Criminal Procedure (Volume II)* (Washington, D.C.: U.S. Institute of Peace Press, 2008). Hereafter: O'Connor/Rausch, *Model Codes: Volume II,* 2008. See also, United Nations Office of the High Commisioner for Human Rights and the International Bar Association, *Human Rights in the Administration of Justice: A Manual on Human Rights for Judges, Prosecutors and Lawyers,* 2002.
220. International Monetary Fund Legal Department, *Plain English Tax Law Drafting,* 2008.
221. UN Sec-Gen, "Secretary-General's Report," 2004.

is harder to draft new provisions that comply with international standards. Those involved in the drafting process should be aware of the international legal standards by which the host nation is bound and integrate them into new laws. Capacity development initiatives, such as training or consultation with outside experts on international standards, would be useful in this regard.[222] It is especially important to integrate key international standards for marginalized groups.

*7.5.21 Forget the common law and civil law debate, and think about hybridization.* Many of those involved in law reform processes think of legal systems in black and white terms: they are either civil law or common law. This may be historically accurate but in a contemporary context, this distinction is less clear. So-called civil law systems vary greatly, as do common law systems. There has been so much borrowing across systems that the divide that once existed is now blurred.[223] Now there is a trend toward hybridization. Drafters should choose and blend features and legal provisions from many traditions that work best in the context of the host nation.

*7.5.22 Consider how to appropriately use foreign laws to inform the process.*[224] Be careful about how foreign laws are used in the law reform process. Where a law is not adapted to local conditions, is imposed through an external process, or is unfamiliar to the population, its acceptance may be weak. Conversely, voluntary borrowing of external provisions, where states make an informed decision to copy them fares much better. Consider alternatives and undertake extensive comparative research in advance of adopting a foreign provision of law.

*7.5.23 Consider the relationship between the formal and informal justice sectors when determining new content.* When undertaking reforms of certain areas of law (e.g., criminal law), consider whether these cases are dealt with through informal systems rather than through the formal system or whether certain new provisions will apply to these systems (e.g., a bill of rights in a constitution). In some instances, it may be appropriate to consider creating or modifying the legislative relationship between the formal and informal justice systems. This may involve deciding what crimes fall under the purview of which system or providing for appeal rights from the informal system to the formal system.[225]

# 7.6 Necessary Condition: Public Order

### 7.6.1 What is public order? Why is it a necessary condition?

Public order is a condition characterized by the absence of widespread criminal and political violence, such as kidnapping, murder, riots, arson, and intimidation against targeted groups or individuals.[226] Under this condition, such activity is reduced to an

---

222. In the realm of criminal justice, there are certain tools that may also assist in this process. See O'Connor/ Rausch, *Model Codes: Volume I*, 2007 and *Model Codes: Volume II*, 2008.

223. USAID, "Guide to ROL," 2008.

224. Alan Watson, *Legal Transplants: An Approach to Comparative Law* (2nd ed.) (Athens, Ga.: The University of Georgia Press, 1993).

225. USAID, "Guide to ROL," 2008.

226. Colette Rausch, ed., *Combating Serious Crimes in Post-Conflict Societies: A Handbook for Policymakers and Practitioners* (Washington, D.C.: U.S. Institute of Peace Press, 2006). Hereafter: Rausch, *Combating Serious Crimes*, 2006.

acceptable minimum, perpetrators are pursued, arrested, and detained, and the local population—no matter which party to the conflict they may belong to—is able to move freely about the country without fear of undue violence. Public disorder can be profoundly destabilizing for societies emerging from conflict. It can instill constant fear in the local population, undercut efforts to strengthen state security institutions, and jeopardize the success of the peace process. Criminal and politically motivated activity is often accompanied by widespread violation of human rights, including torture; rape; cruel, inhuman, or degrading treatment; and arbitrary arrest and detention. The population has few means by which to address these threats—the police are usually in short supply, with a legacy of abuse and corruption. There are few judges, and confidence is low in their ability to adjudicate cases independently. Prisons are overflowing. Without public order, people will never build confidence in the public security system and will seek security from other entities like militias and warlords.[227]

## 7.6.2 Guidance for Public Order

*7.6.3 Approach: A Comprehensive System*
Public order is the domain of police or other policing agencies, courts, prosecution services, and prisons—all of which make up the criminal justice system. Understand that this system is chain-linked—all elements need to work together.

*7.6.4 Take a holistic approach when developing a strategy for public order.* Often, the police are prioritized at the expense of other parts of the criminal justice system, especially criminal defense and corrections.[228] While reconstructing police may be a priority, nest this within a broader strategy. Police require criminal codes, courts, and prisons, and courts require timely delivery of evidence by the police to adjudicate cases. Arbitrary or politicized sentencing, an incompetent or corrupt judiciary, or inhumane prison conditions will undermine the benefits that come from better policing and public order in general.[229] Increased information flow and cooperation among criminal justice actors is critical. The goal is not to simply grow the number of institutions and officials, but to improve the overall delivery of criminal justice.

*7.6.5 Transform systemic threats to public order as a prerequisite.* In these environments, it is unlikely that peace accords will recognize and address all abuses and sources of dysfunction that have afflicted judicial systems. It is also highly unlikely that the parties to accords will comply fully without any need for assistance in dealing with the impunity of spoilers, the legacy of politicization of the legal system, or the risk of institutional criminalization rooted in illicit revenue sources.[230] In this context, local police, judges, and jailers who seek to uphold the law will not survive for long, even with comprehensive vetting, training, and mentoring programs. To enable public order, the mission may need a very broad spectrum of capabilities that goes beyond establishing institutional capacity to include disrupting and dismantling spoiler networks that

---

227. Rausch, *Combating Serious Crimes*, 2006.
228. Hurwitz/Studdard (IPA), "Rule of Law Programs," 2005.
229. Seth G. Jones, Jeremy M. Wilson, Andrew Rathmell, K. Jack Riley, *Establishing Law and Order After Conflict* (Santa Monica, Calif.: RAND Corporation, 2005).
230. Covey/Dziedzic/Hawley, *Quest for Viable Peace*, 2005.

subvert the rule of law. For more on spoilers, see Section 6.5.10; for a discussion on economic-based threats, see Section 9.6.

### 7.6.6 Approach: Interim Law Enforcement

Law enforcement—the capacity to apprehend and arrest suspected criminals—is vital for security and cannot be postponed for months. Because local forces will likely be weak, discredited, or a party to the conflict, assistance from international actors may be necessary to ensure that urgent law enforcement functions are performed while local institutions undergo reform. International police, both individual and formed units, can fill this role.

*7.6.7 Move quickly to prevent criminal elements and political spoilers from cementing their grip on power.*[231] In the lawlessness of these environments, asserting authority early on is essential to securing the trust of the population. Waiting too long to confront violence can permit spoilers, organized crime syndicates, and their militias to perpetuate instability and entrench themselves in the new political system, which allows them to protect their interests and solidify public support through intimidation. A culture of impunity results.

*7.6.8 Be prepared to perform critical law enforcement functions when necessary.* Certain public order functions are critical whether performed by international or host nation actors. Calibrate the international police mandate according to needs on the ground. International police may have to perform critical law enforcement functions on the ground in cases where public disorder is high, local capacity is nonexistent, or local forces are responsible for systemic human rights violations. The performance of law enforcement functions by international forces typically requires an executive mandate for the UN mission or other authority. Key law enforcement functions include the following:[232]

- Street patrols
- Arrests and detention
- Criminal intelligence and surveillance
- Criminal investigations and evidence collection (including war crimes)
- Crowd and riot control
- Public dispute resolution
- Protection of critical infrastructure
- Border security
- Witness protection to address the impunity of political criminals
- High-risk arrest capacity for political violence and extremism.

*7.6.9 Coordinate public order functions between the military and the police and ensure that any gap is filled.* Establishing public order in war-torn societies requires unique capabilities that do not belong solely to either the military or the police. Incidents involving political violence and extremism, for example, may require greater force than the police can employ. Ultimately, military and police capabilities must be coordinated to fill this gap and share critical intelligence, while overcoming differences in culture, capabilities, legal constraints, and command and control structures. For more on intelligence, see Section 6.5.15. The military will likely be first on the scene and

---

231. Dobbins/Jones/Crane/Cole DeGrasse, *Beginner's Guide,* 2007.
232. Ibid.

will probably have to perform some public order functions, but it is not the ideal instrument for the job. Equipped with lethal firepower, the military is better primed to confront threats to the peace process and could actually jeopardize the mission by using excessive force. The police are better trained in the measured use of force, negotiation techniques, and control over lawlessness.[233] In the emergency phase, the military may have to perform critical law enforcement functions. These responsibilities, however, should be transitioned as quickly as possible to an international police force or, if they are reliable, the local security forces. Sound rules of engagement for the military should define the procedures for investigation, arrest, and detention. Public order activities by the military include protecting high-value facilities to prevent looting, run security checkpoints, perform vehicle inspections, regulate public gatherings, undertake high-risk searches, arrest and detain people who disrupt public order, and regulate the freedom of movement, which is further discussed in Section 6.9.3.

*See Trade-off: Section 6.10.4, Public order functions performed by the military vs. the police.*

*7.6.10 Deploy local forces whenever possible without compromising human rights and justice.* As soon as it is prudent and possible, local law enforcement should participate in public order operations to begin building capacity, albeit with extreme caution. The local police force will likely have played a role in human rights abuses. Thorough reforms will have to take place. But shifting public order functions to local forces is the ultimate goal and can also minimize confrontation between international actors and the population.[234] Local forces also speak the language, know the culture, and are more familiar to local populations, which is vital for good policing.[235] Colocating international police with local forces at police stations can improve cooperation, the effectiveness of the mentoring process, and the transfer of skills.[236] It can also help the international police better assess the state of policing. But colocation programs should be used cautiously—extended periods of colocation in isolated areas can lead to internationals losing their objectivity or impartiality. Human rights are further addressed in Section 3.7.3; police vetting is also addressed in Section 6.7.21.

*7.6.11 Address illegal armed groups and informal policing structures.* If illegal armed groups continue to operate, including informal policing structures, this constitutes an unacceptable threat to law and order. Whether militias, vigilante groups, or gangs; state-sponsored, community based, or private security companies; religious, ethnic, or tribal, they must either be demobilized and reintegrated into society or, if they qualify on an individual basis, allowed to be integrated into one of the entities comprising the security sector. In most cases the process for doing this will be stipulated in a peace agreement, but noncompliance will need to be anticipated and dealt with effectively.[237]

*7.6.12 Support the building of host nation police capacity.* Careful decisions need to be made about the type of equipment, infrastructure, training, and ongoing monitoring

---

233. Oakley/Dziedzic/Goldberg, *Policing the New World Disorder*, 2002.
234. Ibid.
235. Dobbins/Jones/Crane/Cole DeGrasse, *Beginner's Guide*, 2007.
236. UK FCO, *Police Personnel*, 2007.
237. Etannibe E.O. Alemika and Innocent C. Chukwuma, *The Poor and Informal Policing in Nigeria: A Report on the Poor's Perceptions and Priorities on Safety, Security and Policing in Access to Justice Focal States in Nigeria* (Lagos: Center for Law Enforcement Education, 2004).

that is provided to the police force and leadership. The law and the rules and regulations around the use of weapons should be analyzed to ensure compliance with international human rights norms and standards.[238] Undertake training to improve the operational law and order skills of the police, organizational management, and supervisory skills of police leadership and education about democratic principles of policing (e.g., representative policing, responsive policing, accountable policing).[239] Police mentors can provide training on the job (e.g., UNPOL or other international police advisers). Promote accountability by drafting, publicizing, and enforcing disciplinary procedures and codes of conduct.[240] Ongoing education and training of police will be required as well as the development of training facilities (e.g., police schools or academies), if not already in place. Further efforts to enhance capacity involve human resources systems, organizational restructuring, budget and asset management, procurement rules, and infrastructure. For more on institutional governance functions, see Sections 8.6.7 to 8.6.9; for more on police reform, see Sections 6.7.21 to 6.7.23.

### 7.6.13 Approach: Interim Judiciary[241]

An interim judiciary should not be an afterthought. In the aftermath of violent conflict when local institutions are still being built or transformed, an interim judiciary may be necessary to handle urgent cases of impunity and political violence and resolve disputes that arise over housing, land, and property.[242] Work must also begin to assess which host nation institutions or actors in the judiciary can perform judicial functions. A weak or politicized judiciary, a prevalent phenomenon in societies recovering from violent conflict, can lead to corruption, extrajudicial murders, and arbitrary or politicized sentencing.

**7.6.14 Deploy core elements for an emergency judiciary.**[243] Prevent arbitrary exercise of power. An interim capacity for administering justice and resolving disputes, particularly highly sensitive cases, may be needed from international actors. This may include the deployment of international judges, prosecutors, defense attorneys, court administrators and court reporters to accompany deployments of international police for law enforcement functions. Without these judiciary elements, the police function will be of little or no value. This holistic judiciary team should help host nation personnel set up hybrid special courts to adjudicate cases of political violence and organized crime until host nation institutions are capable of confronting impunity.
*See Gap/Challenge: Section 6.11.8, Holistic security strategy.*

**7.6.15 Employ informal systems when it makes sense.** Before a formal justice system is functioning or strengthened, it may be necessary to rely on informal mechanisms

38. See United Nations, *Basic Principles on the Use of Force and Firearms by Law Enforcement Officials*, 1990.

39. United Nations Department of Peacekeeping Operations, *Handbook on United Nations Multidimensional Peacekeeping Operations*, 2003. Hereafter: UNDPKO, "Handbook on UN Peacekeeping Operations," 2003.

40. David H. Bayley, *Changing the Guard: Developing Democratic Police Abroad* (Oxford: University Press Oxford, 2006). Hereafter: Bayley, "Changing the Guard," 2006.

41. For the purposes of this manual, the judiciary refers to courts, including judges, court administrative staff (court administrators, court clerks), other staff under the court's control (bailiffs, court guards), and prosecutors (depending on the local context). (USAID. "Guide to ROL," 2008.)

42. United States Army, *Field Manual 3-07: Stability Operations* (Washington, D.C.: Department of the U.S. Army, 2008). Hereafter: U.S. Army, *FM 3-07*, 2008.

43. Rausch, *Combating Serious Crimes*, 2006.

for resolving disputes. These could include independent bodies like complaint commissions or an ombudsmen office or even an informal, non-state justice system. These institutions should be held accountable for their actions.[244] The arbitration of disputes can have many political ramifications in many decisions; be cautious in how the resolution of these cases is communicated to the population.

**7.6.16 Protect the judiciary from physical harm and outside influence.** Three elements of the judiciary must be protected from outside influence and physical harm:

- Facilities, such as courts and auxiliary locations
- Documents and evidence, including both criminal and property records
- Individuals who participate in the system, such as court personnel and witnesses.[245]

Courts must operate with security in mind. Over the long term, security improvements will require significant resources, but interim measures, such as creating a corps of court security officers and clarifying practices about where both victims and witnesses will sit while awaiting proceedings and during court hearings, can also have a high impact. Often mission components can provide some security to the judiciary and affiliated individuals.[246] Also manage court personnel to ensure their impartiality. International staff can assist with judicial functions until host nation personnel are adequately vetted and trained. For more on judicial independence and accountability, see Sections 7.7.7 and 7.7.8.

**7.6.17 Ensure that witnesses and victims are adequately protected and supported.** Key witnesses and their families may be threatened because of their involvement in a trial. Methods to protect witnesses before, during, and after the trial (e.g., close protection, witness protection measures, witness relocation programs) are necessary.[247] Victims, who are potential witnesses, may also be in danger. They may need other types of support, particularly in cases of domestic and gender violence or trafficking.[248] NGOs or legal resource centers can help victims to claim their rights and provide support services.[249]

**7.6.18 Vet the judiciary.** In these environments, some judicial personnel may have committed human rights violations, are corrupt, or are connected to spoilers and criminal elements. Lustration or vetting may be necessary and result in a need to recruit new personnel. These personnel should be strictly vetted for past human rights violations or links to criminal organizations. Ensure that judicial personnel reflect the population in terms of gender, ethnicity, religion, and linguistic groups.

---

244. UK FCO, "Police Personnel," 2007.
245. USAID, "Guide to ROL," 2008.
246. UNDPKO, "Primer for Justice Components," 2006.
247. For a discussion on witness protection, see Articles 147–62, "Model Code of Criminal Procedure" in O'Connor/Rausch, *Model Codes: Volume II*, 2008. See also Rausch, *Serious Crimes Handbook*, 2006.
248. For a discussion on the support of victims of trafficking, see United Nations, *Protocol to Prevent, Suppress and Punish Trafficking in Persons, Especially Women, Supplementing the United Nations Convention against Transnational Organized Crime*, 2000.
249. See United Nations Office of the High Commissioner for Human Rights, *Declaration of Basic Principles of Justice for Victims of Crime and Abuse of Power*, 1985.

*7.6.19 Use mobile courts and paralegals to meet immediate needs.*[250] Where court-houses are destroyed or nonexistent, consider mobile courts that can move around the country to administer justice. Mobile courts can handle more cases than regular courts. Another option is to leverage judicial power (if it exists under the law) to set up a court anywhere. Consider establishing this power under a new law if it is not in the current code. Judges can hear applications for bail and dispense with cases on the spot, demonstrating responsiveness. Mobile investigation, prosecution, and defense teams should complement the mobile courts. A society emerging from conflict will likely have a severe shortage of lawyers and no state-run legal aid programs. In this situation, paralegals can be employed to provide legal advice.

### 7.6.20 Approach: Humane Detention and Imprisonment

Detention and prison management and capacity are critical security priorities that are too often neglected relative to police and judicial functions.[251] The ability to run detention centers and prisons effectively in adherence to international standards has a direct impact on the possibility for lasting peace and security. The capacity to securely incarcerate dangerous spoilers is critical to transform systemic threats to the rule of law. Common challenges include dilapidated facilities, chronic underfunding, lack of training for prison staff, antiquated prison laws, overcrowding, prolonged pretrial detention, and serious violations of human rights.[252] *See Gap/Challenge: Section 6.11.3, Corrections.*

*7.6.21 Meet minimum international standards for treatment of detainees.* Depending on the nature of the mission mandate, detention may be handled early on by either the mission or host nation government. When capacity is low, which is often the case, the mission will have to assume responsibility, in which case a strategy for transitioning prisoners over to the host nation government must be developed.[253] At all stages of this process, detainees must be handled in accordance with international standards. The *UN Standard Minimum Rules for the Treatment of Prisoners* is a good place to start. Some basic principles include the following:[254]

- All persons deprived of liberty shall be treated with humanity and with respect for the inherent dignity of the human person.
- Everyone charged with a criminal offense shall be presumed innocent until proved guilty.
- Pretrial detention shall be the exception rather than the rule.
- No detainee shall be subject to torture or to cruel, inhuman, or degrading treatment or punishment or any form of violence or threats.

---

50. Ibid.
51. For the purposes of this discussion, prisons refer to facilities used to house convicted individuals. Detention refers to any deprivation of personal liberty other than the result of a conviction.
52. United Nations Department of Peacekeeping Operations, *Prison Support Guidance Manual,* 2006. Hereafter: UNDPKO, *Prison Guidance,* 2006.
53. Ibid.
54. United Nations Office of the High Commissioner for Human Rights, *Human Rights and Law Enforcement: A Manual on Human Rights Training for the Police,* http://www.unhchr.ch/html/menu6/2/training.htm (accessed June 18, 2009).

- Detained persons shall be held only in officially recognized places of detention and their families and legal representatives are to receive full information.
- Decisions about duration and legality of detention are to be made by a judicial or equivalent authority.
- Detainees have the right to be informed of the reason for detention and charges against them.
- Detainees have the right to contact the outside world and to visits from family members and the right to communicate privately and in person with a legal representative.
- Detainees shall be kept in humane facilities, designed to preserve health, and shall be provided with adequate water, food, shelter, clothing, medical services, exercise, and items of personal hygiene.
- Every detainee has the right to appear before a judicial authority and to have the legality of his or her detention reviewed.

*7.6.22 Take measures to provide for prison security.* Develop a prison security system that both prevents prisoners from escaping and protects corrections officers from harm. Key issues often include untrained and poorly paid prison staff, who do not have appropriate weapons and equipment, as well as the lack of prison buildings and infrastructure that can be secured. Solutions depend on the degree of damage to existing prison facilities, the proficiency of the prison staff, their affiliation with groups associated with the conflict, the international and host nation resources available, and the political will to implement reform. Establish an adequate level of prison security that meets international human rights standards and can be sustained by a new government. International corrections professionals can improve prison security by securing prison infrastructure and professionalizing staff and procedures after a careful assessment of the national prison law, existing infrastructure, and the capacity of prison staff.[255]

*7.6.23 Address illegal and excessive pretrial detention and prison overcrowding.* Work to ensure that those who are illegally detained are released from detention immediately and address the problem of excessive pretrial detention, a violation of basic human rights that puts a massive strain on overcrowded prisons. If no transportation exists to bring a detainee to court, putting a mobile court in the prison to review the legality of continued detention is an option. Consider creating a case flow management committee, which can be established with civil society participation even in the absence of other justice institutions.[256] The committee can review the status of detainees and recommend release pending trial or the dropping of charges for less serious crimes. Children detained for less serious crimes should be released from custody. Establish mechanisms over the long term to protect the right to liberty,[257] such as a system for bail or other alternatives to detention[258] (e.g., house arrest). If the law allows, the prosecuting authority can simply refrain from pressing charges for less serious crimes.

---

255. International Network to Promote the Rule of Law, "Prison Security in Societies Emerging from Conflict," Consolidated Response (07-007), 2007.

256. United Nations Office on Drugs and Crime and United States Institute of Peace, "DRAFT: Handbook on Criminal Justice Reform," 2009.

257. For a discussion of the right to the presumption of liberty, see "Model Codes of Criminal Procedure," Article 169, in O'Connor/Rausch, *Model Codes: Volume II*, 2008.

258. For a discussion on alternatives to detention, see "Model Codes of Criminal Procedure," Article 184, in O'Connor/Rausch, *Model Codes: Volume II*, 2008.

An official warning or an apology to the victim may be used. In systems that require a formal legal basis for this action, known as diversion, or that require mandatory prosecution of suspected crimes, consider drafting legal provisions on diversion.

*7.6.24 Improve prison conditions.* Prisons and jails in a society ravaged by conflict invariably fall far short of international human rights standards. Improving prison conditions will be an imperative. New structures should conform to international human rights standards, particularly those concerning the use of punishment units, local climatic conditions, ventilation, natural light, the number of toilets and shower units, area for preparing and cooking food, and waste disposal.[259] Former "dark cells" and other punishment units within the prison should be adjusted to conform to international standards or removed entirely.[260] International agencies may be engaged to provide food for prisoners or to set up prison farms. Separate women and children from men as required by international standards by at least housing women and children in a different part of the prison.

*7.6.25 Prevent torture and focus on evidence-based criminal investigation.* Torture by justice actors may have been commonplace prior to and during the conflict. Work to ensure that torture as a practice in criminal investigations is stopped in compliance with international human rights law.[261] Focus on evidence-based investigations and integrate a prohibition on torture into the law.[262] Vertical and horizontal accountability mechanisms, discussed in Section 7.7, can support the monitoring of torture in the justice system. Training of justice officials will be required, including the proper investigation of crimes (e.g., taking of forensic evidence). Finally, support from senior political and justice officials for the prohibition of torture is necessary, along with the ability to ensure there are consequences for violations of the prohibition.

# 7.7 Necessary Condition: Accountability to the Law

### 7.7.1 What is accountability to the law? Why is it a necessary condition?

Accountability refers to the processes, norms, and structures[263] that hold the population and public officials legally responsible for their actions and that impose sanctions if they violate the law. Accountability is essential if systemic threats to the rule of law are to be corrected. This involves ensuring there are consequences for criminal behavior (which is addressed in Section 7.6); mechanisms to address impunity for past crimes; and horizontal accountability (state institutions overseeing the actions of one another) and vertical accountability (citizens overseeing the actions of the state). Without accountability, human rights will be denied, crime will flourish, and impunity for past conflict-related crimes will persist, undermining legitimacy and prospects for reconciliation. The concentration of power in any one branch, institution, or level of

---

259. Ibid.
260. Ibid. See Penal Reform International, *Making Standards Work: An International Handbook on Good Prison Practice*, 2001, for an authoritative commentary on the application of international standards to prisons.
261. See United Nations Office of the High Commissioner for Human Rights, "International Covenant on Civil and Political Rights," Article 7, 1976.
262. United Nations, "Convention Against Torture and Other Cruel, Inhuman or Degrading Treatment or Punishment," Article 15, 1987.
263. United Kingdom Department for International Development, Briefing, "Justice and Accountability," 2008.

government often leads to abuse of power and corruption that horizontal and vertical accountability mechanisms can help prevent. Accountability also aims to mitigate against capture of justice institutions by political and economic spoilers that enables impunity, favoritism, and unequal application of the law.

### 7.7.2 Guidance for Accountability to the Law

#### 7.7.3 Approach: Transitional Justice

Transitional justice aims to end impunity for past crimes associated with the conflict, including genocide, crimes against humanity, mass atrocities, and other war crimes. It is defined as the "full range of processes and mechanisms associated with a society's attempt to come to terms with the legacy of past abuses, in order to ensure accountability, serve justice and achieve reconciliation."[264] In order to make perpetrators accountable for conflict-related crimes, transitional justice mechanisms may be employed, such as tribunals, truth commissions, or traditional approaches. Inter- and intra-group reconciliation is addressed in Section 10.8.3.

*See Trade-off: Section 7.10.3, Peace vs. justice.*

#### 7.7.4 Protect and preserve evidence. 
The gathering and preservation of evidence of genocide, crimes against humanity, and war crimes is essential if there is a decision to prosecute perpetrators. International military forces and civilian actors (including specialists like forensic anthropologists) should be involved in the protection and preservation of evidence. Make this an early priority as the host nation population is often eager to recover evidence and remains of relatives. Recovery by non-professionals can jeopardize the validity of the evidence. Evidence and physical sites (e.g., mass graves) must be protected from both well-intentioned as well as hostile interference and appropriately preserved for future analysis. For more on the protection on war crimes evidence, see Section 6.8.12.

#### 7.7.5 Choose the most appropriate transitional justice options. 
Support a national dialogue on transitional justice, especially with victims and marginalized groups to look at the different options. Each transitional justice process must spring from the particular needs of the country and its religious, moral or cultural norms.[265] The imposition of prepackaged solutions by the international community is not advised.[266] The judicial and nonjudicial options below may be combined or used separately:

- *Special courts or tribunals.* War crimes, genocide, serious human rights violations, and crimes against humanity are typically the purview of special courts. A special court may be purely host nation, purely international, or a hybrid of the two. In establishing special courts and tribunals, international legal professionals such as judges, prosecutors, and lawyers often work with host nation counterparts to co-administer justice. Successful courts and tribunals depend on political will of regional and international actors[267] and significant international funding.

---

264  Ibid.
265. Judy Barsalou and Victoria Baxter, *The Urge to Remember* (Washington, D.C.: U.S. Institute of Peace, 2007).
266. UN Sec-Gen, "Secretary-General's Report," 2004.
267. United States Agency for International Development, Office of Transition Initiatives, *Guide to Program Options in Conflict-Prone Settings,* 2001.

- *Truth and reconciliation commissions.*[268] Truth and reconciliation commissions are official, nonpermanent, nonjudicial, and investigative bodies that can be used to address conflict-related crimes and their impact on society. Their primary purpose is to allow a society emerging from conflict as a whole to understand *what* happened during the conflict as well as *why* it happened and to pursue communal resolution.

- *Customary or traditional approaches.* When incorporating customary or traditional approaches into a rule of law framework, consult knowledgeable host nation actors.[269] Analyze the advantages and disadvantages of incorporating each customary method. Confirm that suggested approaches are valid cultural elements and are not an attempt by factions to create new mechanisms of control. Consideration of international human rights standards and fair play are paramount.[270] Long-standing customary mechanisms may be used as a form of transitional justice. In addition, customary mechanisms that have fallen out of use or completely novel non-state mechanisms may also be established. This may involve establishing new mechanisms or resurrecting those that have fallen out of use.

- *Reparations.*[271] Reparations include redress for harm suffered in the form of restitution, compensation, rehabilitation, and guarantees of non-repetition. They can also include public apologies, commemorations or days of remembrance, exhumation, reburial, erection of tombstones, return of the remains of deceased relatives, issues of death certificates, holding of ceremonies for the disappeared, and teaching school children about past abuses.

- *Lustration.* Lustration bars a class of individuals from public employment, political participation, and the enjoyment of other civil rights based on involvement with a prior regime. Best practice lustration methods make individual determinations, do not treat the whole group as black and white, and establish an administrative system to adjudicate claims for exemption in an impartial and reasonably expeditious manner.[272]

- *Vetting.* Vetting seeks to exclude individuals lacking integrity from public institutions. Integrity refers to a person's ability to serve in accordance with fundamental human rights, professional, and rule of law standards.[273] Vetting requires an administrative system to carefully determine who will be excluded.

---

268. United Nations Office of the High Commissioner for Human Rights, *Rule-of-Law Tools for Post-Conflict States: Truth Commissions,* 2006.
269. For further reference on customary approaches, see United Nations Office on Drugs and Crime, *Handbook on Restorative Justice Programs,* 2006.
270. IPA, "Securing the Rule of Law," 2005.
271. See United Nations Office of the High Commissioner for Human Rights, *Rule-of-Law Tools for Post-Conflict States: Reparations Programs,* 2008.
272. Jens Meierhenrich, "The Ethics of Lustration," *Ethics and International Affairs,* no. 1, 2006.
273. United Nations Office of the High Commissioner for Human Rights, *Rule-of-Law Tools for Post-Conflict States: Vetting,* 2006.

- *International Criminal Court (ICC).* A state can refer a case to the ICC for prosecution. Where a state has ratified the Statute of the International Criminal Court, and where it decides it will not prosecute, the ICC may nonetheless assume jurisdiction where a crime was committed by a national or on the territory of the state.
  *See Trade-off: Section 10.9.7, Restorative vs. retributive justice.*

### 7.7.6 Approach: Horizontal and Vertical Accountability
Accountability of those in power can take many forms: it can either be horizontal, meaning state institutions oversee the actions of one another, or vertical, meaning citizens oversee the actions of the state. It may be proactive or reactive; it may be centralized or decentralized;[274] and it may be formal (written in law) or informal.

**7.7.7 Promote the separation of powers and judicial independence.** The separation of powers, a core element of the rule of law, should ideally be articulated in a newly drafted or reformed constitution, along with judicial independence. The judiciary should function as a check on executive and legislative authority. In the immediate aftermath of violent conflict, the justice system is often the sole means for holding those in power accountable for criminal conduct. Matters such as judicial appointment, judicial qualifications, duration of terms, conditions of promotion, the transfer and cessation of their functions, and judiciary independence from the executive and legislative branches should be written into law and be consistent with international standards.[275] Protecting judges from intimidation or harm and ensuring that judges are adequately remunerated[276] helps prevent improper influence from those seeking to control or undermine the justice system. Medium- to long-term initiatives to strengthen judicial independence include (1) ensuring that there is a sufficient number of judges in relation to case loads and providing the courts with necessary support staff and equipment;[277] (2) passing codes of conduct; (3) providing for self-governance where the judiciary can control its own administrative, oversight, and disciplinary functions through bodies such as a judicial council; and (4) providing for random and automated case assignments, simplified procedures to reduce undue delay, public court hearings, publication of court verdicts, and public information centers.[278]

**7.7.8 Support the use of horizontal accountability mechanisms.** A new constitution can establish such mechanisms but understand they require resources and long-term sustainment. Significant international assistance will be needed to establish and maintain many of these accountability mechanisms after conflict. This includes providing technical assistance in the drafting of related laws, facilitating the sharing of comparative experiences from other societies emerging from conflict, giving initial financial support

---

274. OECD DAC, *SSR Handbook,* 2007.
275. See United Nations Committee on Human Rights, *Equality Before the Courts and the Right to a Fair and Public Hearing by an Independent Court Established by Law,* 1984.
276. UNDPKO, "Primer for Justice Components," 2006. United Nations, *Basic Principles on the Independence of the Judiciary,* Principle 11, 1985.
277. United Nations, *Procedures for the Effective Implementation of the Basic Principles on the Independence of the Judiciary,* Procedure 5, 1989.
278. UNDPKO, "Primer for Justice Components," 2006.

for infrastructure, capacity building, and training and monitoring the performance of those engaged in these mechanisms. Horizontal accountability mechanisms can take many forms:[279]

- Internal accountability through supervision, internal reviews of actions, code(s) of conduct, disciplinary systems, and performance reviews.
- Executive accountability by the head of state, ministries, national justice advisory boards, or coordinating bodies through command authority, setting of basic policies, budget management, and power to investigate claims of abuse.
- Legislative accountability by the parliament or parliamentary oversight bodies through hearings, budget approval, enacting laws, and visiting and inspecting facilities.
- Judicial accountability by courts through adjudicating cases brought against justice actors, protecting human rights, monitoring the powers of justice officials, assessing constitutionality, providing remedies, and inspecting police or prison facilities.
- Accountability by independent bodies (e.g., an ombudsman, national human rights institutions, audit offices, inspectors general) that receive complaints, raise awareness of human rights, investigate claims of failures and abuses, and ensure proper use of public funds and compliance with policy.[280]

**7.7.9 Provide for vertical accountability mechanisms.** Vertical accountability is typically undertaken by civil society and media with the support of the general population. It occurs through analyzing, being part of consultations on new laws, lobbying, providing alternative views to the population, investigative reporting, and monitoring of the justice system and other branches.[281] Promote accountability through involvement in budget formulation, analysis, and tracking of justice sector and other government expenditures; the establishment of watchdog or monitoring functions; public interest litigation; and participatory performance monitoring of public service delivery. The population can support the accountability mechanism by filling out scorecards or surveys rating the performance of the justice sector and that of other government institutions. Vertical accountability requires a well-established civil society and independent media. See Section 8.8 for more on accountability through civil society and the media.

**7.7.10 Consider international engagement as a necessary safeguard for accountability.**[282] The international community often plays an important role in creating effective accountability structures, including those for initial vetting, hiring, and disciplinary processes for criminal justice actors. The international role requires host nation invitation or an international mandate. If an international process is in place, engage host nation actors early and frequently. Consider the establishment of a hybrid international-host nation commission or a host nation commission with an international secretariat. For the transformation from impunity to accountability to take place, host nation members of these institutions must take increasing risks and responsibility for disciplinary

---

279. See United Nations Office of the High Commissioner for Human Rights, *Principles Relating to the Status of National Institutions,* 1993.
280. OECD DAC, *SSR Handbook,* 2007.
281. Ibid.
282. UNDPKO, "Primer for Justice Components," 2006.

action. Those who do so should not be abandoned by the international community. Rather, their success should be guaranteed by a long-standing commitment to ensure the ability of accountability structures to prevent impunity from reasserting itself.

# 7.8 Necessary Condition: Access to Justice

### 7.8.1 What is access to justice? Why is it a necessary condition?
Access to justice is more than improving an individual's access to courts or guaranteeing legal representation.[283] Access to justice is defined as the ability of people to seek and obtain a remedy through formal or informal institutions of justice for grievances[284] in compliance with human rights standards.[285] There is no access to justice where citizens (especially marginalized groups) fear the system, see it as alien, and do not access it; where the justice system is financially inaccessible; where individuals have no lawyers; where they do not have information or knowledge of rights; or where there is a weak justice system. Access to justice involves normative legal protection, legal awareness, legal aid and counsel, adjudication, enforcement, and civil society oversight.[286] Access to justice supports sustainable peace by affording the population a more attractive alternative to violence in resolving personal and political disputes.

### 7.8.2 Guidance for Access to Justice

*7.8.3 Approach: Equal Access[287]*
In societies emerging from conflict, large segments of the population may not have had access justice. Equal access involves extending the reach of formal[288] rule of law institutions to the population by removing barriers to their use. Strengthening access also involves engaging the informal[289] sector to enhance its reach, effectiveness, and compliance with human rights standards.

*7.8.4 Address barriers to both quantity and quality.* In a society recovering from violent conflict, several barriers to justice—financial, geographic, linguistic, logistical, or gender-specific—are present. Improving access is not just about more courtrooms or more staff. It is also about quality of justice. Justice systems that are remote, unaffordable, slow, or incomprehensible to the public effectively deny legal protection.[290] Increase the quantity and quality of justice administration to address these problems.

---

283. UNDP, "Access to Justice," 2004.

284. A grievance is defined as a gross injury or loss that constitutes a violation of a country's criminal or civil law or international human rights norms and standards. Ibid.

285. United Nations Development Programme, *Programming for Justice: Access for All: A Practitioner's Guide to Human Rights-Based Approach to Access to Justice* (Bangkok: UNDP, 2005). Hereafter: UNDP, *Programming for Justice*, 2005.

286. UNDP, "Access to Justice," 2004.

287. United States Agency for International Development, *Rebuilding the Rule of Law in Post-Conflict Environments*, 2006. Hereafter: USAID, *Rebuilding the ROL*, 2006.

288. The formal justice system includes courts, prosecution, police, prisons, and public defense. Ibid.

289. The informal system includes modern processes, (e.g., noncourt mediation and arbitration) and customary justice (e.g., tribal councils, village elder councils, or other local dispute resolution approaches). USAID, "Rebuilding the ROL," 2006.

290. United Kingdom Department for International Development, "Safety, Security, and Accessible Justice," 2002.

Better prepared defense attorneys, more citizen-oriented court staff, more reasonable hours, better information about the justice system are all means for improving quality. The justice system should be linguistically accessible with local language proceedings or provision of interpretation.

***7.8.5 Enhance physical access.*** Courthouses and police stations may only exist in urban, populated areas, leaving the rest of the country without proper access to the formal justice system. Bring judges, prosecutors, defense counsel, court administrative staff (including translators), police, and corrections officials, as well as logistical/security support and public information capacity to areas where the justice system has ceased to function. While mobile courts may be needed in the emergency phase to deal with the most acute needs, they can also provide a long-term solution to endemic access to justice challenges.[291] Efforts to build and staff courthouses and police posts outside of urban areas should also be undertaken to increase access to justice.

***7.8.6 Increase access through provision of legal aid.*** Legal information centers and legal aid offices that offer free or low-cost legal advice and representation, pro se projects that train people to represent themselves, and paralegal-based projects that train and employ people to serve as advocates and mediators, can all increase public knowledge of the legal system.[292] Supplement legal aid schemes with paralegal aid schemes run by NGOs.[293] Paralegals are trained in criminal law and procedure in order to provide legal advice to suspects or accused persons who are brought before the informal justice system. They also sit in on police interviews and go to court to provide advice (but do not represent the accused). Legal assistance can also be provided by law students or recent graduates through their law schools or legal resource centers.

***7.8.7 Promote legal awareness.***[294] For the population to access justice, they must understand their rights and the means for claiming them. For most people in a war-torn state, the laws and the formal justice system are alien institutions they fear or do not understand. Legal awareness helps counter this misunderstanding and promote access to justice. Legal awareness campaigns can be conducted by the state but they are most effective when conducted by civil society at a grassroots level or through the media. Because providing information to huge populations is a significant challenge, trusted and familiar social networks (i.e., community-based formal and informal networks) can be used to enhance legal awareness efforts.[295] Legal awareness of suspects and the accused should also be promoted. Messages should be in local languages and should take into account literacy rates.

***7.8.8 Strengthen civil society as the foundation for promoting access to justice.*** Even though civil society may be shattered after violent conflict, its role in promoting access to justice and for reforming rule of law is important.[296] Civil society organizations should have a legal status to appear in court to undertake public interest litigation. Legal barriers to their work will need to be removed (e.g., laws that prohibit civil

---

291. UNDPKO, "Primer for Justice Components," 2006.
292. Dobbins/Jones/Crane/Cole DeGrasse, *Beginner's Guide,* 2007.
293. UNDP, "Programming for Justice," 2005.
294. Ibid.
295. UNDP, "Access to Justice," 2004.
296. USAID, "Rebuilding the ROL," 2006.

society from criticizing the judiciary). Development of civil society is further addressed in Section 8.8.

***7.8.9 Recognize that increased access to justice depends on public confidence in the justice system.*** The citizen-friendliness and quality of institutions are as important as proximity to the population they serve. Increasing access to justice is not always about quantity—quality is very important when designing legal aid programs because poor legal representation is not necessarily better than lack of legal representation. In war-torn societies, marginalized groups are especially vulnerable to discrimination and unequal treatment. Thus, justice systems must be linguistically and culturally accessible. Try to ensure that staff members are representative of the host nation population. Simplified procedures and widely promulgated laws and decisions help too.[297]

### 7.8.10 Approach: Remedies for Grievances
Maximizing access to justice[298] involves the use of both informal/non-state and formal/state justice mechanisms based on strict compliance with human rights standards. This will likely require harmonizing informal practices with international human rights law.

***7.8.11 Understand informal justice mechanisms.*** These systems derive legitimacy from traditional, customary, or religious sources. In these environments, they often help resolve disputes because the formal, state-based system does not reach the entire population, the population views informal mechanisms as more legitimate and effective, and the volume of cases may be too large for the formal system to process. Informal practices may also continue functioning at the local level in the absence of a formal and codified legal system.[299] Where these systems are ignored or overridden, the result can be the exclusion of large sectors of society from accessible justice.[300]

***7.8.12 Use the local context to determine how and to what extent local practices should be incorporated into the formal legal system.*** During transitional phases, there will inevitably be overlap and contradictions between formal and informal justice mechanisms. Consider the compatibility of local practices with international norms, whether they can be integrated within the formal justice system or have to stand alongside it, and whether the practices serve to divide society or unite it.[301]

***7.8.13 Modify or use informal systems in combination with formal mechanisms to ensure adherence to international human rights standards while maximizing access and public trust in the system.*** Some informal systems violate international human rights standards or promote biases and tensions that are drivers of conflict. Modifications can be made, for example, to allow religious courts to have jurisdiction in certain cases but prevent them from carrying out punishments that would be considered violations of human rights.[302] Determine under what circumstances cases should be referred to the formal system and create mechanisms through which judges in

---

297. USAID, "Guide to ROL," 2008.
298. Eric Scheye, *Pragmatic Realism in Justice and Security Development: Supporting Improvement in the Performance of Non-State/Local Justice and Security Networks* (The Hague: Clingendael Institute, 2009).
299. UNDP/USAID, "First Steps," 2007.
300. UN Sec-Gen, "UN Approach to Rule of Law Assistance," 2008.
301. United Nations, "Law Overruled: Strengthening the Rule of Law in Postconflict States," 2008.
302. USAID, "Guide to ROL," 2008. Dobbins/Jones/Crane/Cole DeGrasse, *Beginner's Guide,* 2007.

the formal system endorse or validate punishments handed down by the informal system.[303] Informal systems should be subject to the same level of oversight and accountability as the formal system in order to promote public trust in their integrity and legitimacy.[304]

*See Gap/Challenge: Section 7.11.5, Engagement with non-state or religious justice systems.*

**7.8.14 Support the adjudication of claims for a remedy through the formal state justice system and civil society.**[305] In order to seek and obtain a remedy, there has to be an adjudication procedure in place. In the early days after conflict, mobile courts may be used. Initiatives that enhance the independence of the judiciary—a cornerstone for access to justice[306]—should also be prioritized. Other means of adjudication include national human rights commissions[307] or alternative dispute resolution mechanisms that can be led by the state, by a non-state justice system (NSJS), or by non-state actors (e.g., civil society) such as through arbitration[308] or mediation/conciliation.[309] The establishment of arbitration or mediation through the state justice system will require both law reform measures and specific mechanisms. This is a long-term venture. Arbitration and mediation through the non-state justice system or by non-state actors may already be ongoing and can be supported in the short term. Mediation or arbitration by civil society works where credible and influential NGOs can be identified.

**7.8.15 Support the adjudication of claims for a remedy through the informal non-state justice system.**[310] The non-state justice system will generally deal with close to 80 percent of disputes in many countries.[311] Non-state justice systems are systems that have some form of non-state authority in providing safety, security, and accessible justice to the population and include traditional, customary, religious, and informal mechanisms.[312] Consider ways to work with these systems, despite challenges such as human rights violations and the fact that NSJSs cannot address crimes outside their communities, such as organized crime, or disputes between communities.[313] In the short term, international and host nation actors should consider some of the following options:

- Restoring internal accountability mechanisms (such as methods for selecting customary justice authorities or ensuring the possibility of appeal) and training non-state justice authorities in mediation techniques and familiarizing them with domestic laws.

---

303. United Kingdom Stabilisation Unit, "ROL and Stablisation," 2008.
304. UK PSO Guide.
305. Ibid.
306. Ibid.
307. UNDP, "Programming for Justice," 2005.
308. Arbitration involves "a simplified version of a trial involving less strict rules of evidence." Decisions are binding and this form of alternative dispute resolution (ADR) "is often used to resolve commercial or business disputes." (UNDP, "Access to Justice," 2004).
309. Mediation/conciliation involves a third-party intervention (the mediator or a panel of mediators) in which the disputing parties meet and negotiate face-to-face and where the mediator may advise on, or determine the process of, mediation (UNDP, "Access to Justice," 2004).
310. UNDP, "Programming for Justice," 2005.
311. United Kingdom Department for International Development, *Non-State Justice and Security Systems,* 2004.
312. Ibid.
313. UNODC/USIP, "DRAFT: Handbook on Criminal Justice Reform," 2009.

- Promoting rights awareness or training community members or paralegals to advocate for women and marginalized groups before the NSJS.
- Encouraging the recording of cases and their resolution to promote consistency of decisions and to provide a basis for appeal to the formal system.
- Improving linkages between the formal and informal systems on criminal matters in the short term and working out criteria for when the NSJS can deal with criminal matters and when they must refer them to the formal system.
- Working with customary authorities, state actors, and civil society to incorporate restorative principles such as compensation and reconciliation, into cases dealt with by the formal justice system.
- Working to mitigate harmful practices such as witchcraft trials. With regard to the latter activity, top-down prohibitions tend to be ineffective and counterproductive.[314] A more effective way is to work with tribal leaders and others to gain their acceptance of change.

*7.8.16 Develop culturally acceptable alternatives to harmful practices.*[315] Dialogue and community initiatives to develop culturally acceptable alternatives to harmful practices are important. Another option is to develop alternatives for those who may potentially be subject to harmful practices by the NSJS by providing them with legal aid or resources to access the formal system. Focus on longer-term initiatives between the formal and informal systems to identify problems and construct solutions. Draw on comparative examples from other countries that have struggled with the integration of the formal and NSJS to help design possible models of integration.
*See Trade-off: Section 7.10.1, Culture vs. human rights.*

*7.8.17 Support the enforcement of remedies.*[316] Remedies are useless if they are not enforced. The enforcement of remedies is the province of the prosecution service, the police, and the prison service. NGOs may also monitor the enforcement of remedies.

*7.8.18 Approach: Fairness*
A society emerging from conflict often suffers severe case backlog and other deficiencies. In spite of this challenge, the justice system must handle cases efficiently and predictably, according to set principles and procedures, including equality before the law and equal application of the law. An efficient system can provide some level of deterrence against criminal acts and discourages delaying cases, such as by bribes from those trying to influence decisions.[317]

*7.8.19 Ensure equal application of the law.*[318] In a society emerging from conflict, individuals with power and marginalized populations may receive unequal treatment. This imbalance in application will likely have caused deep mistrust in the system or may have led to violent resolution of disputes. Applying the law equally regardless of iden-

---

314. Ibid.
315. Ibid.
316. UNDP, "Programming for Justice," 2005.
317. Rachel Belton, *Competing Definitions of the Rule of Law: Implications for Practitioners* (Washington, D.C.: Carnegie Endowment for International Peace, 2005).
318. USAID, "Guide to ROL," 2008.

tity is critical to creating a semblance of fairness and legitimacy. This involves applying laws in a nondiscriminatory manner, treating all parties equally in the courtroom, and having rulings that are consistent with the law regardless of the identity of the parties (gender, class, religion). Ensure the law is consistently and equally applied in both criminal and civil matters (land titling, enforcement of leans, landlord-tenant disputes, and debt collection).

***7.8.20 Promote procedural fairness.***[319] Procedural fairness helps mitigate abuse by police, judges, and prosecutors by establishing fair rules for legal proceedings and adhering to them. For criminal offenses, procedural fairness involves guaranteeing the right of those accused of crimes to know the charges levied against them in a language they understand, the right to obtain or be provided counsel, the right to present evidence in their defense, the opportunity to hear or review the prosecutor's evidence, the opportunity to confront and cross-examine witnesses (where oral proceedings exist), and a right to a speedy trial, particularly if incarcerated. In civil matters, procedural fairness ensures that all parties have a full and equal opportunity to be heard, to present evidence and arguments in support of their position, to have notice of and opportunity to respond to the case presented against them, and to receive timely and adequate notice of all court proceedings. Adequate procedural protection helps ensure that law enforcement cannot violate the rights of individuals.

***7.8.21 Facilitate transparency in all judicial processes.***[320] Transparency throughout the justice system guards against abuse of power by officials, such as court personnel destroying court records or judges altering the outcome of cases or making judgments that contradict evidence. Consider transparent case-tracking mechanisms, which make it difficult to tamper with files, and transparent trial processes, which prevent judges from ruling in favor of power brokers when the evidence should lead to conviction.

***7.8.22 Ensure effective application of the law, ensure adequate authority to enforce judgments, and improve the efficiency of court administration and management.*** Judgments are useless unless they are effectively enforced. Consider the need for sufficient authority for judges and enforcement agents to enforce judgments, including authorities for issuing interim orders to freeze assets.[321] Further, if individuals do not feel that their grievances will be addressed in an efficient and timely manner through a legitimate system, they may resort to violent alternatives. The majority of people should see the judicial system as viable, responsive, and fair. Understand the roots of inefficiency, which may include inadequate procedures, lack of access, and discrimination.[322] Legal reform programs should emphasize case management, budgeting, personnel, and financial policies. Due to the importance of court administrative functions, a specific administrative office is established in some systems. Where possible, automation of records and processes can significantly increase efficiency, enabling other reforms and improving the quality of judicial decisions, even while pursuing longer-term reform and streamlining of processes. Online storage of legal materials, case information, previous decisions, and other materials can improve the quality of judicial decisions.

---

319. Ibid.
320. Ibid.
321. Ibid.
322. USAID, "Guide to ROL," 2008.

These automated solutions can strengthen court statistical and analysis functions, which can assist with more efficient assignment of work and can support budget and staffing decisions.[323]

***7.8.23 Increase the knowledge and professionalization of justice personnel to dispense justice.*** Education and training, as well as increased access to laws, are also critical to ensuring professionalism of justice system personnel.[324] For example, lawyers need to have adequate knowledge of the law and legal procedures to effectively represent parties in court, while judges need to fully understand applicable laws and trial procedures. Judicial and bar associations can serve as a community where good conduct is supported and promoted.

## 7.9 Necessary Condition: Culture of Lawfulness

### 7.9.1 What is a culture of lawfulness? Why is it a necessary condition?

A culture of lawfulness means that the population in general follows the law and has a desire to access the justice system to address their grievances.[325] It does not require that every single individual in that society believe in the feasibility or even the desirability of the rule of law but that the average person believes that formal laws are a fundamental part of justice or can be used to attain justice and that the justice system can enhance his or her life and society in general.[326] Without a culture of lawfulness, the population will have no desire to access the system and may resort to violence to resolve grievances. For the rule of law to be fully realized, the population needs to follow the law and support its application voluntarily rather than through coercion.

### 7.9.2 Guidance for Promoting a Culture of Lawfulness

*7.9.3 Approach: Participation and Communication*
Participation and communication can help build the foundations for a culture of lawfulness, which may not exist in a society emerging from conflict. Participation means that the population feels they are a part of the process and can use the law to improve their lives. Communication means that an open dialogue exists between the rule of law community and the population in general and that the public has the means to obtain information from the government.

*7.9.4 Support legal empowerment of marginalized communities.*[327] Legal empowerment refers to "the use of legal services and related development activities to increase disadvantaged populations' control over their lives." Legal empowerment aims to prevent the poor from being excluded from legally recognized systems, particularly concerning property and labor rights.[328] This involves development that is community-driven and rights-based

---

323. UNDPKO, "Primer for Justice Components," 2006.

324. Ibid.

325. Roy Godson, "A Guide to Developing a Culture of Lawfulness," presented at the Symposium on the Role of Civil Society in Countering Organized Crime: Global Implications of the Palermo, Sicily Renaissance, 2000. Hereafter: Godson, "Culture of Lawfulness," 2000.

326. Ibid.

327. Stephen Golub, *Beyond Rule of Law Orthodoxy: Legal Empowerment Initiative* (Washington, D.C.: Carnegie Endowment for International Peace, 2003).

328. United Nations Commission on the Legal Empowerment of the Poor, *Concept to Action*, 2006.

and is seen as an alternative to more conventional rule of law programs. Specific mechanisms for legal empowerment can include legal services that reduce poverty, promote the rights of marginalized populations, and connect these populations to the rule of law system. Focus on civil society initiatives that strengthen legal capacities and power of marginalized populations, but also engage the government wherever possible.

*7.9.5 Promote public participation.* In many societies emerging from conflict, the population may be afraid to speak out and voice their opinions.[329] They may have little experience with participation. The international community should promote participation in rule of law reforms. When the population starts to feel part of the process, they connect to their society, thus strengthening social cohesion and their investment in promoting the rule of law, and they begin to trust in their government and the justice system,[330] both of which are essential for planting the seeds of a culture of lawfulness and respect for the rule of law.

*7.9.6 Promote communication between the justice system and the population.* In societies emerging from conflict, a lack of mutual understanding and trust commonly exists between the population and the justice system. The international community should support efforts to open the lines of communication to help enhance mutual trust and understanding through dialogue between the public and the justice system. Dialogue can be convened around key issues affecting both the population and the justice system or through permanent communication structures such as local community-police fora. These dialogue sessions can also provide a forum for justice actors and the population to put forward joint proposals for rule of law reforms. Another way to foster communication and understanding is to establish more permanent communication structures such as local community policing boards in which the police meet with the population on a regular basis to discuss issues of concern to both sides.

*7.9.7 Ensure transparency.*[331] For the media or civil society to be able to report on government conduct, there needs to be transparency in government operations that affords the population access to budget information and other government documents. Laws and procedures that provide for transparency (e.g., public budgets, freedom of information legislation) should be put in place to help the media or civil society report on government conduct.

### 7.9.8 Approach: Education and Culture

Building a culture of lawfulness involves civic- and school-based education, centers of moral authority, and mass media and popular culture. Strive to affect the way citizens understand, use, and value the law rather than just building institutions and structures in the society.[332] These activities work to improve community-justice system relations and build knowledge, trust, and respect for the law and the justice system.

---

329. See Deepa Narayan, Robert Chambers, Meera K. Shah, Patti Petesch, *Voices of the Poor: Crying Out for Change* (Oxford: Oxford University Press, 2000). Hereafter: Narayan/Chambers/Shah/Petesch, Voices of the Poor, 2000.

330. Ibid.

331. Godson, "Culture of Lawfulness," 2000.

332. Thomas Carothers, "The Problem of Knowledge," in *Promoting the Rule of Law Abroad* (Washington, D.C.: Carnegie Endowment for International Peace, 2006).

*7.9.9 Support school-based education.*[333] By including rule of law curriculum as part of school education for children, a strong culture of lawfulness message is sent not only to students but to the families and the community. School education programs should help young people understand how the rule of law improves quality of life and why they should follow the law, as well as develop knowledge of the justice system and skills for preventing crime.

*7.9.10 Involve centers of moral authority.*[334] Centers of moral authority might be faith-based institutions and leaders of religious movements, artists, writers, teachers, or locally well-known courageous figures. These individuals or groups can support a culture of lawfulness through their statements, teachings, and pastoral messages. For example, they may send messages to the population about the need to embrace the rule of law and about their roles and responsibilities. They may also mobilize the community against crime and openly condemn it.

*7.9.11 Engage the mass media and popular culture.*[335] The mass media and popular culture are powerful institutions in many countries. They can send strong messages that support a culture of lawfulness and the rule of law. The media can also expose crime and corruption and provide a forum for the population to express their views on the rule of law by covering related issues or topics and by providing a forum for national discussion. Popular culture, through films, popular songs, television, advertising, and art can all convey positive rule of law messages. The role of media outlets is discussed further in Section 8.8.10.

*7.9.12 Work with law enforcement agencies.*[336] Law enforcement agencies are at the front lines and are the first point of contact of the justice system with the population. Law enforcement officials should send a message that rule of law matters, that corruption will not be rewarded, and that officers are expected to ensure responsive, service-oriented policing. Accountability mechanisms also support a culture of lawfulness. Education of law enforcement officials is necessary, as are performance reviews that take into account how the official has upheld the rule of law.[337] Community policing is addressed in Section 6.7.23.

# 7.10 Trade-offs

*7.10.1 Culture vs. human rights.* Rule of law requires that all laws and institutions conform to international human rights norms and standards.[338] But best practice suggests that a state's culture should be respected. Very often, human rights standards are at direct odds with aspects of culture (e.g., treatment of women; cruel, inhuman punishments delivered by the non-state justice system). The international community can take a firm position that the country should work toward achieving international human rights standards, a goal which can be achieved incrementally. Certain core standards such as the

333. Godson, "Culture of Lawfulness," 2000.
334. Ibid.
335. Ibid.
336. Ibid.
337. See in general, http://www.cultureoflawfulness.org/.
338. UN Sec-Gen, "Secretary-General's Report," 2004.

prohibition against torture can be insisted upon in the short term. In other cases, the international community should support dialogue on human rights and culture and support reform constituencies that are pro-human rights.

*7.10.2 Security vs. human rights.* Security and human rights are often pitted against each other in the aftermath of conflict, where insecurity reigns. Some insist that security takes precedence over human rights. The provision of security to the population, however, is a human right, and these are not mutually exclusive concepts. States around the world work to balance the need to protect the security of the population with human rights guarantees. Violations of human rights will have been the hallmark of the prior oppressive regime. In the aftermath of conflict, abandoning human rights principles at the very moment they need to be promoted sends a message to the population that human rights do not matter and they will be harder to build later.

*7.10.3 Peace vs. justice.* There is a strong call for justice after conflict for conflict-related abuses. At the same time, the imperative of peace needs to be protected. In some instances, measures to ensure that justice is administered against certain individuals may ignite tensions and may negatively impact a fragile peace. The question often arises about whether to prosecute and ensure justice or not to prosecute and preserve peace. Some argue that there should be no political considerations taken into account and that justice should prevail at any cost. Others argue that it is more important to preserve peace than to go after individual perpetrators immediately after conflict. Any decision on whether to pursue justice against certain individuals, whose prosecution may impact peace, should be carefully considered.

*7.10.4 Quick fixes vs. a strategic approach.*[339] There is the temptation, coupled with a sense of urgency, to "do" and to start fixing the justice system immediately. This approach has resulted in suboptimal results in the past. There are certainly activities that can promote rule of law in the short term. However, a strategic approach is much more likely to be successful in the long term.

# 7.11 Gaps and Challenges

*7.11.1 Comprehensive, coordinated rule of law assessments.* Assessments need to be taken more seriously and more money, time, and effort need to be invested in them, both immediately after conflict and thereafter. A standard assessment methodology involving the legal and extra-legal components needs to be developed. A greater effort to share assessments among the international community is also required.

*7.11.2 Monitoring and evaluation.* Monitoring and evaluation of rule of law assistance is not taken seriously by the international community; many staff are not trained and funds are not allocated to do it properly. Monitoring and evaluation needs to be prioritized and the results need to be shared widely so that the field as a whole can grow and learn from past experiences.

*7.11.3 Prioritization and sequencing.* There is no methodology or policy guidance on how to sequence and prioritize rule of law assistance. The international community does not fully understand what assistance to provide when and at what juncture that assistance will

---

339. UK Stabilisation Unit, "Rule of Law and Stabilisation," 2006.

be the most effective. This is because it knows little about how positive change occurs and how to support it.[340] There is an urgent need for systematic research and discussions on change and how rule of law is brought about.[341]

***7.11.4 Prioritization of noncriminal justice assistance.*** Criminal justice is often prioritized as the primary focus for rule of law assistance. Other important areas of potential assistance, such as property rights or public administration reform, have not been addressed. Property issues and displacement can affect a large percentage of the population.[342] More people may deal with the state's public administration than with the criminal justice system on matters such as civil registration and health services.[343] Research and the development of best practices in these fields needs to be developed.

***7.11.5 Engagement with non-state or religious justice systems.*** While it is agreed that there needs to be engagement with the non-state justice system to promote the rule of law, the international community does not fully understand these systems, how they operate, what to do with regard to human rights issues, and even less so, what assistance measures promote the rule of law. Empirical, comparative research is needed. In addition, research is needed to look at how to deal with non-state, religious systems of justice and how to integrate religious considerations into rule of law assistance overall.

***7.11.6 Capacity development of international and host nation rule of law staff.*** Rule of law practitioners often go to work in societies emerging from conflict with very little rule of law experience. The rule of law community needs to ensure the highest level of training for rule of law practitioners, coordinate around core content of education and training, and require that practitioners have the requisite skills and knowledge to do their job. Rule of law practitioners could also benefit from a community of practice, where new initiatives, documents, or research can be shared and discussed.[344] The international community should support the training of host nation actors on rule of law to support ownership and capacity development.

***7.11.7 Gender mainstreaming.*** The international community is not adept in mainstreaming gender through rule of law assistance, including ensuring women's needs are met by justice institutions, that women have equal access to justice and fair treatment under the law,[345] and that women participate in the development of rule of law strategies. Many of the crimes committed against women in conflict and after (e.g., domestic violence, rape) are not adequately addressed. Just like human rights, gender should be mainstreamed through all rule of law assistance measures. The international community should develop strategies for this to address sexual- and gender- based violence that occurs during and after violent conflict.

---

340. Samuels (WB), "Rule of Law Reform," 2006.

341. Ibid.

342. Scott Leckie, ed., *Housing Land and Property Rights in Post-Conflict United Nations and Other Peace Operations: A Comparative Survey and Proposal for Reform* (London, UK: Cambridge University Press, 2008).

343. Per Berling, Lars Bejstam, Jenny Ederlöv, Erik Wennerström, and Richard Zajac Sannerholm, *Rule of Law in Public Administration: Problems and Ways Ahead in Peace Building and Development* (Sweden: Folke Bernadotte Academy, 2008).

344. See for example, the International Network to Promote the Rule of Law (www.inprol.org).

345. For a primer on ensuring access to justice for women, see United Nations Development Programme, *Gender Equality and Justice Programming: Equitable Access to Justice for Women,* 2007.

# SECTION 8
# STABLE GOVERNANCE

**Provision of Essential Services**
- Core Service Delivery
- Access and Non-Discrimination
- Host Nation Capacity

**Stewardship of State Resources**
- Restoration of Executive Institutions and Public Administration
- Security Sector Reform
- Protection of State Resources

## STABLE GOVERNANCE
Ability of the people to share, access, or compete for power through nonviolent political processes and to enjoy the collective benefits and services of the state.

**Civic Participation and Empowerment**
- Civil Society Development
- Independent Media and Access to Information
- Inclusive and Participatory Political Parties

**Political Moderation and Accountability**
- National Constituting Processes
- Political Governance and Conflict Management
- Systems of Representation
- Legislative Strengthening

# Stable Governance

*Ability of the people to share, access, or compete for power through nonviolent political processes and to enjoy the collective benefits and services of the state.*

## 8.0 What is stable governance?

Stable governance refers to an end state where the state provides essential services and serves as a responsible steward of state resources; government officials are held accountable through political and legal processes; and the population can participate in governance through civil society organizations, an independent media, and political parties. Stable governance is the mechanism through which the basic human needs of the population are largely met, respect for minority rights is assured, conflicts are managed peacefully through inclusive political processes, and competition for power occurs nonviolently. National and subnational government institutions may work with a range of non-state partners to provide some of the government functions. Essential services—defined here as security, the rule of law, economic governance, and basic human needs services—are addressed fully in Sections 6, 7, 9, and 10, respectively.

## 8.1 What are the key governance challenges in societies emerging from conflict?

Societies emerging from conflict often have debilitated or corrupted governance institutions, lack professional capacity for governance, and require new or reformed legal frameworks for political engagement. State security forces may be degraded, nonexistent or have been co-opted by warring parties. An urgent demand for humanitarian assistance, amplified by a general lack of institutional capacity, often exists, especially for minority or displaced populations. Due to the degradation of security and the rule of law during violent conflict, a culture of fear may have overwhelmed a culture of civic participation, resulting in the collapse of civil society organizations and media.

## 8.2 Why is stable governance a necessary end state?

Without stable governance, political spoilers may rise to fill the governance vacuum and usurp state resources. Their quest to gain authority and control over resources—often aided and abetted by organized criminal groups, terrorist organizations, or other profiteers—can destabilize the state and motivate a return to violence. When the government cannot provide for the population, people will do whatever it takes to put bread on the table and ensure their own security, even if it means supporting opponents to the peace process or engaging in criminal activity.

## 8.3 What are the necessary conditions to achieve stable governance?

- *Provision of Essential Services* is a condition in which the state provides basic security, the rule of law, economic governance and basic human needs services; essential services are provided without discrimination; and the state has the capacity for provision of essential services without significant assistance from the international community.

- *Stewardship of State Resources* is a condition in which national and subnational institutions of governance are restored, funded, and staffed with accountable personnel; the security sector is reformed and brought under accountable civilian control; and state resources are protected through responsible economic management in a manner that benefits the population.

- *Political Moderation and Accountability* is a condition in which the government enables political settlement of disputes; addresses core grievances through debate, compromise, and inclusive national dialogue; and manages change arising from humanitarian, economic, security, and other challenges. A national constituting process results in separation of powers that facilitates checks and balances; the selection of leaders is determined through inclusive and participatory processes; a legislature reflects the interests of the population; and electoral processes are free and fair.

- *Civic Participation and Empowerment* is a condition in which civil society exists and is empowered, protected, and accountable; media are present, professional, and independent of government or political influence; equal access to information and freedom of expression are upheld; and political parties are able to form freely and are protected.

# 8.4 General Guidance for Stable Governance

*8.4.1 Build host nation ownership and capacity.* Stable governance is fundamentally dependent on domestic capacity to perform core administrative, political and economic governance functions.[346] That means helping leaders, government personnel, and civil society acquire the skills and tools needed to govern accountably, participate in political processes, and provide core services for the population. This may often require helping to build the capacity of informal/non-state governance institutions to complement formal/state functions.

*8.4.2 Act only with an understanding of the local context.* Understand the specific and unique governance needs of the host nation. There are few universally applicable approaches for achieving the conditions necessary for stable governance.[347] Programs aimed at strengthening governance must be based on in-depth needs assessments and specific knowledge of the host nation's historical, cultural, societal, economic, and political background. This understanding should include input from the host nation population from various sides of the conflict and marginalized groups such as women, minorities, youth, and the poor. Key considerations include the following:

- What are the core functions the government must perform?
- What role did institutions of governance play in the conflict?
- What is necessary and acceptable to the host nation population given cultural, political, and historical considerations and resources?
- What are the core institutions—state and non-state—that can perform governance functions and in what condition are they?
- What laws and regulations, processes, and procedures, if any, govern these functions?

---

346. U.S. Army, *Field Manual 3-07*, 2008.
347. United Nations Department of Economic and Social Affairs and United Nations Development Programme, *The Challenges of Restoring Governance in Crisis and Post-Conflict Countries*, 2007. Hereafter: UNDESA/UNDP, *Challenges of Restoring Governance*, 2007.

- What is the condition of the basic infrastructure required to perform core functions?
- What financial and human resources exist? Are they adequate to provide essential services to places in need?
- Are there oversight mechanisms for state institutions? Are they empowered to take action?[348]

***8.4.3 Prioritize to stabilize.*** For stability, prioritize governance functions that support the delivery of essential services and contribute to political settlements.[349] Focus on producing political settlements that help resolve conflicts that were not addressed in a peace agreement or a mandate. Think hard about the protection of critical state resources—human, natural, financial, cultural, and infrastructure—that are necessary to prevent and mitigate conflict. Priorities should ultimately be determined by their potential to prevent conflict and increase the strength of nonviolent political settlements.[350]

***8.4.4 Use a conflict lens.*** All choices in governance affect power relationships. The choice of an interim minister, the location of a municipal center, the adoption of a regulation, or the award of a contract to a local business has the ability to exacerbate tensions or address and resolve internal conflicts. Be sure to identify and understand the specific sources of conflict and motivations for violence to ensure that governance reform efforts do not reignite violent conflict.

***8.4.5 Recognize interdependence.*** The widely understood core functions of governance—security, the rule of law, meeting basic human needs, and economic governance—are intertwined like a rope. Failure to provide one will unravel the ability to provide the others. The administration and delivery of humanitarian assistance and basic services to the population, for example, depends on adequate security for civilians and some basic rule of law system that prevents banditry and looting of critical supplies and resources. All of these core services depend on sound economic management and governance.

# 8.5 Necessary Condition: Provision of Essential Services

### 8.5.1 What is the provision of essential services? Why is it a necessary condition?
Providing essential services is the primary function of administrative governance in societies emerging from conflict. These societies are in immediate need of security, the rule of law, economic governance, and basic human needs services such as health and education.[351] In providing these services, the focus must be on the development of host nation capacity, equal access, and nondiscrimination in service delivery, and adequate and timely payment of civil service salaries to make peace pay. Providing essential services boosts the legitimacy of the host nation government and limits the influence of drivers of conflict that exploit the absence of essential services. Experience shows that

---

348. UK Stabilisation Unit, "UK Approach to Stabilisation," 2008.
349. Organisation for Economic Co-operation and Development, *From Fragility to Resilience: Concepts and Dilemmas of Statebuilding in Fragile States,* 2007.
350. UK Stabilisation Unit, "UK Approach to Stabilisation," 2008.
351. Derick W. Brinkerhoff, ed., *Governance in Post-Conflict Societies: Rebuilding Fragile States.* (New York: Routledge, 2007). Hereafter: Brinkerhoff, *Governance in Post-Conflict Societies,* 2007.

people perceive the authority to govern to be contingent upon the provision of security, the rule of law, sound economic governance, and basic human needs services.

### 8.5.2 Guidance for the Provision of Essential Services

### *8.5.3 Approach: Core Service Delivery*

Core service delivery involves providing security, the rule of law, economic governance, and basic human needs services for stabilization and reconstruction. Providing these services involves developing the core administrative and institutional capabilities of government. Accountability and transparency mechanisms, along with adequate resources, are necessary to provide equitable and effective service delivery, minimize corruption, and impede threats to the peace process by those who aim to sabotage delivery.

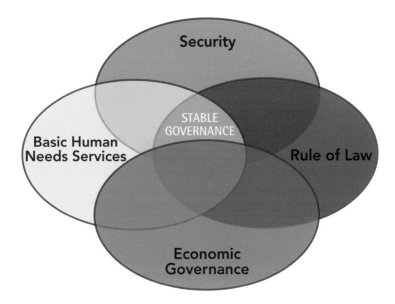

Providing security, the rule of law, economic governance, and basic human needs services are interdependent priorities.

*8.5.4 Focus on providing security, the rule of law, economic governance, and basic human needs services for stability and to provide space for political settlements and development.* Not all government services are immediately essential, and in this resource-constrained, war-shattered environment, not all services can be delivered at once anyway. The priorities will always be security, the rule of law, economic governance, and basic human needs services if not already provided. The military or police, acting in accordance with human rights laws and conventions, must provide security for the host nation population, government employees, and the institutions of the state. Basic human needs—for water, food, shelter, health care, education, and sanitation—must be met. The society needs a system of justice based on the rule of law that holds violators of the peace accountable and offers human rights-based penal institutions for those convicted. When planning and providing these services, their interdependence must be recognized.

*8.5.5 Transparency and accountability mechanisms help ensure that the government delivers essential services effectively and reliably.* In societies emerging from conflict, government policies and use of state assets may have benefited elites and their networks at the expense of the population. Lax budget controls and public management may have led to endemic corruption. Redressing this common pattern of abuse requires, at a minimum, an adequate regulatory framework and budget management executed through some basic professional administration that strictly adheres to human rights conventions and the law. Also needed is a commitment to transparency in developing and implementing government policies, regulations, budgets, contracts, private-public partnerships, and civil service systems for the delivery of essential services.[352] Mechanisms for transparency and accountability help ensure that the government protects the resources it needs to provide services, operates within the bounds of the law, and responds to the population's needs.

*8.5.6 Understand the roles of state and non-state actors in providing services and the impact of those actors on stability.* The host nation government should play a dominant role in providing services by engaging in direct provision of services to the population or by overseeing their provision through contracts. In the latter case, the government sets standards and monitors quality and quantity of service delivery through contracts.[353] But informal actors can fulfill basic functions of governance as well.[354] These actors may include traditional tribal, religious, clan-based networks or those led by warlords and their militias. While these differ from conventional western models of governance, they may have a central role in providing order and social services. These structures could be legitimate or benign and serve as the basis for local governance. Their control over delivery, if completely independent from the state, may have implications for stability, government legitimacy, and the need for nondiscrimination and equal access as they potentially serve only one part of the population (e.g., religious or tribal groups). If they are tied to destabilizing activities, such as arms trafficking

352. Brinkerhoff, *Governance in Post-Conflict Societies,* 2007.
353. United States Agency for International Development, "DRAFT: Guidance for Democracy and Governance Programming in Post-Conflict Countries," 2009. Hereafter: USAID, "DRAFT: Guidance for Democracy and Governance," 2009.
354. Louise Anten, *Strengthening Governance in Post-Conflict Fragile States* (The Hague, The Netherlands: Clingendael Institute, 2009). Hereafter: Anten, "Strengthening Governance," 2009.

or other organized crime activities, their role could undermine peace and should be proscribed or restricted.

*8.5.7 Deliver security as a top priority and provide the cornerstone for stable governance.* Security affords fragile government institutions an opportunity to develop their capacity, ensures the safety of new political leaders and processes, facilitates the effective provision of basic humanitarian services for populations in need, strengthens public support for inclusive and participatory government, and enables and protects critical revenue-generating activities for government operations. The hard lesson learned here is that security is more than the cessation of combat and separation of warring parties. It is about law and order and whether violators of the peace answer to a system of justice based on the rule of law. See also Section 6, Safe and Secure Environment.

*8.5.8 Rebuild and uphold the rule of law as a primary responsibility of the host nation government.* The inability of the justice system to function can allow crime and politically motivated violence to flourish. An integrated system of police, courts, and prisons must not be an afterthought—it is the basis for security. In order to restore the rule of law and banish a culture of impunity, civil and criminal legal codes, law enforcement, judicial institutions, and a penal system are required immediately and will likely need to be restored, rebuilt, or reformed. Equal access to justice should be ensured, particularly for minorities, women, and the poor, and international human rights standards should be upheld.[355] Legal and constitutional frameworks for national and subnational governance need to be established or reformed based on the desires of the host nation population. See also Section 7, Rule of Law.

*8.5.9 Provide good economic governance as a framework for stabilization and reconstruction.* Good economic governance is essential to enable effective provision of basic services and to provide a framework for jumpstarting economic activity in a conflict-affected society. Such a framework for economic governance also addresses the challenges of a war-ravaged market economy, the need to generate employment, the collapse of the public finance system, and management of state of resources.[356] Good economic governance requires a system of laws and regulations, policies and practices, and institutions and individuals that provide a framework for economic recovery.[357] See also Section 9, Sustainable Economy.

*8.5.10 Deliver essential services to meet basic human needs and restore the basis for government legitimacy.* In these environments, there is a potential for large-scale humanitarian crises to threaten a fragile peace and host nation government legitimacy. The role of the government is to create the administrative foundation and infrastructure required to provide these services in a non-discriminatory and effective manner. Nongovernmental or private sector organizations that may help deliver these services should be accountable to national and local authorities with transparent accounting, hiring and management practices, and should adhere to human rights laws and conventions. See also Section 10, Social Well-Being.

---

355. United Nations Development Programme, *Access to Justice Practice Note*, 2004.

356. UNDP/USAID, "First Steps," 2007.

357. United States Agency for International Development, *Economic Governance in War Torn Economies: Lessons Learned from the Marshall Plan to the Reconstruction of Iraq*, 2004.

### 8.5.11 Approach: Access and Nondiscrimination

In societies emerging from conflict, control over the provision of essential services translates into power for those who deliver. Whether it is the government or non-state providers delivering the services, it is necessary that the population have equal access to the services and that the services are provided in a nondiscriminatory manner. Equal access means that administrative, geographic, political, and financial barriers to essential services are removed. Nondiscriminatory service delivery that affords equal treatment regardless of ethnicity, religion, or political affiliation is a requirement for stability.

### 8.5.12 How essential services are provided is just as important as the delivery itself.

Because the provision of essential services empowers and bestows authority upon providers, those responsible for decisions must think about which institutions will provide the services, which political officials will be responsible for oversight, how the services will be provided, and by what standards. The dialogue on restoring services and accompanying infrastructure should begin before a peace agreement is signed and should include both providers and intended beneficiaries. Identify the appropriate individuals for managing resources, developing institutional capacity and monitoring service delivery, and be sure that implementation is carried out by legitimate national and subnational agencies.[358] An effective monitoring system that engages the host nation population and civil society will enhance service provision.

### 8.5.13 Provide equal access to services and nondiscrimination in delivery to enhance the government's legitimacy, support the peace process, and help prevent a renewal of conflict.

Before or during violent conflict, essential services may have been denied to certain segments of the population either as a means for punishing some and rewarding others or because the collapse of government institutions prevented delivery. Restoration of service delivery is directly connected to securing peace and preventing renewal of conflict. In service delivery, money, personnel, and infrastructure need to be distributed across the population. In doing so, ensure that all communities, regardless of ethnic, religious, or political affiliation, are provided for and that access is guaranteed.[359] If equal access is not assured or the population perceives that access is preferential, resentment and frustration with the government will likely increase and be capitalized on by spoilers. Impartiality is a legal obligation, regardless of considerations of political necessity.

### 8.5.14 Approach: Host Nation Capacity

Developing host nation capacity is the exit strategy for international actors and the path for peace for the host nation population. Host nation capacity for service delivery means that services are largely implemented and managed by the host nation population. This approach is more affordable and sustainable than using international actors, enhances the government's legitimacy, and boosts the economy by putting resources into the hands of the host nation population. Weak capacity is better than no capacity.

See Trade-off: Section 8.9.1, Rapid and effective delivery of essential services vs. legitimacy for nascent government institutions.

See Trade-off: Section 10.9.1, Delivering assistance through host nation vs. international capacity.

---

358. UNDESA/UNDP, "Challenges of Restoring Governance," 2007.

359. Organisation for Economic Co-operation and Development, *Fragile States: Policy Commitment and Principles for Good International Engagement in Fragile States and Situations*, 2007.

*8.5.15 Build host nation capacity to deliver essential services in a professional, account-able, and sustainable manner.* This requirement places a heavy burden on the need to find, train, mentor, and pay local personnel. Accountability mechanisms to ensure delivery and equal access and to prevent destabilizing corruption are key to building sustainable local capacity. If international assistance is required while capacity is built, typical approaches include (1) temporary substitution for these governments, (2) direct assistance for capacity-building to these governments, (3) support for public-private partnerships, and (4) assistance through nongovernmental organizations.[360] Even when government capacity to provide services is very weak, delivering services "with" rather than "for" local government improves prospects for legitimacy and stability.[361]

*8.5.16 Make peace pay through effective personnel management.* For peace to last, it has to pay. Making peace pay means that government employees responsible for essential services are provided quick employment and are paid. In the immediate aftermath of violent conflict, fair systems are needed for vetting those who perpetrated war crimes or who might use government positions to continue violence. To ensure reasonable guar-antee of service delivery, prevent the rise of pervasive corruption, build constituencies for peace, and make it a priority to pay the salaries of essential service providers on a regular and timely basis.[362] This means that significant resources for salaries should be commit-ted to the central budget, and a transparent and efficient system should be in place for disbursement, including local banking or payment mechanisms. Accounting and tracking procedures should ensure that the money goes to the providers who earn it.
*See Gap/Challenge: Section 8.10.1, Making peace pay and civil service reform.*

*8.5.17 Manage expectations of the population through communication about service delivery.* The population's expectations for services should match reality. This is especially important when a peace accord generates high expectations among the former warring parties and the population.[363] Spoilers are quick to capitalize on unmet expectations and can use the population's frustration to their advantage. National and subnational government institutions should conduct strategic communications cam-paigns about service delivery to keep expectations aligned with the ability to provide.[364] Consultative structures, particularly for local government, should be created to facili-tate dialogue about service needs and delivery between the population and providers.[365]

# 8.6 Necessary Condition: Stewardship of State Resources

### 8.6.1 What is stewardship of state resources? Why is it a necessary condition?
Stewardship of state resources refers to a condition in which the government serves as an effective manager and responsible protector of critical state resources. Achieving this condition in the aftermath of violent conflict entails restoring national and subna-tional institutions of governance; ensuring civilian control, management, and oversight of security services; and protecting state resources. Audit and oversight capabilities,

360. UNDESA/UNDP, "Challenges of Restoring Governance," 2007.
361. UK Stabilisation Unit, "UK Approach to Stabilisation," 2008.
362. UNDP/USAID, "First Steps," 2007.
363. Shari Bryan, *Engaging Political Parties in Post-Conflict Parliaments,* presented at the International Conference on Parliaments, Crisis Prevention and Recovery, 2006. Hereafter: Bryan, *Engaging Political Parties,* 2006.
364. UNDP/USAID, "First Steps," 2007.
365. UK Stabilisation Unit, "UK Approach to Stabilisation," 2008.

both within the government and civil society, are required for effective stewardship of state resources. Since competition for state resources can motivate violence, effective stewardship of those resources helps prevent renewal of violent conflict. Responsible stewardship of state resources also enhances legitimacy and protects and generates critical revenue to provide essential services. In societies emerging from conflict, state resources will likely include substantial contributions from external sources. Protecting those funds is an essential element of stewardship.

## 8.6.2 Guidance for the Stewardship of State Resources

*8.6.3 Approach: Restoration of Executive Institutions and Public Administration*
For the purposes of the manual, executive institutions refer to national and subnational agencies that carry out the main functions of government at the direction of appointed or elected leaders. They often exist in the form of ministries or agencies. Public administration refers to the personnel, systems, and infrastructure in these institutions that are needed to manage budgets, implement government policies, and deliver services. Reform of public administration entails identifying the roles, responsibilities, regulations, and processes involved in providing government services.

*8.6.4 Understand the terrain.* Needs assessments help to determine how to restore government institutions. If the design of former institutions contributed to the collapse of the state or fueled violent conflict, they may need to be reformed rather than simply rebuilt. Critical questions include the following:

- Did the government institutionalize discrimination, violate human rights, promote economic inequality, or foster violence prior to or during conflict?
- Have spoilers captured the institutions of the state?
- What is the relationship between national and subnational government institutions (formal and informal)?
- To what degree does corruption exist in government? Is there a nexus between government officials and perpetrators of violent conflict?
- What resources does the government have (personnel, budgets, infrastructure, facilities)?
- How are government employees selected, trained, paid, promoted, and managed?

*8.6.5 Prepare for transitional governance, but keep a focus on permanent governance.*
Interim governance institutions led by international staff may temporarily substitute for host nation institutions in the immediate aftermath of violent conflict, either due to a lack of host nation capacity or because the peace agreement or mandate demands a period of transition. Transitional structures are most successful when they have access to substantial resources, maintain coercive enforcement capabilities, incorporate host nation personnel, provide essential services, and focus on training government officials and employees.[366] Transitional administrators often have to take quick action on a number of priority issues involving human rights, property rights, and elections.[367] Transitional authorities should make provisions for transferring responsibilities to the

---

366. Karen Guttieri and Jessica Piombo, eds.,. *Interim Governments: Institutional Bridges to Peace and Democracy?* (Washington D.C.: United States Institute of Peace Press, 2007).

367. United Nations Development Programme and Christian Michelsen Institute, *Governance in Post-Conflict Situations*, 2004. Hereafter: UNDP/Michelsen, *Governance in Post-Conflict Situations*, 2004.

institutions that should be designed and built largely by the host nation.[368] International actors may also help develop the design, mandates, and oversight mechanisms of permanent executive, legislative, and judicial institutions.[369]

**8.6.6 Ensure local participation within transitional governance structures through consultation or co-administration.** Engage local leaders, civil society groups, and the general population through consultative or co-administrative mechanisms to ensure legitimacy of transitional governing structures.[370] Consider creating a political advisory council comprising host nation leaders who advise on political decisions, a joint military committee composed of senior commanders from different factions who provide input on security matters, or a joint functional committee of civilians to consult on or help oversee domestic governance functions.[371] Consultative or co-administrative structures should be given sufficient resources and authority. They should enable host nation leaders to participate in decision-making and implementation, give the population a voice in transitional governance, help develop cooperation among representative groups, and train the country's future leaders.[372]

**8.6.7 Restore managerial capacity for governance.** Managerial capacity for governance involves recruitment, appointment, training, and mentoring of ministers, deputy ministers, and other senior public administration personnel. Merit-based criteria for selection may be ideal, but in an S&R environment, the host nation's ability to provide this level of talent may be degraded. Warlords and other faction leaders may need to be included in a new administration, and the diaspora may be brought into positions of leadership, whether for political reasons or because they are most qualified for service. If political considerations dictate the need for inclusion of power brokers and potential spoilers, consider time-restricted appointments and strict oversight of these positions.[373] Build capacity early through advanced training and mentoring and consider placing advisers with some authorities for direct oversight.[374]

**8.6.8 Reform national ministries and public administration to ensure accountable use of public resources and use of regulatory power in a nondiscriminatory manner.** Executive institutions of governance in societies emerging from conflict may have a history of favoritism, cronyism, lax budget controls, corruption, and the use of government policies and regulations to benefit the powerful. Incentives for conflict abound with these situations and the reform of these institutions is a focus for governance in most S&R missions. Ministry restoration and reform is a time- and resource-intensive undertaking that involves defining clear lines of responsibility and parameters for political engagement of personnel and developing organization charts, job descriptions, procedures and

368. UK Stabilisation Unit, "UK Approach to Stabilisation," 2008.

369. UNDP/Michelsen, *Governance in Post-Conflict Situations,* 2004.

370. Beth Cole DeGrasse and Christina Caan, *Transitional Governance: From Bullets to Ballots* (Washington, D.C.: United States Institute of Peace, 2006). Hereafter: Cole DeGrasse/Caan, "Bullets to Ballots," 2006.

371. Jack Covey, Michael J. Dziedzic, and Leonard Hawley, eds., *The Quest for Viable Peace: International Intervention and Strategies for Conflict Transformation* (Washington, D.C.: United States Institute of Peace Press, 2005). Hereafter: Covey/Dziedzic/Hawley, *Quest for Viable Peace,* 2005.

372. Dobbins/Jones/Crane/Cole DeGrasse, *Beginner's Guide,* 2007.

373. USAID, "DRAFT Guidance for Democracy and Governance," 2009.

374. Governance and Economic Management Assistance Program, "Overview," http://www.gemaliberia.org/pages/overview (accessed June 17, 2009).

processes, and structures for administrative control and oversight.[375] Based on decades of experience, trying to establish and legitimize a range of institutions at once is unrealistic and can result in underperformance in multiple institutions.[376] Understand that the host nation must work out its own sequencing of institutional development that is responsive to the needs of its citizens. This should not be imposed by outsiders.

**8.6.9 Focus on civil servants.** A professional and ideally meritocratic civil service[377] promotes effectiveness and accountability. To build trust and credibility, the civil service should be inclusive of marginalized groups and representative of the society as a whole. Build upon existing institutional capacity and start by conducting a census of civil servants.[378] Understand the statutory basis for the civil service and the rights and duties of civil servants. Determine how the service is organized, including grades, salaries, benefits, recruitment, promotion, disciplinary, and termination procedures. Appropriate boundaries between the political and administrative spheres should be established.[379] Create monitoring mechanisms of civil service personnel to mitigate corruption, inefficiency, and discrimination that might exacerbate conflict.[380] Ensuring civil servants are paid in a timely fashion and receive sufficient training and resources contributes to accountability.
See Gap/Challenge: Section 8.10.1, Making peace pay and civil service reform.

**8.6.10 Develop the top-down and bottom-up political processes and institutional structures that are required for stable governance.** Stable governance is a product of successful interaction between functioning and accountable national and subnational institutions and an empowered civil society. Top-down processes aimed at building national governance must also be matched step-by-step with bottom-up processes that develop subnational governance, political parties, and civic participation. Progress at the national level requires that subnational government institutions gain legitimacy and authority, which in turn depends on the ability of the national government to extend resources and services beyond the capital city.

**8.6.11 Strengthen subnational governance capacity.** Developing and strengthening the institutional capacity of subnational governance can lead to increased responsiveness to local concerns, create a venue for conflict management of local disputes, and present opportunities for emerging leaders or previously marginalized groups to enter government.[381] These aspects of decentralization can enable more effective service delivery and

375. USAID, "DRAFT Guidance for Democracy and Governance," 2009.

376. Brinkerhoff, *Governance in Post-Conflict Societies*, 2007.

377. For the purposes of this manual, the "civil service" refers to public servants (national and subnational), whose salaries come from the government, who are hired and managed in accordance with civil service laws, and who are protected from political interference in hiring or removal and the conduct of their duties. See http://web.worldbank.org/WBSITE/EXTERNAL/TOPICS/EXTPUBLIC SECTORANDGOVERNANCE for more information.

378. National Academy of Public Administration, *Civil Service Reforms and International Assistance: An Initial Framework of Lessons Learned*, 2007.

379. World Bank, Conflict Prevention and Reconstruction Unit, *Rebuilding the Civil Service in a Post-Conflict Setting: Key Issues and Lessons of Experience*, 2002. Hereafter: WB, *Rebuilding the Civil Service*, 2002. UNDP/Michelsen, "Governance in Post-Conflict Situations," 2004.

380. Harry Blair, "Rebuilding and Reforming Civil Services in Post-Conflict Societies," in *Governance in Post-Conflict Societies: Rebuilding Fragile States* (New York. NY: Routledge, 2007).

381. U.S. Agency for International Development, *Decentralization and Democratic Local Governance Programming Handbook*, 2000. Hereafter: USAID, *Decentralization and Democratic Local Governance*, 2000.

inter-group political discussion that strengthens bonds within and across communities after conflict.[382] Subnational institutions typically require real decision-making power and authority, control over budgets and resources, the institutional capacity to deliver services, and adequate and timely pay to be effective.[383] Decentralized governance, the degree and forms of which should be a host nation decision, can create rapid and visible results to garner legitimacy within local communities through responsiveness and transparency and emphasize revenue generation as a key priority.[384] Mechanisms to coordinate and communicate between national and subnational institutions facilitate success. Oversight mechanisms for subnational institutions help to ensure inclusivity, transparency, and accountability to the rule of law and may mitigate against factional struggles for control of local governance and resources.

***8.6.12 Consider the impact of different forms of decentralization on stabilization.*** Peace agreements and mandates may include provisions for decentralization, regardless of the local conditions. Understand the potential consequences of decentralization, however, particularly when insecurity or threats to the central government persist and emanate from specific regions. In unstable environments, the potential for spoilers to control local governments raises concerns for continued conflict. Plan for the effects of different forms of decentralization, which may include the following:

- Deconcentration (assigning responsibility to local offices of national ministries);
- Delegation (involving a contractual relationship for the performance of certain functions that may include national, subnational, and nongovernmental institutions)
- Devolution (endowing subnational governments with freedom for autonomous action, accomplished typically through subnational elections).[385]

When possible, align decentralization options to reflect local conditions and increase accountability and stability. Experience in stabilization environments reveals that incremental steps toward decentralization may be most effective. These steps can involve starting with administrative responsibilities for delivering essential services, continuing with fiscal authorities for spending and raising revenue, and concluding with the endowment of political authorities.[386]
*See Gap/Challenge: Section 8.10.2, Subnational governance.*

***8.6.13 Approach: Security Sector Reform***
In a society emerging from conflict, stable governance requires a legitimate state monopoly over the means of violence, which can be developed through security sector reform. SSR seeks to strengthen civilian control, management, and oversight[387] of security forces to ensure that the forces are liable for their conduct and held accountable for abuse of

---

382. Paul Jackson and Zoe Scott, *Local Government in Post-Conflict Environments* (Oslo, Norway: United Nations Development Programme and Oslo Governance Centre, Democratic Governance Group, 2008).

383. UNDP/Michelsen, "Governance in Post-Conflict Situations," 2004.

384. USAID, "Decentralization and Democratic Local Governance," 2000.

385. USAID, "DRAFT Guidance for Democracy and Governance," 2009.

386. Ibid.

387. For the purposes of this manual, "oversight" encompasses supervision, inspection, responsibility, and control, as defined in *Organisation of Economic Co-operation and Development* (Development Assistance Committee), *Handbook on Security System Reform* (Paris: OECD Publishing, 2007). Hereafter: OECD DAC, *Handbook on SSR,* 2007.

power. SSR also involves developing formal security policy that is often absent in governments after violent conflict and may be neglected by S&R actors. Security policies are necessary to govern when and how forces are to be used, how they are managed, and how abuse of authority will be dealt with. These policies should be promulgated by the legislative branch, addressed in a constitution reform process, and implemented by executive institutions. Other aspects of SSR are discussed in Section 6.7.18.

**8.6.14 Prioritize good governance of the security sector.** An effective and accountable security sector relies on good governance. Good governance includes policies and laws that ensure security forces are accountable to legitimate civilian authority, including executive, legislative, judicial, and civil society structures and processes with the necessary checks and balances to prevent abuse. Peace agreements often mandate the reform of security bodies without a concomitant mandate for civilian governance of those bodies. Focus on developing accountable and capable civilian government authorities and nurturing specific civil society involvement in oversight.[388] Monitoring the development and implementation of security policy may be effectively accomplished with the help of community advisory, review, and oversight boards. A functioning judicial system should provide legal recourse when abuses occur.[389]
*See Gap/Challenge: Section 8.10.3, Security sector governance.*

**8.6.15 Establish accountable civilian authority over the security sector to protect human rights and prevent the renewal of conflict.** Placing security forces under effective and legitimate civilian authority can provide accountability to the population for the conduct of the security forces, based on the rule of law and protection of human rights. Civilian authorities should exercise oversight and transparency in appointment, budget, and administrative processes through such mechanisms as internal financial controls; disciplinary procedures; performance reviews; and legitimate selection, retention, and promotion policies. Authority and oversight should be multilayered and involve internal controls within security forces, parliamentary and civil society monitoring, review and reporting mechanisms, and review by the judiciary. Independent oversight bodies may include human rights commissions, audit and inspector general offices, ombudsmen, and public complaint commissions that offer specific mechanisms for oversight and accountability.[390]

**8.6.16 Strengthen legislative, judicial and civil society participation and oversight to prevent abuse of power.** Accumulation of excessive power by the executive branch is often a factor in conflict and may not be resolved in its aftermath. A largely discredited government may also remain in conflict's wake. Oversight that is external to the executive branch can offer an immediate path for accountability and a check on official abuse of power, while lengthy reform processes within executive ministries unfold. Legislative approaches include holding hearings and using subpoena powers to compel testimony from ministry officials, commanders, and others; exercising budget review and approval

---

388. See example, Articles 17–51, "Agreement on the Strengthening of Civilian Power and on the Role of the Armed Forces in a Democratic Society," Guatemala (September 19, 1996), http://www.usip.org/files/file/resources/collections/peace_agreements/guat_960919.pdf (accessed June 17, 2009).

389. Nicole Ball, "Democratic Governance and the Security Sector in Conflict-Affected Countries," in *Governance in Post-Conflict Societies: Rebuilding Fragile States* (New York: Routledge, 2007). Hereafter: Ball, "Democratic Governance and the Security Sector," 2007.

390. OECD DAC, "Handbook on SSR," 2007.

authorities; and creating new laws for governance of the security sector. Inspections of facilities and investigations of alleged abuse are additional parliamentary tools for oversight. The judiciary also plays an important role by adjudicating cases involving members of security forces, performing judicial review of policies and special powers, and providing remedies in accordance with human rights.[391] Civil society organizations (CSO) may have official mandates to help oversee the security sector. CSOs with expertise in security issues are also sources for training new or reformed forces and providing policy advice and/or staff for new or reformed ministries or parliamentary oversight committees.[392] For more on oversight mechanisms, see Section 7.7.6.

*8.6.17 Ensure that the host nation population drives governance reform of the security sector, as it is an inherently political process.* Reform of the security sector begins with a comprehensive assessment of the specific context of security needs and what the population expects and will accept. Understand that since the control of security forces likely enabled conflict, the reform of those forces is among the most sensitive and dangerous issues that will confront society. Resistance to change from those who stand to lose control in a reform process may become violent. Significant and lasting reform can only result from a process of active dialogue with key stakeholders in government, security bodies, and civil and political society, led by legitimate host nation actors. If significant change is to occur, these local stakeholders need to support reforms. International actors can help facilitate this politically sensitive process with the understanding that reform is a long-term effort.[393]

## 8.6.18 Approach: Protection of State Resources

The resources of the state belong to the population. It is the responsibility of the government to protect those resources and ensure they are collected, managed, and spent in a manner that meets the social and economic needs of the population. Protecting state resources requires sound public financial management based on transparency in revenue collection, taxation, and budgetary processes. It also means preventing corrupt government officials from abusing their positions of power for personal gain, thereby impeding efforts for good governance and economic development. If they are mismanaged, these resources can serve as a source of instability for societies emerging from conflict.[394]

*8.6.19 Promote good economic governance to enable recovery and generate confidence in the government's ability to manage public finances.* After violent conflict, the need to reform political governance often overshadows the need for good economic governance. But the latter is vital to strengthen public trust in the government and enable long-term development.[395] Good economic governance relies on a system of laws and regulations, policies and practices, and institutions and individuals that provide the

---

391. Ibid.
392. South African Defense and Security Management Network, "SADSEM: The South African Defense and Security Management Network," http://sadsem.org (accessed June 17, 2009).
393. Ball, "Democratic Governance and the Security Sector," 2007.
394. Paul Collier, ed. *Breaking the Conflict Trap: Civil War and Development Policy* (Washington, D.C.: The International Bank for Reconstruction and Development and The World Bank, 2003). Hereafter: Collier, *Breaking the Conflict Trap,* 2003.
395. United Nations Economic Commission for Africa, 2005 African Governance Report, 2005. Hereafter: UNECA, *African Governance Report,* 2005.

framework for economic recovery.[396] The system should enable the government to perform its financial responsibilities—including licensing, tax collection, central banking, concessions, and trade and investment policies—with accountability and transparency to ensure those resources benefit the general population and do not end up in the pockets of corrupt government officials. Fiscal management is further discussed in Section 9.5.12.

***8.6.20 Address low-level corruption that deprives the government of badly needed resources.*** The government is frequently the largest single employer in societies emerging from conflict. During and after conflict, many employees will have engaged in various degrees of corruption, from extortion to nepotism, to accepting bribes in exchange for ignoring traffic, tax, or customs violations.[397] While this level of corruption may seem minimal, it can have detrimental consequences. Low-level corruption deprives the population of their tax money and hinders critical investments in electricity, education, roads, and other infrastructure. It can also reinforce inequities, alienate parts of the population, and undermine public trust in the government's ability to manage finances. Addressing these activities requires developing anticorruption laws and regulations and enforcing them by consistently investigating complaints about corruption, punishing convicted officials, and denying government contracts to companies that fail to demonstrate tax compliance.[398] It should also involve streamlining government processes and limiting discretion. To protect customs and import revenue, pay close attention to improving border management by reforming customs procedures and equipment.[399] Also ensure that tax policies and systems are perceived as equitable and nondiscriminatory, as perceptions of inequities can also encourage tax evasion.

***8.6.21 Sever the nexus between government officials and illicit sources of revenue.*** During violent conflict, many government officials will have engaged in high-level corruption to entrench their power at the expense of the public good. One of the biggest threats to stable governance arises from this political-economic nexus, in which political actors maintain power by receiving royalties from extractive industries or by taxing organized crime syndicates or actors who control, exploit, and capture trade networks, remittances, and other assets.[400] Pay close attention to this reality and resist pressures from these groups to simply restore long-standing political structures that facilitate corruption. An important means of preempting the entrenchment of vested interests is to address corruption early on when the government is being designed.[401] This can include specifically addressing corruption in the peace agreement. Whenever possible, keep out officials who have been well-known

---

396. United States Agency for International Development, *Economic Governance in War Torn Economies: Lessons Learned from the Marshall Plan to the Reconstruction of Iraq*, 2004.

397. RAND, *Guidebook for Economic Development in Stability Operations* (Santa Monica, Calif.: RAND Corporation, 2009).

398. United Nations Development Programme, *Anti-Corruption Practice Note*, 2004; Emil Bolongaita, "Controlling Corruption in Post-Conflict Countries," presented at the Distinguished Lecture Series, Joan B. Kroc Institute for International Peace Studies, January 2005; UNECA, "African Governance Report," 2005.

399. United States Agency for International Development, *Guide to Economic Growth in Post-Conflict Countries*, 2009. Hereafter: USAID, "Guide to Economic Growth."

400. Karen Ballentine and Heiko Nitzschke, *The Political Economy of Civil War and Conflict Transformation* (Berlin: Berghof Handbook for Conflict Transformation, 2005). Hereafter: Ballentine/Nitzschke, *Political Economy*, 2005.

401. USAID, "DRAFT Guidance for Democracy and Governance," 2009.

for corrupt behavior to avoid setting the wrong standard for the future. Permitting the impunity of political-criminal actors can seriously hamper prospects for good political and economic governance and undermine government legitimacy. Confronting vested interests requires strong political will. Severing the criminal-political nexus is further discussed in Section 9.6.

**8.6.22 Establish oversight mechanisms in government processes to ensure accountability.** Robust systems of oversight will most likely be needed to ensure that public funds are collected and spent with integrity. Oversight mechanisms may include internal controllers and auditors who reside within executive institutions or exist in the form of parliamentary commissions, civil society commissions, and external auditors.[402] These bodies should be independent of executive branch authorities and fully staffed and resourced to do their jobs effectively, even if they are part of the executive branch (e.g., inspector generals). Oversight units should monitor government institutions and employees to ensure that all financial conduct adheres to laws, regulations, instructions, and directives related to the management of public funds. Activities subject to monitoring should include meeting reporting requirements, observing budget limits, and determining recipients of government contracts. Enforcement mechanisms are also critical to give teeth to oversight units and ensure their effectiveness in keeping public officials accountable for their actions. In extreme cases, colocating international finance experts in host nation financial institutions may be useful to provide training and build capacity for transparent financial management systems. Giving these international actors co-signing authorities also ensures that all major transactions are reviewed by both a host nation manager and an international adviser.[403] Ultimately, the success of any oversight mechanism depends on strong political will for government reform. Fiscal management is discussed further in Section 9.5.12.
*See Gap/Challenge: Section 8.10.4, Oversight and accountability.*

**8.6.23 Make government financial data and activities as clear and open as possible for the population.** Publishing government financial information and giving the population to access to it helps build the trust in the government's ability to manage resources well.[404] Keep the budgetary process open and widely publicized, including its preparation, execution, and expenditure reporting processes. The legislature should hold public hearings to force ministers to justify budget requests. Information on all domestic and international debt should also be made publicly available. Ensure that all information published is consistent with actual activities in government.

**8.6.24 Keep budget deficits under control by mobilizing revenue and increasing the efficiency of the tax system.** Shortfalls in revenue are often a major cause of budget deficits, so pay attention to generating sufficient funds to finance critical social and economic development programs.[405] In societies emerging from conflict, key sources for revenue will likely be indirect taxes, rents from nonrenewable resources, and ex-

---

402. UNECA, "African Governance Report," 2005.

403. Governance and Economic Management Assistance Program, "Overview," http://www.gempliberia.org/pages/overview (accessed June 17, 2009).

404. UNECA, "African Governance Report," 2005.

405. Ibid..

ternal grants, so focus on protecting those revenue streams. Keep tax regulations and procedures open and accessible and educate the public about the system to increase efficiency and make it easier for taxpayers to comply. Other aspects of the tax system are discussed in Sections 9.5.14 to 9.5.16.

***8.6.25 Protect natural resources as fundamental state assets that are integral to economic recovery and political stability.*** Lucrative nonrenewable natural resources such as oil, diamonds, and timber are a common endowment in societies emerging from conflict. Depending on how they are managed, these resources can serve as either a major source of wealth or a destabilizing force that engenders corruption, economic instability, and conflict over control and distribution of assets.[406] Ensuring that wealth generated from profits or rents fully benefits the population requires protecting natural resource extraction sites and related infrastructure, managing the revenue generated, and establishing transparent and accountable processes for letting resources concessions. Clear rules and procedures for public procurement should ensure that government contracts are awarded based on merit rather than parochial or personal interests. Protect the integrity of the revenue stream through the aforementioned mechanisms for prevention through good public financial management and enforcement through prosecutions and the judiciary. Additionally, natural resource wealth management issues should be addressed in peace agreements, constitutions, and other aspects of the political settlement process.[407] Natural resource wealth management is also discussed in Section 9.6.11.

# 8.7 Necessary Condition: Political Moderation and Accountability

### 8.7.1 What is political moderation and accountability? Why is it a necessary condition?

Political moderation and accountability refer to the condition where the government provides the official fora and processes for settling core political grievances through debate, compromise, and inclusive national dialogue and manages change arising from humanitarian, economic, security, and other challenges through a renegotiation of rules and policies. Achieving this condition involves a national constituting process that provides for the institutional design and constitutional framework for governance, the selection of leadership for national and subnational government institutions that is determined through inclusive and participatory processes and that is representative of society as a whole, a legislative or parliamentary system that reflects the interests of the population, and electoral processes that are free and fair. After major conflict ends, fierce confrontations between and within factions for control of government often continue.[408] Intimidation, targeted acts of violence such as arson, and revenge killings become tools of those who oppose a new political order. Dealing with these threats and transforming this violent struggle into a peaceful one is the charter for the political governance of the host nation. Good political governance affords the host nation the opportunity to move beyond violent conflict so that disputes can be moderated and resolved peacefully.

---

406. Collier, "Breaking the Conflict Trap," 2003; Jill Shankleman, *Managing Natural Resource Wealth* (Washington, D.C.: United States Institute of Peace, 2006). Hereafter: Shankleman, *Managing Natural Resource Wealth*, 2006.

407. Shankleman, "Managing Natural Resource Wealth," 2006.

408. Covey/Dziedzic/Hawley, *Quest for Viable Peace*, 2005.

## 8.7.2 Guidance for Political Moderation and Accountability

### 8.7.3 Approach: National Constituting Processes

Societies emerging from conflict often find a new path for the country's political future. This new path may be discovered through inclusive and participatory national constituting processes that generate consensus for political progress and define the political arrangements[409] for the host nation based on a shared vision. National constituting processes broadly involve the population in the shaping, drafting, and approval of a document that shapes the country. Processes can include drafting sessions, debates, and referenda through which the population defines the institutions of governance; the duties, rights, and relationships of the host nation and its citizens; and a vision for the identity of the host nation.[410]

**8.7.4 Build broad-based consensus on the country's political future through inclusive and participatory national constituting processes.** Constituting processes, ranging from national dialogue to constitutional conventions, seek to foster broad-based agreement on the political future and government structure of the host nation.[411] The provision of technical support and resources, the training of dialogue facilitators, and the identification of media outlets to disseminate information to the population helps to ensure national constituting processes are effective, gain momentum, and are capable of engaging a range of participants.[412] Elites play a particularly important and powerful role in this form of political settlement, and their buy-in and support is critical.[413] The inclusion of women, minorities, and non-state traditional institutions is fundamental to the success of national constituting processes. Guarantee their participation through quotas, appointments, or other necessary measures to ensure representation.[414]

**8.7.5 Help generate agreement on central issues for governance to prevent the renewal of violent conflict.** Constitution-making processes afford the host nation population a major opportunity to make fairly momentous decisions about the shape of the state following violent conflict. Agreement may emerge on issues concerning religion and language, the secular or religious identity of the state, the degree of centralization or subnational distribution of power and authorities, the role of the armed forces, political and civil rights and liberties, minority rights, the type of and rules for electoral and legislative systems—in short, the issues that shape the kind of state that will govern a society that has undergone conflict severe enough to warrant the amending or replacement of a constitution.[415]

**8.7.6 Focus on the process for writing the constitution as much as what the constitution says.** The UN has recognized that the International Covenant on Civil and Political

---

409. Anten, "Strengthening Governance," 2009.

410. Vivien Hart, *Democratic Constitution-Making* (Washington, D.C.: United States Institute of Peace, 2003).

411. Robert Orr, "Governing When Chaos Rules: Enhancing Governance and Participation," in *Winning the Peace: An American Strategy for Post-Conflict Reconstruction* (Washington, D.C.: The Center for Strategic and International Studies Press, 2004).

412. UNDP/Michelsen, "Governance in Post-Conflict Situations," 2004.

413. Alan Whaites, *States in Development: Understanding State-building* (London, UK: Department for International Development, Governance and Social Development Group, 2008).

414. Conaway, *The Role of Women*, 2006.

415. USAID, "DRAFT Guidance for Democracy and Governance," 2009.

Rights affords the population the right to choose their form of constitution.[416] Inclusive and broad-based public participation in the constitution-making process is an international standard that is key to developing a constitution that is widely supported.[417] Often, these processes are more important than the document that is produced.[418] Options for public participation in the constitution-making process can include electing a constitutional convention, generating a public dialogue on the draft content of the constitution, or holding a referendum on the adoption of the constitution. To hold a participatory constitution-making process, sufficient resources, attention, and time are critical to ensure that the result is based on consensus rather than externally imposed deadlines.[419] This process can also play a powerful role in transforming conflict and generating legitimacy for the host nation government, because it helps the population articulate their common values, societal norms, and hopes for the future.[420] Understand that the process may also be deemed as lacking legitimacy if leaders control commission appointments, block participation from segments of the population, or refuse to abide by term limits or other restrictions on power that are frequently part of constitutions.

### 8.7.7 Approach: Political Governance and Conflict Management

In a society emerging from conflict, institutions of governance that provide for political moderation and conflict management and structure competition to transform wartime objectives into nonviolent political objectives hold the key to stabilization. Issues not resolved by peace accords or that are left to be negotiated after violent conflict ceases typically fall to nascent structures that attempt to moderate differences and produce agreements. This approach refers to those aspects of political systems that offer official, regular, and inclusive forums and processes for debate over core grievances and ongoing challenges facing a government. Interim structures such as special assemblies and transitional governing councils—and ones more characteristic of permanent government systems such as regular meetings of the cabinet and other inter-ministerial processes—and parliamentary sessions and committee processes can combine to facilitate peaceful debate and resolution of grievances and challenges. Traditional means of resolving core issues of particular national contention can be extremely important and add legitimacy for acceptance of results by the population.

### 8.7.8 Help former warring factions to reframe their interests through non-violent political processes.[421] Help parties with conflict aims to view their interests differently through a political process. This will require time and patience and will typically not be amenable to any script or external control. Attitudes and demands, fortified by conflict and perceived sacrifice, may require years to transform into productive, peaceful ends. In these settings, former armed groups do sometimes transform themselves into political parties. Rejection of violence; acceptance of competitive elections; and respect for freedom of speech, association, and other fundamental human rights must

416. United Nations, "International Covenant on Civil and Political Rights," http://www.unhchr.ch/html/menu3/b/a_ccpr.htm (accessed June 17, 2009).

417. UNDESA/UNDP, "Challenges of Restoring Governance," 2007.

418. Noah Feldman, "Agreeing to Disagree in Iraq," *New York Times*, August 30, 2005.

419. Lakhdar Brahimi, *State Building in Crisis and Post-Conflict Countries*, 2007. Hereafter: Brahimi, *State Building*, 2007.

420. A.B. Inbal and H. Lerner, "Constitutional Design, Identity, and Legitimacy in Post-Conflict Reconstruction," in *Governance in Post-Conflict Societies: Rebuilding Fragile States* (New York: Routledge, 2007).

421. Covey/Dziedzic/Hawley, *Quest for Viable Peace*, 2005.

be the price for entry into politics. When this decision occurs, consider the need for campaign training, platform development, and party law development, in addition to disarmament, demobilization, and reintegration. Understand that setbacks and protests in political governance may frequently occur and include temporary withdrawal or walk-outs of parties from parliamentary structures, boycotts of sessions or elections, and threats of or actual resignation by ministers.[422] Protection for those who enter the political process, whether by peacekeeping or close protection police forces, is often required to confront threats from those who oppose their participation.

*8.7.9 Bring the widest range of leaders into the political process and seek to include voices of moderation.* Addressing problems of exclusion that characterized the period of violent conflict by including those who were marginalized and victimized because of ethnic, political, or religious identity offers hope for lasting stability. Many times, including previously marginalized or excluded groups in power sharing arrangements has formed a central objective of peace agreements. Creating all-parties councils, or *Loya Jirgas,* for example, can enhance the goal of having former opponents see their interests promoted through working cooperatively with the other.[423] Understand, however, that in highly divisive societies, governmental decision-making may be inhibited by periods of paralysis and be hampered by patronage arrangements as a result of including very different views and interests.[424] Power-sharing among identity-based groups that command allegiance over followers can dampen prospects for democratization and potentially exclude other groups, emboldening or even creating spoilers.

*8.7.10 Reinforce issue-based politics over identity politics.* Encourage and support collaboration among parties through coalitions or caucuses that seek to appeal to the population through issues that cut across identity groups. Issue-based politics focus on the interests of the population writ large, such as health care and housing, rather than the interests of ethnic, religious, or other identity groups.
*See Gap/Challenge: Section 8.10.8, Identity and issue politics.*

### 8.7.11 Approach: Systems of Representation
Governments should represent the interests of their population through a regular and fair process that allows the population to select their legislators and chief executive and remove them if they fail to perform. Creating effective representation involves uprooting embedded power imbalances that may have caused conflict, enabling the participation of marginalized populations in political processes, and holding free and fair elections when conditions are favorable. Legislators should reflect the needs of their constituencies and act as a counterbalance to the executive branch to ensure accountability.

*8.7.12 Meet requirements for free and fair elections in order to reflect the population's interests.* The ability to elect political leaders is a fundamental human right recognized by the UN.[425] It is also one of the most important mechanisms the population has for ensuring their interests and needs are represented by the government. Free and fair elections require agreement on the election laws and systems; available assistance with

422. USAID, "DRAFT Guidance for Democracy and Governance," 2009.
423. Covey/Dziedzic/Hawley, *Quest for Viable Peace,* 2005.
424. USAID, "DRAFT Guidance for Democracy and Governance," 2009.
425. United Nations, "Article 21, Universal Declaration on Human Rights," http://www.un.org/Overview/rights.html (accessed June 17, 2009). Hereafter: UN, "Article 21, UDHR."

election administration; and adequate oversight of the process.[426] In addition, the following daunting requirements are typically needed: a safe and secure environment, a functioning justice system, a media sector, accurate census data and voter registration, inclusive and participatory political parties, civic education, campaign rules, balloting logistics, disarmament and demobilization of armed groups, and trained and funded election staff.[427] An independent national electoral commission is normally created to assist in the establishment of legal procedures and basic electoral rules, including the requirements for voting and the means to verify the voter registry.[428] The inclusion of refugees, internally displaced populations, women, and minorities is important for effective elections after conflict and for stable governance. Broad participatory processes can also pose challenges—logistics, security, resource constraints, and management of public expectations—so understand and plan for these.

### 8.7.13 Consider the timing and impact of elections on the stability of the host nation.[429]
Elections are not just an exit strategy for the international presence or an antidote for violent conflict, they can produce negative consequences if not properly managed. While elections can increase the government's legitimacy, they can also reignite tension and escalate motivations for violence if held under improper conditions. These may occur when adequate security conditions are not met, not all stakeholders and potential spoilers are engaged in the political process, institutions and laws such as electoral commissions or voter registries are not in place, and civil or political rights are not assured. Consider holding local elections prior to national elections to allow time for the proper conditions to emerge across the host nation. Consider the impact of the electoral system on the development of political parties when selecting the format for elections. Also, understand the impact on the operation of the legislature and of local government vs. national government when selecting the format for elections. Finally, understand and prepare for the role of the diaspora.
See Trade-off: Section 8.9.5, Early elections vs. maturation of politics and processes.

### 8.7.14 Approach: Legislative Strengthening
Legislatures and parliaments[430] can play a critical role in conflict management by offering a forum for debate and dispute resolution, ratifying peace settlements and political accords, working across divisions to enact laws and manage resources, representing the diverse interests of constituents, and providing a check on power of the executive. Parliaments also serve as the primary vehicle through which the opposition presents its views and opinions.[431] Legislative strengthening involves establishment or reform of procedures and process, training and support for members of the parliament and staff, development of committee and other administrative support systems for legislative activities, and building of necessary infrastructure.

---

426. United States Department of State, Office of the Coordinator for Reconstruction and Stabilization, *Transition Elections and Political Processes in Reconstruction and Stabilization Operations: Lessons Learned*, 2007. Hereafter: S/CRS, *Transition Elections*, 2007.

427. UNDP/Michelsen, "Governance in Post-Conflict Situations," 2004; UNDP/USAID, "First Steps," 2007.

428. United Nations *Development Programme, Electoral Systems and Processes Practice Note*, 2004; Cole DeGrasse/Caan, "Bullets to Ballots," 2006.

429. Brahimi, "State Building," 2007.

430. For the purposes of this manual, legislatures and parliaments are used interchangeably.

431. USAID, "DRAFT Guidance for Democracy and Governance," 2009.

**8.7.15 Consider the design and structure of the legislature to aid in stabilization.** The type of legislative system that exists will depend on the electoral system the host nation chooses. The system may involve either proportional representation, where parties or individuals are elected based on their share of the vote, or majoritarian systems that award victory to those with overwhelming majorities. Understand the impact of both systems on prospects for stabilization and strive to ensure that, whatever system is used, the broadest representation from across the political spectrum exists in formal legislatures.

**8.7.16 Strengthen legislative bodies to counterbalance the executive branch and help bolster representative and accountable governance.** Develop effective legislative bodies, including national parliaments, assemblies, senates, or other elected legislative chambers, for sustainable governance. Legislative bodies are a vehicle for the representation of public interests in government and are the foundation for government legitimacy and accountability. They are needed to enact critical laws and reforms required for successful conflict transformation. Initial needs assessments help determine the institutional, professional, financial, and legal assistance required for progress. Assessments should analyze the political context of parliamentary development.[432] Parliamentary development should also be included in the constitutional and electoral design.[433] Technical assistance is often necessary for the institutional design and rules of conduct for legislative bodies, training for legislators and administrative personnel, and assistance with ensuring effective budget oversight and transparency. Specific attention to the competencies of political groups to perform their responsibilities within parliamentary processes strengthens legislative performance.[434] A strong committee system that enhances lawmaking, oversight, and representation is a typical feature in effective legislative bodies.[435] Transparency and accountability are served by holding open legislative sessions, publishing records of chamber and committee sessions, and ensuring legislators and their staff are accountable to the rule of law.

**8.7.17 Train and mentor legislators and staff for conflict management.** Legislatures typically mirror major divisions in society and without specific training and support for conflict management and mitigation skills and processes, those divisions may be enhanced, not ameliorated. Facilitation, mediation, and negotiation skills emerge from experience and are often not sufficient in S&R environments. Prioritize the strengthening of these skills. Help develop and sustain a community of support outside of the formal parliament in the form of civil society organizations, media, and academic institutions to provide analysis of issues, advise members and staff on process, offer training, and provide forums for constituents to channel concerns.[436]

432. United Nations Development Programme, *Parliamentary Development Practice Note*, 2003.
433. United Nations Development Programme, *Parliaments, Crisis Prevention, and Recovery: Guidelines for the International Community*, 2006.
434. United Nations Development Programme, *Lessons Learned in Parliamentary Development*, 2002.
435. Ibid.
436. USAID, "DRAFT Guidance for Democracy and Governance," 2009.

## 8.8 Necessary Condition: Civic Participation and Empowerment

### 8.8.1 What is civic participation and empowerment? Why is it a necessary condition?

Civic participation and empowerment refer to a condition in which every citizen has the means to actively engage in the public sphere, including political processes.[437] Under this condition, civil society is empowered, protected, and accountable; the media are present, professional, and independent of government influence; equal access to information and freedom of expression is upheld; and political parties are able to form freely and are protected. Civil society, the media, and political parties can mitigate the potential for violent conflict by providing legitimate public forums and mechanisms for peaceful debate.[438] Through these means, the population can also peacefully participate in politics, provide a check on the government, and influence government policy. Without opportunities for civic engagement, motivations for violence may be more likely to increase, as the population seeks to ensure their voice is heard and their needs are met. Civic participation and empowerment also require respect for fundamental civil and political rights[439] of minority groups, including the perception that these rights can be freely exercised without fear of retribution.[440]

### 8.8.2 Guidance for Civic Participation and Empowerment

#### 8.8.3 Approach: Civil Society Development

Civil society occupies the political space between the individual and government. It is a public sphere where citizens and voluntary organizations can engage freely outside of the government, family, and the private sector.[441] Civil society organizations can include a wide range of nongovernmental organizations, advocacy groups, charities, faith-based organizations, civic education organizations, business and professional associations, or community groups, among many others.[442] These organizations embody an active citizenry that reflects the values of those it represents, based on cultural, ethical, political, or other such considerations. They often serve as a link between the state and population, helping to influence and monitor government decisions; mobilize the population and educate them on their rights, responsibilities, and opportunities to influence government policies and lobby for reform; assist in public service delivery; and facilitate intergroup dialogue and other means for social reconciliation.[443] The important role of a vibrant civil society in S&R environments is widely accepted.

---

437. World Bank, Social Development Department, Civil Society and *Peacebuilding: Potential, Limitations and Critical Factors,* 2006. Hereafter: WB, *Civil Society and Peacebuilding,* 2006.

438. Dobbins/Jones/Crane/Cole DeGrasse, *Beginner's Guide,* 2007.

439. Refers to the freedom of religion, assembly, press, speech, association, and movement. Dziedzic/Sotirin/ Agoglia, "Measuring Progress in Conflict Environments," 2008.)

440. Ibid.

441. London School of Economics, "Centre for Civil Society," http://www.lse.ac.uk/collections/CCS/ (accessed June 17, 2009); WB, "Civil Society and Peacebuilding," 2006.

442. Dobbins/Jones/Crane/Cole DeGrasse, *Beginner's Guide,* 2007; London School of Economics, Centre for Civil Society, "What Is Civil Society?" http://www.lse.ac.uk/collections/CCS/what_is_civil_society.htm (accessed June 17, 2009).

443. Michael Lund, Peter Uvin, and Sarah Cohen, *Building Civil Society in Post-Conflict Environments: From the Micro to the Macro* (Washington, D.C.: Woodrow Wilson International Center for Scholars, 2006). The World Bank identifies seven key functions of CSOs: (1) protection, (2) monitoring and early warning, (3) advocacy and public communication, (4) socialization, (5) social cohesion, (6) intermediation and facilitation, and (7) service provision (World Bank, "Civil Society and Peacebuilding," 2006). Dziedzic/Sotirin/ Agoglia, "Measuring Progress in Conflict Environments," 2008.

***8.8.4 Leverage existing capacities in developing civil society.***[444] Understand that many forms of civil society will have existed prior to or during the conflict, filling the vacuum of service delivery that the state failed to provide. Many of these civil society groups or networks emerge in refugee camps and other environments where communities are forced to reorganize themselves as a means of survival. Often, these organizations may not resemble westernized civil society structures and may include community councils, church groups, community social networks, or other traditional structures that seek to strengthen social bonds in response to conflict. While there may be a tendency to favor partnerships with more familiar NGO structures, do not neglect these traditional groups and the resources they bring to the table.[445] To leverage existing capacity, conduct rigorous assessments and analyses of the diverse landscape of organizations that are already present and identify those with the potential to play a positive role, as well as those that have played a negative role.[446] Understanding the historical relationship between the state and population is also an important step in maximizing the potential of civil society in ensuring lasting peace and promoting good governance, among other peacebuilding objectives.

***8.8.5 Establish a legal and regulatory framework to protect CSOs and ensure they are allowed to form and operate freely.***[447] Because some of these organizations may be unfamiliar forces in societies emerging from conflict, they may need special protections. Establishing legal and regulatory frameworks for the formation and operation of CSOs ensures they have a basis in law. Laws should guarantee the right of association, expression, information, and participation; and regulations should address rules for financing, tax status, and registration.[448] Legal standing can enhance the contribution of CSOs to society by legitimizing their activities, decreasing potential public mistrust in them, and ensuring their accountability.[449] No statutory or regulatory framework, however, should encroach upon the independence or freedoms of these organizations, which is paramount to their effectiveness. Civil society activists should not be threatened or harmed and should not be imprisoned without reason.[450] They should be able to freely assemble and file complaints against the government for abuses.

***8.8.6 Foster ownership of host nation CSOs by providing necessary support to boost capacity.*** Societies emerging from conflict often experience a sudden expansion in CSOs, as the space for civic engagement opens up. This mushrooming of organizations may include both an influx of international CSOs and the emergence of new local organizations, in addition to those that existed before or during the conflict. International CSOs should be careful not to supplant or undermine local resources.[451] Focus on empowering domestic organizations whose sustainability will be vital to lasting peace

---

444. Dobbins/Jones/Crane/Cole DeGrasse, *Beginner's Guide,* 2007
445. Beatrice Pouligny, "Civil Society and Post-Conflict Peacebuilding: Ambiguities of International Programmes Aimed at Building 'New' Societies," Security Dialogue, vol. 26, no. 4 495-510 (2005).
446. WB, "Civil Society and Peacebuilding," 2006.
447. Dobbins/Jones/Crane/Cole DeGrasse, *Beginner's Guide,* 2007.
448. WB, "Civil Society and Peacebuilding," 2006.
449. International Center for Not-for-Profit Law, "Enabling Organizational Development: NGO Legal Reform in Post-Conflict Settings," *The International Journal of Not-for-Profit Law* 9, issue 4 (2007).
450. Dziedzic/Sotirin/Agoglia, "Measuring Progress in Conflict Environments," 2008.
451. Dobbins/Jones/Crane/Cole DeGrasse, *Beginner's Guide,* 2007.

and development. Many local organizations may lack the necessary skills and resources to perform their functions, and will likely be hampered by weak membership bases and a lack of national visibility. The lack of sustainable funding is another recurring challenge for new local CSOs, so assist them with budget management and administration through skills training and mentoring programs.[452] Consider innovative funding approaches that have been used before, such as granting tax-exemptions for donations to CSOs or creating a foundation where funds are invested to provide a continuous source of funding over the long term. Top-down approaches in developing civil society can encourage dependency, rather than empowering local actors to drive their own agendas and seek out innovative sources of funding and support.[453] See also Sections 7.8.8 and 7.8.14 for the role of civil society in justice.

*8.8.7 Promote inclusivity in developing CSOs.* If they are not diversified, civil society organizations can be perceived as exclusionary. Emphasize inclusivity in CSOs to ensure that their work fully represents the interests and values of what may be a very diverse population. In societies where divisions run deep, encourage CSOs to build bridges across social groups and avoid reinforcing divisions based on identity. Pay close attention to marginalized groups, particularly women, given their demonstrated potential for contributing to lasting peace. The civic engagement of women may help ensure, for example, that there is support for laws that address women's issues. These laws may include protecting women from domestic violence, safeguarding their inheritance rights if their husbands die, and ensuring their rights in customary marriage, which is important for rural women.[454] Assess diversity of CSOs by examining the funding sources, member demographics, and the range of issues or interests represented.[455]

*8.8.8 Foster and support community-based development to broaden civic participation and enhance opportunities for developing leadership in civil society.*[456] Community-based development involves partnering with the host nation population to design and implement programs aimed at meeting the needs of communities.[457] Such programs have an inherent and profound benefit for civil society development because they cultivate local leadership and broaden civic participation in political processes. They also teach people basic organizational and management skills, such as resource management, budgeting and accounting, and project evaluation.

*8.8.9 Promote accountability of CSOs through regulatory oversight mechanisms.* The boom in CSOs after violent conflict can serve as an entry point for organizations controlled by those who oppose the peace process or seek to manipulate the population. Other CSOs may form simply to take advantage of robust flow of donor funds. Promote accountability of these organizations by establishing CSO registration proce-

452. Ibid.
453. Initiative for Peacebuilding (International Alert and European Commission), *Building Inclusive Post-Conflict Governance*, 2009.
454. Ibid.
455. Dziedzic/Sotirin/Agoglia, "Measuring Progress in Conflict Environments," 2008.
456. World Bank, "Strengthening Local Governance and Promoting Community Based Development in Afghanistan," http://web.worldbank.org/WBSITE/EXTERNAL/EXTABOUTUS/IDA/0..contentMDK:21296643~menuPK:3266877~pagePK:51236175~piPK:437394~theSitePK:73154.00.html (accessed June 17, 2009). Hereafter: WB, "Strengthening Local Governance."
457. U.S. Agency for International Development, *Community-Based Development in Conflict-Affected Areas*, 2007.

dures and encouraging development of important corporate governance mechanisms—boards of directors, audits, and bylaws—to ensure that CSOs operate within the law and with respect for human rights.[458]

### 8.8.10 Approach: Independent Media and Access to Information

An independent media sector includes print, broadcast, or Web-based outlets that serve the public interest by disseminating information to the population about social, economic, and political developments. Journalists in the media sector typically include publishers, editors, producers, and reporters. In societies emerging from conflict, the primary function of the media is to report on the actions of the government and provide a public forum through which the population can debate issues peacefully and voice its concerns about the government. Without a functioning media sector that is free from censorship, the population cannot fully participate in political processes, exercise their civic rights and responsibilities, or express their needs to political officials. Access to information is a basic human right and entails that information is available in a format and language that is usable and understood by the population.

***8.8.11 Nurture and sustain a media sector that is pluralistic, transparent, sustainable, and independent.*** These characteristics are vital if the media sector is to perform its key function of ensuring government accountability for its actions by keeping the population abreast of key political developments. A pluralistic media sector includes a diverse array of voices with competing perspectives, including marginalized populations such as women and minorities. A transparent media sector prizes truth and credibility in the reporting of information. A sustainable media sector is one that comprises local staff with the capacity to generate and manage revenue needed to finance its operations. Assessing fully the media landscape and the enabling environment in which it operates is a necessary first step in developing a sustainable media sector.[459] An independent media is free from government control or political influence and enjoys the freedom of speech. Assess the media's independence and capacity to oversee government actions by examining the extent of editorial criticism against the government, the number of opposition media outlets that exist, and the severity of cases involving government efforts to threaten journalists or censor information.[460]

***8.8.12 Consider creating media monitoring mechanisms to prevent incendiary or hate speech from destabilizing the country.*** During violent conflict, warring parties may have dominated major media outlets as a means for disseminating propaganda, delivering hate messages, or reinforcing societal divisions. Consider establishing an outlet for the UN or other UN Security Council-mandated mission, that can counter these messages and communicate the peacebuilding objectives of the mission. The mission-owned outlet may be used to raise awareness about public information such as where the population can access essential services, how to vote, and what rights the population has, among others. Another mechanism for preventing media abuses can involve creating an independent regulatory commission that sets standards, monitors media abuses, and

---

458. Dobbins/Jones/Crane/Cole DeGrasse, *Beginner's Guide*, 2007.
459. Eron Frankel and Sheldon Himelfarb, *DRAFT Peacebrief: Purpose and Possibility, A Formative Media Assessment Template*, (Washington, D.C.: United States Institute of Peace, 2009). Yll Bajraktari and Emily Hsu, *Developing Media in Stabilization and Reconstruction Operations* (Washington, D.C.: United States Institute of Peace, 2007). Hereafter: Bajraktari/Hsu, *Developing Media*, 2007.
460. Dziedzic/Sotirin/Agoglia, "Measuring Progress in Conflict Environments," 2008.

addresses complaints.[461] A commission should operate with fairness and transparency, within a clearly defined set of rules. While cracking down on spoilers, also be sure to identify and promote the voices of moderate organizations and individuals.

*8.8.13 Ensure that media outlets are representative of and accessible to the population.* The ability to access information on political processes, basic rights, and public services is recognized by the United Nations as a human right.[462] In planning for new media outlets, maximize the population's access to information by carefully assessing the demographics of the country. Large rural populations may be illiterate, which may render print outlets ineffective. Limited access to television sets may also mean radios are a more appropriate medium for information. Also consider the languages in which information is published to ensure that all segments of the population have a means for consuming the information. Create a diverse array of outlets that includes the voices of women, minorities, and other marginalized groups. A pluralistic market can elevate competing views while diluting incendiary ones.

*8.8.14 Define media broadly but distinguish carefully between media sector development and strategic communications.* Adopt an expansive definition of media sector support to include both information and communications technology (ICT) thereby spanning traditional media (radio, tv, print), new media (text messaging, internet) as well as telecommunications. However, conflating strategic communications and media development diminishes the efficacy of both. The former is about controlling the message; the latter about developing a media sector (radio, tv, print, internet, telecom) that is valued by the body politic and pluralistic. This is not to say that the media sector is unable to engage in social marketing types of messages, but that those messages need to be clearly labeled as such (originating sponsor/funder) for credibility and usefulness.

*8.8.15 Develop a strong legal framework to protect the rights of journalists.* During conflict, many journalists are persecuted, kidnapped, or murdered for their views and activities by the government or by opposition groups. Other serious offenses against media may involve ransacking of offices; denial of registration or funding; libel suits and other forms of harassment; and death threats targeted at reporters, editors, and owners. To safeguard the greatest possible freedoms for the press, a strong legal framework for media is needed to clearly define media freedoms and prevent the government or other groups in society from unlawfully censoring information. Laws, however, are worthless without an effective judiciary that is willing and capable of administering justice to violators of the law.

*8.8.16 Encourage the development of journalism training and education programs to promote journalistic standards and potential for long-term success.* Professional training and education programs should underscore journalistic concepts such as truth, impartiality, and public service. Before and during violent conflict, many journalists will have worked in isolation under an authoritarian regime and may not have been exposed to international standards for journalism. Journalism education should go beyond ethnical principles to include comprehensive education on critical business concepts that are

---

461. Bajraktari/Hsu, *Developing Media*, 2007.

462. UN, "Article 21, UDHR"; UNDP/Michelsen, "Governance in Post-Conflict Situations," 2004; United Nations Development Programme, *Access to Information Practice Note*, 2003.

key to sustainability of outlets—competition in the media market, management of sales and advertisement activities, and administrative capacities.

**8.8.17 Complement education programs by creating professional associations for journalists to connect host nation actors with the international media network.** Establishing associations can help cultivate leadership and promote accountability and compliance with journalistic standards in professional integrity and ethics. Promulgating widely accepted standards can help to control inflammatory rhetoric in the media. Engaging in a wider network of foreign journalists helps domestic journalists avoid isolation and provides greater support for those who continue to face persecution or manipulation by the state or other opposition groups. Domestic journalists as well as the general population should have access to international media, including foreign newspapers, magazines, and broadcast stations, along with unfiltered access to the Internet.[463]

**8.8.18 Approach: Inclusive and Participatory Political Parties**
The right to participate in the political arena is a central element of stable governance. Political parties are the basis for participatory governance and serve as the vehicles through which groups with political differences can compete non-violently for power. Through these groups, political opponents can engage each other in a constructive way, forging relationships across party lines and establishing lines of communication.[464] Political parties are responsible for developing positions on key public issues and cultivating candidates who compete for elected office during election season.[465] They also help to facilitate and stimulate public debate and structure political competition and participation.[466]

**8.8.19 In developing political parties, foster inclusivity but prioritize the commitment to peace.**[467] Engaging as many warring parties and potential spoilers as possible in the political process may help develop a lasting peace. But while inclusivity is ideal, it is most important that participating parties be fully committed to peace. Be wary of criminals, human rights abusers, or former leaders, who may seek to legitimize themselves through elections only to abuse their positions for personal gain. Carefully assess each group's record of past crimes, the level of popular support, and their commitment to peace when deciding cases where certain individuals may have to be prohibited from engaging in the political process. Continue to monitor abuses during the campaign process to minimize violent or unethical practices through election commissions or other CSOs. Emphasize issue-based politics, rather than politics based solely on ethnicity, religion, or other potentially divisive lines, which can increase the potential for conflict.

**8.8.20 Pay special attention to engaging women, minority ethnic groups, and other marginalized populations in the development of political parties.** In societies emerging from conflict, certain groups may have historically been excluded from forming political parties or otherwise participating in the political process. Take special care to ensure that all groups have access to the political process and can promote candidates

463. Dziedzic/Sotirin/Agoglia, "Measuring Progress in Conflict Environments," 2008.
464. Bryan, "Engaging Political Parties," 2006.
465. United States Agency for International Development, *Political Party Assistance Policy,* 2003.
466. Eric Bjornlund, Glenn Cowan, and William Gallery, "Elections Systems and Political Parties in Post-Conflict and Fragile States," in *Governance in Post-Conflict Societies: Rebuilding Fragile States"* (New York: Routledge, 2007).
467. S/CRS, "Transition Elections," 2007.

to run for office. Ensuring representation of marginalized groups is a fundamental aspect of ensuring broad-based public involvement and support for political processes. Recognize and empower women in these activities, as they often make up the strongest constituency for peace.[468] UN Security Council Resolution 1325 recognizes and mandates the participation of women in the political process.[469] Consult and inform women's organizations about political processes, support women's participation in government administration, and provide training and resources aimed at developing female leadership.[470] Depending on the situation, quotas or other such mechanisms may be an effective way to help correct power imbalances and ensure full participation of marginalized groups.[471]

**8.8.21 Provide political parties with necessary training and support, but ensure neutrality in delivering that support.**[472] Many political parties will have limited know-how in civic processes. Assist parties in strengthening their voter bases by training them to be responsive to the needs of their constituencies. Help smaller parties increase their impact by building coalitions across society. Ensure equal access to media outlets, opportunities for campaigning, and training forums to inform party members about their roles and responsibilities. Financial support is also critical for the viability of political parties. While some states may be prohibited from providing direct assistance to political parties, create public financing laws or an international fund through which political parties can legitimately access financial support. But keep in mind that the neutrality of international actors and the existence of equitable access to support are critical to perceptions of legitimacy and the appearance of a balanced playing field.[473] Regulate the flow of money in the political sphere by means such as limiting campaign and party contributions, banning donations from foreign nationals, placing spending limits on campaigns, creating time limits for the campaign period, ensuring public disclosure of expenditures, and providing some public campaign financing to limit dependence on donors.[474]

# 8.9 Trade-offs

**8.9.1 Rapid and effective delivery of essential services vs. legitimacy for nascent government institutions.** International actors may be the only ones capable of providing essential services to the population in the early stages of recovery. But having international actors provide critical services can sacrifice legitimacy for nascent government institutions, even though they lack the capacity to provide those services. Carefully balance urgency to deliver with the need to build local capacity.

**8.9.2 Hiring host nation actors to assist international organizations vs. staffing domestic institutions.** International organizations often attract some of the most educated and experienced host nation actors. While this temporarily boosts the economic well-being

468. Ibid.
469. United Nations Security Council, "United Nations Security Council Resolution 1325," available from http://www.peacewomen.org/un/sc/res1325.pdf (accessed June 17, 2009).
470. Conaway, "The Role of Women," 2006.
471. S/CRS, "Transition Elections," 2007.
472. Ibid.
473. United States Agency for International Development, *Money in Politics Handbook: A Guide to Increasing Transparency in Emerging Democracies*, 2003. Hereafter: USAID, *Money in Politics*, 2003.
474. Ibid.

of those individuals and helps international organizations achieve their goals, it can also deprive domestic institutions and organizations of domestic talent that is badly needed.

*8.9.3 Rapid service delivery and resource procurement vs. empowerment of spoilers or criminal elements.* International humanitarian organizations and military forces spend vast sums of money on projects that can have a substantial political and economic impact. In the quest to provide rapid delivery of services, internationals or domestic government bodies may need to use or purchase resources from spoilers, which can inadvertently empower them and undermine the legitimacy of the state.

*8.9.4 Responsible fiscal management vs. the need to provide immediate services.* Under pressure to provide services, nascent governments may spend significant amounts of money that require robust oversight to ensure that the funds are properly spent. Fiscal management reform, however, can take years to build, and capacity will likely be weak. The government will have to carefully maneuver between the need for short-term results and the reform of public expenditure management.[475]

*8.9.5 Early elections vs. maturation of politics and processes.* Elections are necessary to provide representative governance and bestow legitimacy on a new government. Running the country for too long with government appointees can reduce domestic and international legitimacy for governance institutions. However, rushing to hold elections before the necessary conditions exist can undermine the political process and create barriers to future political development. Carefully balance the pressures to hold elections with the patience needed to do the job right.

*8.9.6 Political appointments vs. meritocracy.* Appointing warlords and other power brokers who played a role in violent conflict, but who may have no qualifications, is often a necessary step to facilitate an end to hostilities. Meritocratic appointments, conversely, offer opportunities to bring in qualified individuals to govern effectively based on talent and technical skills. One way to manage this trade-off is to limit the time period for political appointments during a transition phase after violent conflict ends and increase meritocratic appointments gradually.[476]

# 8.10 Gaps and Challenges

*8.10.1 Making peace pay and civil service reform.* The failure to adequately resource personnel budgets and pay service providers regularly and on time are recurring challenges in S&R environments. This shortfall has a direct impact on the legitimacy of the host nation government, corruption, and security, as warlords and other spoilers step into the vacuum. Reinstituting a government payroll with adequate donor assistance and oversight in the initial stages and a major reform and rebuilding effort to create an effective civil service are required.[477]

*8.10.2 Subnational governance.* Decentralizing governance by strengthening and empowering subnational institutions can have destabilizing effects, particularly when insecurity or threats to the central government persist and emanate from specific regions. The potential for spoilers to control local governments raises concerns for continued conflict.

475. USAID, "Guide to Economic Growth Program Planning," 2009.
476. Ibid.
477. UNDP/USAID, "First Steps," 2007.

Address this challenge through greater accountability and oversight of subnational governance institutions, incremental steps toward decentralization, and choosing decentralization options based on local conditions.[478]

***8.10.3 Security sector governance.*** Security sector reform tends to be focused on the vetting, training, and funding of the security forces, with less attention on the need for effective governance over the security sector. This has led to the misuse or theft of equipment and funds, corruption in the forces, and collusion of security forces with spoilers and opponents to the peace process. The need to focus on developing accountable and capable civilian government authorities, nurturing specific civil society involvement in oversight, and providing judicial checks on abuse could not be more necessary.[479]

***8.10.4 Oversight and accountability.*** Government leaders and personnel may divert public funds for private use, accept bribes from spoilers in exchange for lucrative contracts, and engage in other forms of corruption. The absence of mechanisms for oversight and accountability poses serious governance problems for societies emerging from conflict. Oversight mechanisms should be implemented early and may include controllers and auditors within executive institutions and parliamentary or civil society commissions that work externally.[480]

***8.10.5 Human capital for basic governance functions.*** Many war-torn societies face high levels of illiteracy and lack professional skills for governance due to inadequate education and training programs during prolonged conflict. In the face of this challenge, international donors provide direct technical assistance in the form of international personnel or turn to private contractors, NGOs, or informal providers on the local level. The costs for technical assistance absorb high percentages of central budgets, capacity for self-government remains weak, and ineffective administration for governance results. Investments in training and education across many professions should be a central priority.[481]

***8.10.6 Democracy in societies emerging from conflict.*** The establishment of democracy after violent conflict has proven to be immensely challenging. Bad actors emerge under the cloak of democratic elections; traditional or informal sources of power assert control and challenge those legitimately elected to lead; and the demands and complexity of democratic systems overwhelm decimated states. The extraordinary difficulties may be overcome with time and resources and development of the foundation for sustainable democratic self-government.[482]

***8.10.7 Transition from international to host nation actors.*** Immediately after large-scale violence ends, international actors may have to perform the bulk of governance functions because capacity among local actors will be weak. The inability to transition these functions effectively from international to host nation control impedes capacity development

478. USAID, "Guide to Economic Growth Program Planning," 2009.
479. See example, Articles 17–51, "Agreement on the Strengthening of Civilian Power and on the Role of the Armed Forces in a Democratic Society," Guatemala (September 19, 1996) http://www.usip.org/files/file/resources/collections/peace_agreements/guat_960919.pdf (accessed June 17, 2009).
480. UNECA, "African Governance Report," 2005.
481. Ashraf Ghani and Clare Lockhart, *Fixing Failed States: A Framework for Rebuilding a Fractured World* (Oxford: Oxford University Press, 2008).
482. Brinkerhoff, *Governance in Post-Conflict Societies,* 2007.

of leadership and staff and results in dependencies that are difficult to reverse.[483] As soon as possible, these responsibilities should be transitioned to local actors, with appropriate safeguards, in order to promote capacity and ownership and to ensure legitimacy over the long term. Managing this transition has proven to be extremely challenging.

***8.10.8 Identity and issue politics.*** Identity politics will likely be both divisive and prevalent in societies emerging from conflict and will challenge those who seek political moderation and accommodation. Issue politics—those built around concerns such as economic progress, health care, education, and human rights—offer a more lasting remedy to prevent renewed conflict. They avoid creating divisions along ethnic, religious, or other forms of identity that likely precipitated the conflict. Building political processes to recognize this reality and sustain peace will involve managing the trade-offs between the two forms of politics. Dealing effectively with issue and identity politics is also a gap in current knowledge and a challenge in practice.

---

483. Anten, "Strengthening Governance," 2009.

# Section 9
# Sustainable Economy

**Macroeconomic Stabilization**
- Monetary Stability
- Fiscal Management
- Legislative and Regulatory Framework

**Control Over the Illicit Economy and Economic-Based Threats to Peace**
- Control Over Illicit Economic Activity
- Management of Natural Resource Wealth
- Reintegration of Ex-Combatants

## SUSTAINABLE ECONOMY
Ability of the people to pursue opportunities for livelihoods within a system of economic governance bound by law.

**Employment Generation**
- Quick Impact
- Agricultural Rehabilitation
- Livelihood Development

**Market Economy Sustainability**
- Infrastructure Development
- Private Sector Development
- Human Capital Development
- Financial Sector Development

# Sustainable Economy
*Ability of the people to pursue opportunities for livelihoods within a system of economic governance bound by law.*

## 9.0 What is a sustainable economy?
A sustainable economy[484] is one in which people can pursue opportunities for livelihoods within a predictable system of economic governance bound by law. Such an end state is characterized by market-based macroeconomic stability, control over the illicit economy and economic-based threats to the peace, development of a market economy, and employment generation. Economic governance refers to the collection of policies, laws, regulations, institutions, practices, and individuals that shape the context in which a country's economic activity takes place.[485]

## 9.1 What are the key economic challenges in societies emerging from conflict?[486]
Violent conflict can severely devastate an economy. Large-scale violence disrupts market activity by destroying infrastructure and critical production and processing facilities. Common features of a war-torn economy include macroeconomic instability, fragmented markets, limited access to credit, reduced confidence, depleted human capital, increased illicit economic activity, mine-littered lands, and debilitated economic institutions that are vulnerable to capture by predatory economic actors[487] or spoilers. States may be captured by a political-criminal nexus sustained through hidden economic transactions, which threaten peace, governance, and development. Major hostilities also deplete the labor market by driving families from their homes and killing, traumatizing, or disabling millions of others. An overall decline in the well-being of the population is common, as the government diverts public service investments to finance military operations or the state collapses and is unable to make necessary investments.

## 9.2 Why is a sustainable economy a necessary end state?
Once violent conflict has ended, countries still face alarming risks of falling back into conflict. Broad consensus exists that sustainable welfare-enhancing economic growth has the potential to mitigate these risks by improving living standards, reducing inequalities among groups, increasing affordability of basic goods and services, and expanding overall opportunity.[488] Economic opportunity and growth give the population a stake in peace,

---

484. "Sustainable economy" is a term of art used in existing literature. For the purposes of this manual, this term is intended to broadly encompass the ability of the people to pursue opportunities for livelihoods within a system of economic governance bound by law.

485. United States Agency for International Development, *Economic Governance in War Torn Economies: Lessons Learned from the Marshall Plan to the Reconstruction of Iraq,* 2004. Hereafter: USAID, *Economic Governance in War Torn Economies,* 2004.

486. Dobbins/Jones/Crane/Cole DeGrasse, *Beginner's Guide,* 2007.

487. For the purpose of this manual, "predatory actors" broadly refer to any group or individual that engages in or directly benefits from illegal economic activity that promotes violence and/or undermines efforts for good governance and economic development. These actors can exist inside or outside of government.

488. United States Agency for International Development, *Guide to Economic Growth in Post-Conflict Countries,* 2009. Hereafter: USAID, *Guide to Economic Growth,* 2009. Paul Collier, Post-Conflict Recovery: How Should Policies Be Distinctive? 2007. Hereafter: Collier, *Post-Conflict Recovery,* 2007.

particularly local entrepreneurs. Although it is rarely the sole precipitating cause of violent conflict, economic failure has proven to be a key factor that can mobilize political and social grievances into large-scale violence. Without broad improvements in economic performance, peace is not sustainable.

# 9.3 What are the necessary conditions to achieve a sustainable economy?

- *Macroeconomic Stabilization* is a condition in which monetary and fiscal policies are established to align the currency to market levels, manage inflation, and create transparent and accountable systems for public finance management. This condition requires a robust and enforceable legislative and regulatory framework to govern issues such as property rights, commerce, fiscal operations, and foreign direct investment.

- *Control Over the Illicit Economy and Economic-Based Threats to Peace* is a condition in which illicit wealth no longer determines who governs, predatory actors are prevented from looting state resources, ex-combatants are reintegrated and provided jobs or benefits, and natural resource wealth is accountably managed.

- *Market Economy Sustainability* is a condition in which a market-based economy is enabled and encouraged to thrive. Infrastructure is built or rehabilitated, and the private sector and the human capital and financial sectors are nurtured and strengthened.

- *Employment Generation* is a condition in which job opportunities are created to yield quick impact to demonstrate progress and employ military-age youths, and a foundation is established for sustainable livelihoods.

# 9.4 General Guidance for Sustainable Economy

*9.4.1 Build host nation ownership and capacity.* Consult broadly and create coordination mechanisms with the host nation population to build trust, prevent dependency, and ensure ownership, paying particular attention to women and minorities who may have special needs. Recognize that the civil service in line ministries makes up the core of the government workforce and must be trained and paid. Small business development—particularly in the agricultural sector—should build on and enhance host nation capacity. Even while peace negotiations are ongoing, start a dialogue with civil society and private sector representatives to build political consensus for the economic recovery program.[489] Also be certain to recognize work that is accomplished by the population through strategic communications.[490]

*9.4.2 Act only with an understanding of the local context.* War-torn economies may share many characteristics, such as physical insecurity, weak state capacity to enforce taxes or regulate the economy, inability to adjudicate economic disputes, macroeconomic instability (volatile currency, high inflation), decreased production, a distorted labor market, a loss of human capital, informal economic activity, a drop in GDP, and

---

489. Organisation for Economic Co-Operation and Development, *Economic Reconstruction in Post-Conflict Transitions: Lessons for the Democratic Republic of Congo*, 2003. Hereafter, OECD, *Congo*, 2003. USAID, "Guide to Economic Growth," 2009.

490. JICA, "Handbook for Transition Assistance," 2006. Jill Shankleman, *Managing Natural Resource Wealth* (Washington, D.C.: U.S. Institute of Peace, 2006). Hereafter: Shankleman, *Managing Natural Resource Wealth*, 2006.

a return to subsistence agriculture.[491] But there is no single strategy that can be applied across the board. Tailored, conflict-sensitive approaches are necessary to account for unique characteristics in the political and economic landscape.[492] The economic assessment should investigate key aspects of the specific context:[493]

- What is the extent of the disruption to commerce and general economic activity?
- What is the extent of damage done to physical infrastructure and social and political institutions?
- What is the competitive advantage of economic structures predating the conflict?
- What is the legacy of conflict-related economies?
- What is the state of livelihoods, including skills, capacity, motives, and access to resources?
- What is the state of macroeconomic policies and institutions and government resources?
- What is the state of industries, investment, trade, and markets?
- What is the potential impact of international actors on the domestic economy?

*9.4.3 Prioritize to stabilize.* Economic recovery programming should not be development as usual. Political imperatives and the need to maintain peace should trump goals of economic efficiency in the immediate aftermath of violent conflict.[494] Principles of inclusivity and balance can avoid perceptions of inequality in wealth distribution. While no consensus exists on the exact sequencing of economic reforms, most agree that more attention must be paid to macroeconomic stabilization, alongside emergency activities such as infrastructure rehabilitation or the reintegration of ex-combatants.[495] S&R missions have typically postponed fiscal and monetary reform, which is key to creating favorable conditions for growth.[496] Acting early in these reforms is vital, when political resistance tends to be low.[497] Other economic priorities in these environments include addressing property rights by developing dispute resolution mechanisms and enforcing laws to combat organized crime and other destabilizing economic activity.

*See Trade-off: Section 9.9.1, Economic efficiency vs. political stability.*

*9.4.4 Use a conflict lens.* Be cautious that economic growth strategies do not reinforce or empower predatory economic actors. After violent conflict is over, these are often the key economic players that emerge and are frequently associated with crime and corruption. Also recognize that all economic recovery activity is fundamentally politi-

---

491. JICA, "Handbook for Transition Assistance," 2006. USAID, "Guide to Economic Growth," 2009. Jonathan Haughton, *The Reconstruction of War-Torn Economies and Peace-Building Operations*, 2002. Hereafter: Haughton, *Reconstruction of War-Torn Economies*, 2002.

492. USAID, "Guide to Economic Growth," 2009. United States Agency for International Development, "Accelerating the Transition From Conflict to Sustainable Growth," 2008. Hereafter: USAID, "Accelerating the Transition," 2008. Haughton, *Reconstruction of War-Torn Economies*, 2002.

493. JICA, "Handbook for Transition Assistance," 2006.

494. OECD, "Congo," 2003.

495. USAID, "Economic Governance in War Torn Economies," 2004.

496. UNDP/USAID, "First Steps," 2007. Haughton, "Reconstruction of War-Torn Economies," 2002.

497. USAID, "Accelerating the Transition," 2008.

cal in these societies. Understanding all actors and their complex political-economic relationships helps to avoid strengthening historical inequities that may have led to violent conflict in the first place.[498] Every decision, from choosing which roads to rehabilitate first to choosing a currency, can have political ramifications. Always consider political impacts before taking action.

***9.4.5 Recognize interdependence.*** Successful economic recovery depends on multiple aspects of the S&R mission, so be sure to address it comprehensively. For example, security is essential for expanding economic activity and allowing farmers or merchants to travel safely to the market place. A predictable legal framework for resolving property rights or contract disputes is key to encouraging business investments and preventing renewed conflict. Good governance over natural resource wealth is vital for boosting the effectiveness and credibility of the state and removing a persistent source of conflict. Recognize these linkages and coordinate economic strategies with those of security, the rule of law, governance, and social well-being.

# 9.5 Necessary Condition: Macroeconomic Stabilization

### 9.5.1 What is macroeconomic stabilization? Why is it a necessary condition?

Macroeconomic stabilization is a condition in which a complex framework for monetary and fiscal institutions and policies is established to reduce volatility and encourage welfare-enhancing growth. Achieving this condition requires aligning currency to market levels, managing inflation, establishing foreign exchange facilities, developing a national budget, generating revenue, creating a transparent system of public expenditure, and preventing predatory actors from controlling the country's resources.[499] It also requires a framework of economic laws and regulations that govern budgetary processes, central bank operations, international trade, domestic commerce, and economic governance institutions. Stabilization of the economy is a prerequisite for economic growth. Empirical evidence shows that creating an environment that is conducive to higher rates of investment can reduce the likelihood of violence, while economic growth has a positive correlation with job creation and higher living standards.[500]

### 9.5.2 Guidance for Macroeconomic Stabilization

#### 9.5.3 Approach: Monetary Stability

Monetary stability is a subjective approach as there are varying degrees to which people seek to achieve it. In the early phases of recovery, this approach may involve stabilizing the currency, bringing inflation and foreign-exchange rates to levels consistent with sustainable growth, promoting predictability and good management in the banking system, and managing foreign debt.[501] The primary authority is usually an independent central

---

498. Raymond Gilpin, "Toward Conflict-Sensitive Macroeconomic Growth: Unraveling Challenges for Practitioners," presented at Building Capacity in Stability Operations: Security Sector Reform, Governance and Economics, *United States Army Peacekeeping and Stability Operations Institute and Center for Naval Analysis,* 2009. Hereafter: Gilpin, "Conflict-Sensitive Macroeconomic Growth," 2009.

499. UNDP/USAID, "First Steps," 2007.

500. Gilpin, "Conflict-Sensitive Macroeconomic Growth," 2009.

501. USAID, "Economic Governance in War Torn Economies," 2004.

bank that controls or stimulates the overall economy by manipulating the money supply and interest rates, within the parameters of monetary policy.[502]

**9.5.4 Assess the state of monetary stability.** An important step in achieving monetary stability is to assess current and past monetary conditions, including the state of the money supply and inflation, currency use, budget deficits, and debt. This assessment, typically performed by the International Monetary Fund (IMF) and World Bank, should also gauge the functionality of various government institutions and staff. Key questions to ask include the following:

- What is causing inflation?
- How much money is in circulation in both the formal and informal economies?
- How deep are the financial markets?
- Are interest rates realistic?
- Are banking institutions intermediating effectively?
- What is the effect of informal finance and remittances?
- What is the condition of nonbank financial institutions?

**9.5.5 Inform monetary decisions by setting up a system for collecting economic data.** The ability to collect and analyze economic data is key to sound monetary policymaking process. Although statistics offices are often ignored in war-torn countries, the host nation government and international actors need to understand what is actually happening in the economy. In the emergency phase, assist the host nation government in establishing an interim mechanism to collect timely information on consumer prices, balance of payments, and other monetary statistics.[503] Late attention to statistics offices could force finance ministries to conduct ad hoc statistical analyses to construct the consumer price index, GDP estimates, and national accounts.[504]

**9.5.6 Address macroeconomic stabilization early on; it is an oft-overlooked priority.**[505] While no consensus exists on the exact sequencing of economic reforms, there is agreement that more attention must be paid to macroeconomic stabilization early on. This is critical for establishing a payment system, managing inflation, and laying down a basis for economic growth. S&R missions have typically prioritized emergency measures such as infrastructure rehabilitation, while postponing the reform of monetary and fiscal institutions and policies that are key to creating favorable conditions for growth.[506] Some macroeconomic measures that may happen early on include opening up to trade, finding an appropriate exchange rate, managing inflation, and bringing the budget deficit to a manageable level.[507]

*See Trade-off: Section 9.9.4, Macroeconomic reforms vs. political stability.*

---

502. JICA, "Handbook for Transition Assistance," 2006.

503. JICA, "Handbook for Transition Assistance," 2006.

504. USAID, "Economic Governance in War Torn Economies," 2004.

505. Ibid. Haughton, "The Reconstruction of War-Torn Economies," 2002.

506. UNDP/USAID, "First Steps," 2007. International Peace Academy and Center for International Security and Cooperation, *Economic Priorities for Peace Implementation*, 2002. Hereafter: IPA, *Economic Priorities*, 2002.

507. Haughton, "Reconstruction of War-Torn Economies," 2002. IPA, "Economic Priorities," 2002. Paul Collier, "Introduction," in *Demobilization and Insecurity—A Study in the Economics of the Transition from War to Peace*, 1994.

***9.5.7 Build public confidence by stabilizing domestic currency.*** An unstable currency is bad for the economy because it is inflationary and can cause scarcity and depletion of resources. As a result, many people may convert their savings into foreign currencies during and after conflict, usually euros or dollars. Others will hoard cash in their homes.[508] Suppressing this trend is often unsuccessful and may not be a priority—with time, domestic currency will eventually be used in local transactions and in paying taxes to the government.[509] Host nation governments have a number of options for stabilizing their currencies, including using preexisting currency, introducing a new national currency, or borrowing foreign currency from another country.[510] The most suitable approach will depend on the political situation but should seek to address supply bottlenecks, shore up reserves, strengthen institutions, and create a domestic market.

***9.5.8 Stabilize the exchange rate through a foreign exchange market.***[511] An organized foreign exchange market that allows countries to buy and sell currency aids stabilization. Develop transparent policies for participation in foreign exchange auctions. Following violent conflict, the exchange rate is often overvalued because of restrictions on imports and other distortions that favor those with access to the foreign exchange at the official rate. There are several policy choices for foreign exchange. When the value of the currency is known, countries can either peg their currency to a major international currency or continue to let their currency float. By submitting to external discipline, pegging a currency foregoes autonomous monetary policy, which can be beneficial in countries trying to stabilize inflation and restore credibility after the conflict.[512] An open exchange rate, however, may make sense for countries with insufficient reserves to maintain a fixed exchange rate.[513]

***9.5.9 Set realistic targets for inflation rates.*** Inflation is often high in war-torn economies. This may be the case because the government resorted to printing money to fund its military costs, among other factors. Stabilizing inflation is important to restore public confidence in the value of domestic currency, invite greater investment, and provide businesses with a guide for what to produce and in what quantities.[514] However, it is important not to go too far. Focusing on managing reserves and debt may be more realistic and effective. Imposing traditional economic reform agendas used in ordinary developing countries may not be appropriate for a country that has just undergone violent conflict. The effect could be to exacerbate social polarization and political disintegration.[515] Neither actors nor institutions in these countries tend to respond to traditional policy prescriptions the way one might expect in a country that is already on a strong path to development.

***9.5.10 Build the institutional capacity of an independent and credible monetary authority.*** A credible monetary authority typically exists in the form of a central bank that is able to

---

508. JICA, "Handbook for Transition Assistance," 2006.
509. Haughton, "Reconstruction of War-Torn Economies," 2002.
510. USAID, "Economic Governance in War Torn Economies," 2004.
511. USAID, "Guide to Economic Growth," 2009.
512. Haughton, "Reconstruction of War-Torn Economies," 2002.
513. Dobbins/Jones/Crane/Cole DeGrasse, *Beginner's Guide,* 2007.
514. Ibid.
515. Gilpin, "Conflict-Sensitive Macroeconomic Growth," 2009.

implement monetary policy decisions without political influence. In cases where it is necessary to develop a central bank, think about reducing the printing of money, replenishing foreign currency, jumpstarting foreign exchange operations and setting up accounting and statistical systems. Training and technical assistance are also important for both high-level officials and central bank staff.[516] The primary functions of a central bank include the following:

- Controlling the emission of domestic currency
- Restoring the payments system
- Facilitating or serving as a market for foreign exchange
- Supervising commercial banks.

**9.5.11 Strive for relevance, transparency, and effectiveness when developing a banking system.** In the early stages, focus on creating a relevant, transparent, and effective banking regime that is capable of mediating between savers and investors. Do not focus too heavily on creating a sophisticated financial sector. Banking policies should focus on establishing rules for transparency, preventing bad loans, and avoiding political lending.

### 9.5.12 Approach: Fiscal Management

Effective fiscal management requires building a transparent and accountable system for collecting revenue, spending public funds, and managing domestic debt. Fiscal policy is the use of the state budget to affect an economy through revenue collection and payments for goods and services and must be established early. A fiscal authority is needed to implement policy and manage fiscal operations, all of which will be a challenge when there is very limited administrative capacity. See Section 8.6 for a discussion on the stewardship of state resources.

*See Gap/Challenge: Section 9.10.6, Public finance management.*

*See Trade-off: Section 8.9.4, Responsible fiscal management vs. the need to provide immediate services.*

**9.5.13 The fiscal authority should be effective and transparent.** A finance ministry is typically the authority responsible for managing fiscal operations. While the precise institutional structure, powers, and responsibilities of that authority will vary depending on the country, the goals are often the same: ensuring that fiscal decisions are made in a predictable rather than ad hoc manner, establishing transparency in fiscal operations, collecting revenue, and ensuring that public spending matches the national priorities. These are fundamental for stabilization. Given weak administrative and technical capacity, simplicity is key. The fiscal authority usually includes four departments with the following functions:[517]

- A budget department to coordinate the spending program and create the budget
- A treasury to control spending, ensure funds are accounted for, transfer state revenues into bank accounts, and record transactions transparently;
- Customs and domestic tax departments for implementing tax policy and collecting tax revenues.

---

516. USAID, "Guide to Economic Growth," 2009.
517. United Nations University, *Strategy for Rebuilding Fiscal Institutions*, 2007.

Donors should coordinate a technical assistance strategy at the outset and provide long-term advisers to account for weak capacity.[518]
*See Gap/Challenge: Section 8.10.4, Oversight and accountability.*

**9.5.14 Do not ignore revenue generation strategies to meet urgent needs in these environments.** After violent conflict, the government will need revenue to resume the provision of basic goods and services, finance key reconstruction projects, and address large macroeconomic imbalances. Significant revenue mobilization, however, will be challenging because of a shrunken tax base, complex or discriminatory tax policies, weak institutional capacity, and competing illicit economies. One of the primary means for collecting revenue is getting the tax system up and running by securing the necessary infrastructure, technical assistance, and monitoring or oversight mechanisms. Another means for generating revenue quickly is through transparent and accountable management of natural resource wealth. Natural resource wealth management is also discussed in Sections 8.6.25 and 9.6.11.

**9.5.15 Stress simplicity in developing tax systems and policies, given limited administrative capacity.** In these environments, there typically is limited capacity to administer a complex tax system. Rather than imposing direct taxes on personal income that could be difficult to implement, taxation could start with simple, indirect taxes on sales at hotels or restaurants. Simple taxes on international trade—sales taxes on exports and excise taxes on imports—may also be relatively easy sources of revenue. The concept of simplicity should be applied to tax administration as well, focusing primarily on the most basic aspects of operation in early phases, such as procedures for filing and paying taxes and registration checks. With time, the focus of attention should shift toward improving the capacity for tax efforts and broadening the tax base.
*See Trade-off: Section 9.9.2, Sophistication vs. simplicity in the income tax system.*

**9.5.16 Accept low tax rates on earned income in the emergency phase.** Sustainable tax revenue requires long-term investment in nurturing the formal economy and fostering a culture of compliance in paying taxes.[519] While revenue collection programs are necessary, they can also be counterproductive when pursued too aggressively in the immediate aftermath of violent conflict—raising taxes too heavily contradicts the central goal of economic recovery and can undermine the credibility of the government. Prepare to accept a prolonged period in which tax rates on earned income are low. The focus instead should be on jumpstarting economic activity by breaking down barriers, establishing new farms or businesses, and expanding operations. How the economy expands will shape the strategy for taxing different sectors.[520]

**9.5.17 Consider debt relief programs to achieve debt sustainability.** Many governments in countries emerging from violent conflict will have accumulated unsustainable debt burdens while immersed in the conflict. In these cases, debt service relief may be a critical element to recovery.[521] The design and implementation of debt relief programs

518. International Monetary Fund, *Rebuilding Fiscal Institutions in Post-Conflict Countries*, 2004. Hereafter: IMF, "Fiscal Institutions," 2004.
519. Collier, "Post-Conflict Recovery," 2007.
520. Dobbins/Jones/Crane/Cole DeGrasse, *Beginner's Guide*, 2007.
521. Raymond Gilpin, "Debt Relief in Fragile States," presented at Debt Relief and Beyond: A World Bank Conference on Debt and Development, The World Bank, April/May 2009.

should be tailored to account for the unique complexities of each country's political economy. These variations can include the speed of delivery, the scope of resources, performance triggers, and the exit strategy. Debt relief should be viewed as part of a long-term effort that includes a comprehensive and robust debt management strategy, and should address all conflict-era debts and forestall commercial borrowing.

*9.5.18 Be prepared to fill the gap between revenue and government costs with funding from international actors.* Inevitably, the host nation government will come up short on revenue in the emergency phases because stabilization costs are high and capacity is low. In these emergency stages, international actors should be prepared to serve as the primary source of funds. But as the host nation government begins to strengthen its taxation capacity, international actors should shift their role to filling funding gaps. Making this shift is challenging. International actors should help the host nation government in this transition by carefully assessing recurrent costs for both salaries and capital expenditure programs and establishing clear goals for achieving self-sufficiency.

*9.5.19 Strengthen public expenditure management (PEM) of the host nation government.* Getting a PEM system up and running requires transparent processes and sound institutions, policies, and regulations. Strengthen budget execution by enhancing administrative and technical capacities of ministries. The ministries will have to draft budget documents and develop executive expenditure authorization procedures to monitor and control spending across the government. Audit capacities are essential and should be strengthened, alongside reforms in the fiscal conduct code, to limit corruption, waste, and misappropriation of public funds.[522] Address bottlenecks in spending and generate controls within the executive branch, legislature, international community, and civil society, all of which play critical roles in ensuring accountability of public spending.[523] Payment for government salaries and essential services (police, schools, clinics, or other operating units) should come from the finance ministry and should not be under the control of the heads of each operating unit.

*9.5.20 Prioritize transparency in contracting and procurement practices to combat corruption.* Contracting processes are one of the greatest sources of corruption in many countries. The best ways for curbing corruption in contracting processes are to establish simple and practical rules and procedures, accompanied by impartial and consistent decisions and a means for holding the contracting agency and contractors accountable for their actions. Implementing controls such as requiring dual authorization of expenditures and audits (i.e., from the manager and accounting clerk), can help restrict grafting practices.[524] The World Bank has developed guidelines on how to standardize the establishment of open, transparent, and competitive contracting procedures.[525] At stake are critical resources, necessary services, and the financial credibility of the operation, all of which outweigh the need to be more efficient. Other aspects of corruption are discussed in Sections 8.6.20 to 8.6.22 and 9.6.

522. IMF, "Fiscal Institutions," 2004.
523. Ghani/Lockhart, Fixing Failed States, 2008.
524. Dobbins/Jones/Crane/Cole DeGrasse, *Beginner's Guide,* 2007.
525. World Bank, "Contracting and Procurement Guidelines," 2004. http://web.worldbank.org/WBSITE/EXTERNAL/TOPICS/CSO/0,,contentMDK:20094613~menuPK:220448~pagePK:220503~piPK:220476~theSitePK:228717,00.html, accessed June 22, 2009.

**9.5.21 Reflect national interests in budget and state spending.** Although administrative capacity is weak, the host nation government should begin keeping budgetary records and ensuring that the national budget is aligned with citizens' interests, including civil service pay and infrastructure investments.[526] Before preparing a budget, the government needs a mechanism by which to execute the budget—a treasury system and spending information management system that allows the state to monitor all expenditures. The treasury should promote predictability, transparency, and timeliness in paying civil servants and procuring goods and services.[527] Improving budget management can help prevent state funds from being siphoned off for illegitimate purposes and promote spending that is consistent with the official budget. Some budgetary execution challenges are rooted in inexperience and unrealistic estimates about the capacity to implement projects in the budget.

*See Trade-off: Section 9.9.3, Creating donor trust funds vs. strengthening the host nation budget process.*

**9.5.22 Approach: Legislative and Regulatory Framework**
A legal, institutional, and regulatory framework is necessary to guarantee proper operation of economic institutions to address stabilization challenges such as property rights.[528] This framework must be simple, transparent, and easily enforceable, and it should address a range of laws governing commerce, labor, and property rights and mechanisms for institutional oversight and fiscal operations. Economic laws are worthless in this environment unless an effective legal system is capable of enforcing the law. This framework, together with broader economic recovery, can provide a foundation for greater investment and growth.[529]

**9.5.23 Assess legal conditions and simplify wherever possible.** In reviewing existing legislation, the goal should be to redress discriminatory practices linked to the conflict and simplify wherever possible to account for what will likely be weak administrative capacity. There is often a mismatch between the administrative capacity of host nation actors and the complexities of laws, particularly tax laws and administrative procedures. Consult widely in both the public and private sectors (informal and formal, on all sides of the conflict) to identify barriers to economic activity.[530] As soon as possible, remove those barriers, including onerous business registration procedures or restrictions on who may apply for import licenses. Laws may need to be drafted or imported and must be understood by domestic courts and the population. See also Section 7.5 for more on assessing and reforming legal frameworks.

**9.5.24 Promote predictability, open markets, and fair competition through commercial laws.**[531] Having a strong national policy and regulatory environment that embraces these tenets is key to creating favorable conditions for a market economy. Stability and predictability are critical to markets, enterprises, and foreign direct investment. Remove ambiguities in the investment code to allow foreign firms to borrow locally,

---

526. Ghani/Lockhart, *Fixing Failed States,* 2008. JICA, "Handbook for Transition Assistance," 2006.

527. Ghani/Lockhart, *Fixing Failed States,* 2008.

528. Covey/Dziedzic/Hawley, *Quest for Viable Peace,* 2005.

529. OECD, "Congo," 2003.

530. USAID, "Guide to Economic Growth," 2009.

531. Johanna Mendelson Forman and Merriam Mashatt, *Employment Generation and Economic Development in Stabilization and Reconstruction Operations* (Washington, D.C.: U.S. Institute of Peace, 2007). Hereafter: Mendelson Forman/Mashatt, *Employment Generation,* 2007.

allow expatriates to get work permits, and avoid corruption and red tape. Create laws that govern contracts (pledges, loans, and mortgages), bankruptcy (for companies that reorganize or liquidate themselves), and commercial and financial transactions. Establish rules of the game by regulating quality standards in major industries and establishing processes for business license registration, whether for partnerships or corporations, domestic or foreign.[532] The legal regime for commerce should also be perceived as favoring free and open markets and ensuring a level playing field for firms. Address market failures and prevent any special privileges or advantages for some sectors. These policies will likely contrast with the conflict-era or pre-conflict era environment in which the privileged few had access to economic opportunity. In cases where ownership was concentrated or state-held, privatization and competition laws are needed.

***9.5.25 Develop a customs, tax, and budget legal framework to govern fiscal operations.*** Laws governing fiscal operations have two main sources: the constitution and tax and budget laws. The constitution typically specifies the division of government taxing powers while tax laws authorize the state to collect taxes and enforce the law when taxes are evaded. Financial regulations are also necessary to authorize the fiscal authority to manage public spending. The goal in creating tax regulations and laws should be to simplify them, make them more transparent, and make them easier to administer. A budget law should set out clear budget classification structures that establish guidelines for executing the budget, such as prohibiting unbudgeted spending, creating a framework for internal control and audit, and providing a means for financing budget deficits. New laws should also address how to deal with situations involving "off-budget transactions," the absence of clear classification of budgetary spending, and the absence of procedures for managing foreign aid.

***9.5.26 Prioritize dispute resolution mechanisms to address property and contract issues.*** Land and property rights disputes dominate in these scenarios. During violent conflict, the state often seizes property or other assets to support its efforts. People flee, land is abandoned, and others take control. The inflow of returnees looking to reclaim land creates a major problem. A national dialogue should commence as soon as possible over this issue of disputed or unclear property rights.[533] The absence of a credible system for resolving property disputes and enforcing contracts will inflame conflict, especially when ethnic cleansing forced one group out and another took possession, or if unequal access to land was an issue that motivated the conflict. Ambiguity can also deter investors when potential investments involve land-intensive projects in areas where outstanding claims still persist. Resolution systems should not exclude customary laws that are already in place or alternative forums (e.g., local government or traditional institutions) that may be able to help manage conflicts within or between groups. These can resolve disputes that do not require a full court proceeding.[534] For more on property dispute resolution, see Section 10.7.10.

532. USAID, "Accelerating the Transition," 2008.

533. USAID, "Guide to Economic Growth," 2009.

534. Michael Bhatia and Jonathan Goodhand, *Profit and Poverty: Aid, Livelihoods and Conflict in Afghanistan* (London: Overseas Development Institute Humanitarian Policy Group, 2003).

*9.5.27 Focus on laws to combat organized crime and other illicit economic activity.* Laws that seek to combat predatory economic actors must be backed up by the means to investigate, prosecute, and convict those actors. This is a tall order. Laws should prevent money-laundering activity and provide ways for financial institutions and actors to report suspicious activity. Create a legal and administrative system to monitor and adjudicate such activity and seize assets when enforcing financial transaction laws. Legal safeguards should prevent predatory actors from capturing public entities when they are privatized. A transparency framework is needed to enable public posting of public property, bids and tenders for buying the property, identity of purchasers, financing of sales, and codicils on use of the property (the right of resale, restriction on use of assets) to ensure that sales are compliant with the transparency regime. The framework should also require public disclosure of transfers with the book and market values of the assets being transferred and the buyer of those assets. Also, state regulations and enforcement mechanisms are needed for enabling internal enterprise governance, maintaining relations with state entities, and reporting financial status and operations.

*9.5.28 Engage the private sector on advocacy for policies and regulatory reform.* Include the broader society in dialogue on policies and regulatory reform to achieve buy-in for economic recovery. But be cautious with regard to some business owners, who may have obtained their power and status during the conflict as a result of rent-seeking or predatory behavior. A public-private forum for dialogue on policies and regulations could benefit the private sector and jumpstart economic growth.[535]

## 9.6 Necessary Condition: Control Over the Illicit Economy and Economic-Based Threats to Peace

### 9.6.1 What is control over the illicit economy and economic-based threats to peace? Why is it a necessary condition?

Control over the illicit economy and economic-based threats to peace is a condition in which predatory economic actors are prevented from perpetuating conflict or hindering good governance and economic development, while the formal economy is strengthened to boost the legitimacy of the host nation government. One of the biggest economic threats to peace arises from the political-economic nexus, where resources acquired from illegal trafficking, smuggling, extortion, and hijacking of state and private enterprises are used to acquire and maintain both formal and informal power. The actors involved this economy may use coercion, terror, intelligence activities, and paramilitary operations to threaten the peace process. Allowing them to operate can hamper prospects for good governance and peace by promoting violence against civilians when acquiring control over assets, or exploiting and capturing trade networks and remittances.[536]

---

535. USAID, "Accelerating the Transition," 2008.

536. Karen Ballentine and Heiko Nitzschke, "The Political Economy of Civil War and Conflict Transformation," in *Transforming War Economies: Dilemmas and Challenges, No. 3 in Dialogue Series* (Berlin, Germany: Berghof Research Center for Constructive Conflict Management, 2006). Hereafter: Ballentine/Nitzschke, "Political Economy," 2006.

### 9.6.2 Guidance for Control Over the Illicit Economy and Economic-Based Threats to Peace

*9.6.3 Approach: Control Over Illicit Economic Activity*
During and after violent conflict, illicit economic activity will likely be pervasive and diverse and may include both benign and predatory actors. Gaining control over these activities requires addressing the problem on many different levels, including severing the nexus between political power and ill-gotten wealth, eliminating economic incentives for continued conflict, and cracking down on criminal trades that violate human rights and contribute to instability. There is also an illegal informal economy that ordinary citizens may resort to as a means of survival during violent conflict. While it may not present a threat to peace, it may be so broad that it threatens government legitimacy and badly needed sources of revenue.

*9.6.4 Understand the different economic channels that emerge from violent conflict.*
Prolonged violent conflict can fragment economic markets into several channels. While market fragmentation is broken down in many different ways, it is addressed in this manual to include four main elements: (1) the official or formal economy that is controlled or supervised by the government and the three following elements of the illicit economy, (2) the informal economy that citizens resort to as a means of survival during violent conflict, (3) the war economy that directly fuels conflict, and (4) the black economy, involving serious crimes and criminal networks that violate human rights and may directly or indirectly prolong the conflict. The lines between these groups are not always distinct—actors may operate across them, making it a complex challenge to address. The illicit elements of the economy are addressed in further detail below. *See Gap/Challenge: Section 9.10.3, Managing the informal sector without hurting ordinary citizens.*

*9.6.5 Understand the legacy of the war economy and its effects on stabilization and reconstruction.* War economies finance conflict in many ways, primarily through violent control over assets and resources. Warring factions often gain control over certain industries or networks and use them to transport military supplies or to generate funding that directly fuels violence. This control can also threaten peace, undermine the legal economy, and enable predatory relationships.[537] Key characteristics of a war economy are the following:[538]

- A criminalized political economy where political power is derived from access to illicit sources of revenue
- The destruction of the formal economy and the growth of black markets
- Extortion and violence against civilians to seize control over high-value assets (such as oil, diamonds, and timber), trade networks, remittances, and labor
- Presence of networks linking transnational organized crime, corrupt government officials, extralegal intelligence entities, spoilers, and external and internal terrorist organizations.

*9.6.6 Prioritize the identification and disruption of finance networks of local power brokers, insurgent groups, transnational organized crime, and terrorist organizations.*[539]

---

537. JICA, "Handbook for Transition Assistance," 2006.
538. Ballentine/Nitzschke, "Political Economy," 2006.
539. USAID, "Economic Governance in War Torn Economies," 2004. Covey/Dziedzic/Hawley, *Quest for a*

During violent conflict, many sophisticated crime networks often emerge for the trafficking of narcotics, humans, weapons, or lootable natural resources. These serious crimes make up what is broadly referred to in this manual as the black economy and often result in violence and serious violations of human rights. While many of these hostile economic activities may have existed in some form prior to the conflict, the actors who initiate them often exploit the security vacuum that follows violent conflict and expand their trades into the formal economy that are difficult to dismantle. These networks are also often linked to corrupt political leaders, who use the illicit revenue to sustain political power.[540] This political-economic nexus constitutes a pervasive incentive and a driving mechanism for violent conflict. These networks should be broken up through aggressive law enforcement. States that are captured by a political-criminal elite can create an environment in which peace settlements seldom prosper. Predatory economic activities can corrupt governance and cripple the economic environment, making it impossible for legitimate business and foreign investors to operate. The integrity of the revenue stream that allows essential state services to be provided must also be protected for the political economy to be sustainable. These and other spoilers are also addressed in Section 6.5.10.
*See Gap/Challenge: Section 9.10.1, Political-economic nexus.*

**9.6.7 Consider the consequences of aggressively curbing the informal economy.** Violent conflict can severely weaken the official economy through corruption, inefficiencies, and falling revenue, which can increase the cost of doing business in this sector.[541] This reality often drives entrepreneurs to establish informal or parallel channels of commerce that may be illegal but represent the de facto economy during conflict. Because other normal distribution systems will have been disrupted, many ordinary citizens will rely on the informal economy for goods and services.[542] Any strategy to curb the informal economy, therefore, should avoid harm to ordinary entrepreneurs and should seek to leverage the economic activities that have emerged as the people's innovative and spontaneous response to difficult times.[543] But encouraging people to participate in the formal economy is still essential to promote a base of taxpayers who have a stake in the country's future and enjoy benefits of good governance.[544] Encourage integration of the informal market structures by making formal channels more accessible, affordable, and nurturing for entrepreneurs. Transform financial instruments to better accommodate the informal sector, through microfinance programs, trade credits, and extension services.[545]

**9.6.8 Understand the consequences of predatory local actors in managing economic recovery programs.** Safeguards against this should include real-time oversight, audits, and payroll mechanisms that limit infiltration and corruption.[546] An important decision is whether to retain existing civil servants who have engaged in corruption in the past.

*Viable Peace*, 2005.

540. Gilpin, "Conflict-Sensitive Macroeconomic Growth," 2009.
541. Ibid.
542. Dobbins/Jones/Crane/Cole DeGrasse, Beginner's Guide, 2007.
543. Hernando DeSoto, *The Other Path: The Invisible Revolution in the Third World* (New York: Harper & Row, 1989).
544. Mendelson Forman/Mashatt, "Employment Generation," 2007.
545. Gilpin, "Conflict-Sensitive Macroeconomic Growth," 2009.
546. Mendelson Forman/Mashatt, "Employment Generation," 2007.

Retention may be attractive because the individuals have the skills to run the programs, but doing so may also pose great risks of destabilizing corruption.

*9.6.9 Recognize that the public sector can be a major source of corruption.*[547] Corruption is the misuse of entrusted power for private gain and is a major challenge in these environments. Spoilers often develop ties to the government during conflict and entrench their power by putting supporters on government payrolls.[548] This is distinct from low-level officials, who partake in petty corruption by looking the other way in enforcing business regulations in exchange for payments. Bribes are often attractive for civil servants because their salaries are low. Corruption undermines public confidence in the political system, impedes the development of strong political leadership and hampers economic growth by distorting competition and market conditions. Mitigating the harmful effects of corruption can involve developing and implementing anti-corruption laws, public education campaigns, and civil society watchdog organizations to pressure the state for good economic governance. Regular and adequate payment of civil service workers is a priority.

*9.6.10 Deal with the harmful use of remittances.* During violent conflict, remittances serve multiple purposes, making them difficult to address. Remittances often constitute a major source of livelihood security for many conflict-affected countries; provide a safety net for communities; and have been invested in social infrastructure, services, and income. At the same time, remittances are also often used to provide weapons and material support to violent groups. These dual purposes make remittances very difficult to address. Tracking and control of these flows is also very difficult because they flow into the country through informal channels. Improving the channeling of remittances to competitive industries that can help economically marginalized parts of population is an unmet challenge.[549]
*See Gap/Challenge: Section 9.10.2, Monitoring diaspora remittances.*

*9.6.11 Approach: Management of Natural Resource Wealth*
Natural resources include renewable and nonrenewable assets such as minerals, oil and gas, land, forestry, marine resources, and water. They can also include illegal commodities such as poppy and coca. Often, the battle for control over natural resources is a cause of violent conflict to begin with. Effectively managing the wealth derived from these resources involves equitably distributing the money to benefit the population, rather than corrupt individuals who are able to siphon the money into their own pockets. Doing so requires establishing the laws, institutions, and capacity to manage wealth in a transparent and accountable manner. Efforts must be made to avoid "resource curses," which include corruption, economic instability, inequitable distribution, and control of resource wealth and areas. These curses undermine the sustainability of peace and long-term economic growth. But when natural resource wealth is used effectively, it can jumpstart revenue generation and have a positive effect on economic recovery. Natural resource wealth management is also discussed in Section 8.6.25.

---

547. Covey/Dziedzic/Hawley, *Quest for a Viable Peace,* 2005.
548. Dobbins/Jones/Crane/Cole DeGrasse, *Beginner's Guide,* 2007.
549. USAID, "Accelerating the Transition," 2008.

*9.6.12 Understand the context before designing a strategy to manage natural resources.*[550] These investigations should center on issues that are unique to the case.[551] The assessment should include the following:[552]

- An examination of the conditions of resources. What resources exist? How is resource wealth monetized and controlled?
- An assessment of the role of resource wealth in the war economy and the connections with government officials and violent spoilers.
- An assessment of how much control the government has over natural resource wealth and areas, including facilities (pipelines, oilfields, mines, airstrips for exporting minerals, etc.).
- A gap analysis of good resource revenue management systems (e.g., transparency, accountability, budget controls to handle volatility).
- Requirements for a stable, transparent, and accountable system for letting concessions.
- Identification of actual or potential subnational conflicts over revenue allocation.
- Identification of relevant work already being undertaken by international economic institutions.

*9.6.13 Prevent control over natural resources, resource-rich areas, and relevant facilities by predatory actors.* Ensuring that legitimate actors have full access to these areas is key to management of natural resources for the benefit of the population. International actors should help the host nation government to establish financial controls for ensuring that revenue is spent in proper budgetary channels. Setting up national funds for revenue deposits from natural resources have been somewhat successful, as well as certification schemes for natural resources. Setting these systems up rapidly is best to prevent political leaders from entrenching their power.[553]

*9.6.14 Draw from past approaches for improving the management of resource wealth and cutting off financing for hostile actors.* Solutions include a mix of carrots and sticks aimed at influencing state behavior and building civil society capacity to pressure its government for better management of natural resources.[554] Sanctions are a means to drain support from states or violent groups that use natural resources to fuel conflict. Interdiction seeks to intercept illicit commodities in transit that drive conflict. The Extractive Industries Transparency Initiative is a voluntary measure that seeks to enhance transparency in natural resource management and collaboration among government, donors, and civil society. The Kimberley Diamond Certification Regime, which shuts out violent actors from the market, and the Publish What You Pay campaign are other well-known programs that have sought to encourage good management of resource wealth. Civil

---

550. United Nations Environment Programme, *From Conflict to Peacebuilding: The Role of Natural Resources and the Environment,* 2009. Hereafter: UNEP, *Role of Natural Resources,* 2009.

551. Some available resources include U.S. government agencies like the Energy Information Administration, U.S. Geological Service, USAID, and the State Department, as well as the World Bank and IMF; UN agencies such as UNDP; NGOs active in natural resource wealth management such as Global Witness, Human Rights Watch; resource companies; and country specialists and experts such as the U.S. National Defense University's Africa Center for Strategic Studies.

552. Shankleman, "Managing Natural Resource Wealth," 2006.

553. Dobbins/Jones/Crane/Cole DeGrasse, *Beginner's Guide,* 2007.

554. Shankleman, "Managing Natural Resource Wealth," 2006.

society can also help curtail corruption in natural resource management by collecting information on illegal resource exploitation and related government corruption.[555]

**9.6.15 Strengthen governance practices to improve natural resource wealth management.[556]** The destabilizing effects of corruption related to natural resource wealth must be tackled at all levels of government. Proper natural resource wealth management depends on governance that is participatory and has a transparent and accountable system of revenue and spending. It also relies on solid corporate governance within an environment of government regulatory structures that promote good behavior. This requires confronting vested interests, involving civil society, and deploying specialized staff trained in following the path of illicit money.

**9.6.16 Maximize participation from all players to ensure effective management.** This includes participation of extractive industries, their bankers, the international financial institutions, regional organizations, international donors, and civil society. A problem in the past has been getting commercial banks and some states to cooperate in international efforts to restrict business with governments that are not transparent or accountable in their natural resource management. Coordination among financial institutions, governments, and international law enforcement agencies should address the linkages between money laundering, corruption, international crime, and sometimes terrorist financing.[557] Successful management of resources also requires strong political leadership and a media sector and civil society willing to pressure the government for good governance.[558] The natural resource issue should also be addressed in peace agreements, DDR programs, and peacekeeping mandates.[559] Since World War II, resource management mechanisms have been addressed in fewer than 25 percent of peace agreements for conflicts involving natural resources.[560] *See Gap/Challenge: Section 9.10.5, Addressing economic factors in the peace agreement.*

**9.6.17 Approach: Reintegration of Ex-Combatants[561]**
Reintegration is a social and economic process in which ex-combatants return to community life and engage in livelihood alternatives to violence.[562] Ex-combatants can present an economic-based threat to peace if they are not successfully reintegrated into the social and economic fabric of society. Integrating ex-combatants into civilian life gives them a stake in the peace and reduces the likelihood that they will turn to insurgent or criminal activity to support themselves if they cannot find gainful employment. Reintegration activities include creating micro-enterprises, providing education and training, and preparing communities to receive ex-combatants.[563] Reintegration is attached to the DDR process, but in reality it requires the attention, resources, and expertise of a very specific set of social and economic actors. It is a big gap for peacebuilders. See Section 6.7.14 for more on reintegration. *See Trade-off: Section 9.9.5, Employment opportunities for ex-combatants vs. women and minorities.*

---

555. Ballentine/Nitzschke, "Political Economy," 2006.
556. Shankleman, "Managing Natural Resource Wealth," 2006.
557. Ballentine/Nitzschke, "Political Economy," 2006.
558. Shankleman, "Managing Natural Resource Wealth," 2006. United Nations Expert Group, National Resources and *Conflict in Africa: Transforming a Peace Liability into a Peace Asset*, 2006.
559. UNEP, "Role of Natural Resources," 2009.
560. Ibid.
561. U.S. Army, *FM 3-07*, 2008.
562. United Nations Secretary-General, *Note to the General Assembly, A/C.5/59/31*, 2005.
563. UN DDR, *Integrated DDR*, 2006.

*9.6.18 Assess the social and economic situation to identify the best options for reintegrating ex-combatants.*[564] To make sound economic decisions, it is imperative to answer: What are the development opportunities? What is the capacity for economic absorption and what does the labor market look like? What is the local demand for goods and services? What is the condition of key economic infrastructure, such as access to markets or the availability of communications? It is critical to ensure that education and training, micro-credit services, and other business development services match the demands of the economy in question.[565] Good employment options for ex-combatants will often engage them in strong, competitive, and profitable pursuits so they can contribute to economic growth.[566] Additionally, it is important to understand the social services and institutions that are available, such as trauma and abuse support services and disability rehabilitation services.

*9.6.19 Be sure to address the needs of communities receiving ex-combatants.*[567] It may be difficult to get communities to accept ex-combatants, especially perpetrators of atrocities. Most will have little to offer by way of education, employment, or training. Most soldiers are traumatized by their experience and could resort to criminal activities, rather than making solid contributions to communities.[568] To quell trepidation, address the needs of the communities that will receive ex-combatants and communicate the goals and importance of the process. Successful reintegration depends on the support of communities, families, local leaders, and women's and youth groups. Encourage these groups to get involved in planning for the return of ex-combatants. Implement a strong public information campaign to spread awareness about the goals of reintegration. Consider funding a period of community service when ex-combatants settle in an area to promote their acceptance.

## 9.7 Necessary Condition: Market Economy Sustainability

### 9.7.1 What is market economy sustainability? Why is it a necessary condition?

A sustainable market-based economy leverages the power of markets to stimulate economic growth and reverse the negative effects of violent conflict.[569] The revitalization of a market economy involves restoring the flow of goods and services within the country and across the border, through infrastructure, private sector, human capital, and financial sector development. In most cases, violent conflict will have caused production, consumption, and wealth to plummet. This slows goods and capital to a halt, keeping people from accessing much-needed food and basic necessities and developing their business. A sustainable market-based economy (1) facilitates equitable movement of goods and services, (2) creates a rewards-based meritocracy, and (3) focuses on efficiency and ultimately connections to global markets.

### 9.7.2 Guidance for Market Economy Sustainability

564. USAID, "Accelerating the Transition," 2008.
565. UN DDR, "Integrated DDR," 2006.
566. Mendelson Forman/Mashatt, "Employment Generation," 2007.
567. European Union, Concept for DDR, 2006.
568. UN DDR, "Integrated DDR," 2006.
569. United States Agency for International Development, *Market Development in Crisis-Affected Environments: Emerging Lessons for Achieving Pro-Poor Economic Reconstruction*, 2007. Hereafter: USAID, "Market Development," 2007.

### 9.7.3 Approach: Infrastructure Development
This section refers primarily to economic infrastructure: transportation (roads, bridges, rail lines), water works, electric power, telecommunications, oil and gas pipelines, government/public administration buildings, and other facilities required for an industrial economy to function. Infrastructure is vital for social, economic, physical and political cohesion.[570] During violent conflict or through looting in its aftermath, infrastructure is often severely damaged or destroyed. Without physical infrastructure, access remains restricted among suppliers, service providers, and consumers, which poses a major constraint on economic development.[571]

### 9.7.4 Establish infrastructure priorities according to broader strategic imperatives.[572]
In prioritizing infrastructure investments, remember that all investment projects are part of a larger reform package that should support the national strategic approach to development. Limited resources require that all investment decisions be made with this broader context in mind. Consider social, economic, and political factors in prioritizing investments, including group-based economic disparities that may have been integral to the conflict. The sequencing of investments should also make sense—reconstructing ports, for example, should not be done until the transportation systems leading to those ports are repaired. Refrain from building too many schools before there is a plan for trained teachers, materials, curriculum, and building maintenance that are required for a school to function.

### 9.7.5 Consider social, political, and environmental impacts in designing infrastructure projects.
As in all economic recovery initiatives, the designers of infrastructure projects must always consider first and foremost the impact of their work on political stability and the potential to exacerbate conflict between different ethnic or religious groups. Infrastructure projects can have immense implications for migration and resettlement, the use of land, the environment, and perceptions of inequity.[573] Infrastructure projects can often be used to promote peaceful relations by cultivating mutual interests among different groups in society and encouraging intercommunal cooperation. Divided communities that have made a commitment to support the peace process should be considered priorities for investment in infrastructure. Consider collateral issues presented with schools, including gender discrimination, inability to pay school fees, or decisions to send children to work rather than school. Other aspects of community-based development and reconciliation are discussed in Section 10.8.

### 9.7.6 Prioritize power, roads, ports, and telecommunications.
Power is a precondition for formal economic development. Roads and waterways are essential for linking the rural economy to the urban market. City streets are vital when the private sector grows and begins to invest more heavily in vehicles, resulting in traffic congestion.[574] Seaports and airports are critical for the movement of goods and people. Telecommunications is also a priority because social, economic, and political recovery depends on

---

570. JICA, "Handbook for Transition Assistance," 2006.
571. Infrastructure often includes social infrastructure, which refers to public institutions, schools, health facilities, post offices, and libraries. Some of these institutions are addressed in Section 10, Social Well-Being.
572. JICA, "Handbook for Transition Assistance," 2006.
573. JICA, "Handbook for Transition Assistance," 2006.
574. Collier, "Post-Conflict Recovery," 2007.

communications.[575]

***9.7.7 Protect infrastructure to ensure peace and economic growth.*** Critical infrastructure is often a strategic target during or after conflict for people who seek to disrupt the peace process or instill fear. Police or military are often deployed to protect the infrastructure. Since transportation is the artery of the economy, it should receive priority protection. This includes roads, bridges, ports, and airports that have immense strategic value for enabling the flow of goods and people. See Section 6.8.9 for more on the protection of infrastructure.

***9.7.8 Focus on infrastructure management, not just infrastructure itself.*** Much attention has been paid to the physical rehabilitation or construction of infrastructure, but it is just as important to strengthen the institutions responsible for managing and maintaining the infrastructure once it is established. These institutions include those that manage electricity companies; the road networks; the rail system, if it exists; and air, land, and seaports. Building institutional capacity is typically achieved by training staff and establishing mechanisms for corporate governance, management, and basic administration capabilities.[576] The host nation population will be responsible for maintaining the systems, so their capacity will be the one that matters.

***9.7.9 Rebuild only what should be rebuilt.*** Refrain from simply reconstructing the services that were destroyed during the conflict. Many practices before and during the conflict were designed for a few people to exploit wealth for their own gain, rather than for the benefit of the country. There may be pressures from certain groups or individuals to preserve these models, but careful assessments should identify which services will actually enhance economic growth. The equitable distribution of goods and services should guide careful consideration for longer-term structural changes.[577] See also Section 8.5.11 for a discussion on equitable service delivery.

***9.7.10 Recognize the wider benefits of infrastructure repair beyond its physical value.***[578] These benefits include demonstrating visible benefits of peace and quantifiable progress relatively quickly. Infrastructure development is also a key source of employment. Better roads reduce travel time and costs, which encourages farmers to travel to the market and produce more. Improved water supplies promote hygiene and reduce health problems, while improved irrigation increases agricultural productivity. Always think about these catalytic impacts when deciding what investments to make. Use infrastructure projects to strengthen administrative capacity and promote reconciliation by having former adversaries work side by side toward mutual community goals. See Section 10.8.12 for more on using infrastructure projects to benefit reconciliation.

---

575. Antonio Carvalho and Samia Melhem, *Attracting Investment in Post-Conflict Countries: The Importance of Telecommunications,* (Washington, D.C.: World Bank, 2005).

576. USAID, "Guide to Economic Growth," 2009. JICA, "Handbook for Transition Assistance," 2006.

577. USAID, "Guide to Economic Growth," 2009.

578. JICA, "Handbook for Transition Assistance," 2006.

### 9.7.11 Approach: Private Sector Development

The private sector is very diverse and can include everyone from farmers and micro-entrepreneurs to domestic manufacturing companies and multinational enterprises.[579] A thriving private sector can provide numerous jobs for the population, serve as the main source of tax revenue, and enable the country to reduce its dependency on international assistance. Nurturing a healthy private sector requires that the enterprising class of individuals and firms have a means for saving money, have access to credit and financial services, have access to infrastructure, and have confidence in property rights. Perhaps most importantly, entrepreneurs need a predictable regulatory environment that enables them to pursue rational business plans.

*9.7.12 Look to local investment and resources; don't wait for foreign investment.*[580] There is no question that foreign direct investment (FDI) brings much-needed assets into the country, including entrepreneurship, management, skills, and top-notch technology. But in the immediate aftermath of violent conflict, it is neither practical nor realistic to rely on this source of investment. Generally, FDI may not begin to flow until political, economic, and social risks are reduced and a level of predictability and stability restored. In the meantime, the host nation population should focus on domestic investments, including remittances from the diaspora.[581] Remittances sometimes make up a large bulk of domestic resources in the emergency phase, which can be invested in critical projects. The host nation government will also rely on international credit and technical assistance in these phases.

*9.7.13 Provide access to immediate credit and financial services for micro, small, and medium enterprises.* Providing people with access to loans for their small and medium enterprises is critical to jumpstarting economic activity and creating jobs. While loans are often available for large government reconstruction projects, they are less readily available for grassroots projects led by self-employed entrepreneurs or those working as part of small or medium enterprises. Many informal lending arrangements at the microlevel begin in refugee camps or on the streets as informal contracts between two parties.[582] But developing microcredit programs and institutions can get people together to exchange experiences, build capacity, and repair social capital.[583] Microfinance is also key to promoting private sector activities by providing access to savings, insurance money transfers, and other banking needs of the population. Microfinance programs should target groups most affected by the conflict, including displaced persons, returning refugees, ex-combatants, and women.[584] Strategies should go beyond the provision of credit to include systems for accrediting microfinance suppliers and monitoring and measuring impact.[585] *See Gap/Challenge: Section 9.10.4, Microfinance and effective intermediation.*

579. United Nations Development Program, *The Role of Private Sector Development in Post-Conflict Economic Recovery,* 2007. Hereafter: UNDP, "Private Sector Development," 2007.

580. USAID, "Guide to Economic Growth," 2009. OECD, "Congo," 2003.

581. UNDP, "Private Sector Development," 2007.

582. Mendelson Forman/Mashatt, "Employment Generation," 2007.

583. International Labor Organization and United Nations High Commissioner on Refugees, *Micro-finance in Post-Conflict Situations: Towards Guiding Principles for Action,* 1999. Hereafter: ILO/UNHCR, *Microfinance,* 1999.

584. Kathleen Kuehnast, "Innovative Approaches to Microfinance in Post-Conflict Situations: Bosnia Local Initiatives Project," 2001.

585. ILO/UNHCR, "Micro-finance," 1999.

*9.7.14 Create an enabling environment that lowers risks, promotes business activity, and attracts FDI.*[586] There are two great hindrances to doing business in these environments: uncertainty about the rules of the game (laws and regulations) and the government's inability to enforce these rules fairly and impartially. Any increase in business activity will depend on an increase in the stability and predictability of the business environment in these regards. Before investing in a project, business owners and managers want to know that their properties will not be seized and that their contracts will be upheld. Other deterrent factors for investment include corruption, insecurity, and poor infrastructure.[587] Mitigating these concerns will require undertaking difficult economic reforms, setting up a foreign investment code, and demonstrating that disputes over property rights can be resolved efficiently through dispute resolution mechanisms. A legal framework of economic laws and regulations is needed to evenly enforce business and trade regulations to ensure equitable compliance with taxes, licensing restrictions, and customs duties, etc.[588]

*9.7.15 Leverage key markets as economic opportunities.* The jobs available in relief operations can begin to create skills and services that could be useful for more sustainable industries. For example, a program that teaches women to make grass mats for refugee shelters could also train women in basket weaving to cater to handicrafts markets.[589] Other examples include training local blacksmiths to craft fuel-efficient stoves used in refugee camps as well as agricultural tools, supporting local carpenters to supply school benches and desks, and supporting local tailors to supply school uniforms. These opportunities are often identified through a value chain analysis that helps focus attention on what markets to leverage.

*9.7.16 Maximize the peacebuilding benefits of private sector activity.* The marketing of some products may emphasize the experience of conflict and current living conditions of the producers. The success of Rwandan coffee in the past decade illustrates this phenomenon. The Rwandan coffee industry's official Web site prominently features a section on "Rebuilding and Reconciliation," refers to the country's recent genocide, and indicates that the development of the coffee industry is bringing "hope for a better future."[590] Such marketing has helped Rwandan coffee producers to benefit even as global coffee markets have constricted over the last few years.[591] Additionally, the industry has become a force for economic integration between Hutus and Tutsis through cross-employment and collaboration in joint coffee, contributing to social cohesion and minimizing risks of a return to conflict.

*9.7.17 Approach: Human Capital Development*
Human capital refers to the stock of skills and knowledge embodied in a population of an economy.[592] Violent conflict depletes human capital through death, disability, trauma,

---

586. USAID, "Guide to Economic Growth," 2009. Mendelson Forman/Mashatt, "Employment Generation," 2007.
587. UNDP, "Private Sector Development," 2007.
588. USAID, "Guide to Economic Growth," 2009.
589. USAID, "Accelerating the Transition," 2008.
590. Coffee Rwanda, "Coffee Rwanda," http://www.coffeerwanda.com/coffee.html, accessed June 22, 2009.
591. Carter Dougherty, "Rwanda Savors the Rewards of Coffee," *The New York Times*, 2004.
592. See human capital entry in Deardorff's Glossary of International Economics, http://www-personal.umich.edu/~alandear/glossary/h.html, accessed June 22, 2009.

displacement, and migration of skilled workers. Even prior to the conflict, many countries suffer from an endemic lack of education, training and opportunities. Restoring human capital will require diverse training programs to account for all kinds of groups, including demobilized combatants, disabled persons, women, and children, as well as for entire communities. See Section 10.6 for more on the development of education.

*9.7.18 Give all a stake in the peace process, including the most vulnerable.* Inclusiveness and equity should be the aim when designing training and vocational programs. Focus on key political and social constituencies that require the most assistance, such as the poor, women, veterans, and demobilized soldiers. Finding ways to empower youth through human capital development is also critical as some have primarily been involved in violent conflict and will not have had access to education or skills training. Training for youth should also be integrated with remedial education.[593]
*See Gap/Challenge: Section 10.10.5, Youth in recovery efforts.*

*9.7.19 Establish a means for collecting labor market data as the basis for human capital development.* Human capital development programs need to be dynamic to respond to changes in the market. Collection of labor market data is essential for planning and should also be continuous thereafter, in communities, among public and private employers, in training programs, and in demobilization camps.[594] It should include past and present data on life and peace skills of the population, vocational training, small and micro-enterprise development, and labor-intensive infrastructure works. The information allows the government to identify broad trends in labor supply and demand and see shifts in employment opportunities and demand for skills across the country. It can also help with the evaluation of program effectiveness.

*9.7.20 Do not neglect the need to impart "life skills."* Conflicts result in a dearth of skills for work and in "life skills" as well. Life skills include the personal capacity to adjust socially in society and the work place, reconcile tensions, and come to terms with the conflict. Life skills training should always be included in education programs[595] and be delivered in schoolhouses, demobilization camps, career centers, and community settings. The programs should be inclusive, innovative, practical, personal, and flexible so they can be tailored for individuals. Life skills are key to improving sustainable employment.

*9.7.21 Begin training and education on the job and look to long-term educational capacity.* Training for operational skills in the immediate aftermath of conflict may be done on the job, such as processing business licenses or managing a road project. Longer-term educational investments will be necessary to sustain economic growth. Doing this will require developing a true professional class of macroeconomic analysts and policy-makers trained in graduate-level programs in-country or abroad. Operational training in areas like treasury operations or tax administration has proven successful, but development of monetary and fiscal analysts has been more challenging because of the requirement for formal education in economics and policy analysis. Professional caliber

593. Johanna Mendelson Forman, "Achieving Socioeconomic Well-Being in Postconflict Settings," *The Washington Quarterly,* Autumn 2002. Hereafter: Mendelson Forman, "Achieving Socioeconomic Well-Being," 2002.
594. International Labour Organisation, *Local Economic Development: Operational Guidelines,* 1997. Hereafter: ILO, *Local Economic Development,* 1997.
595. Ibid.

will differ from case to case, which will impact the level of training needed.[596]

### 9.7.22 Approach: Financial Sector Development

The financial sector refers to the system of commercial banks and lending institutions supervised by an independent central bank that provide much-needed credit to businesses and individuals in the aftermath of conflict. Enabling access to microcredit and the ability to perform financial transactions beyond the simple cash and barter economy is critical for economic growth.[597] Two major functions of banks are to provide a trusted institution for people to deposit financial savings and to provide a means to pay for goods and services to promote commerce.

**9.7.23 Be prepared for a banking system that is severely debilitated.** During violent conflict, the central bank and many commercial banks may have ceased to function. Politically directed loans at concessionary interest rates and insider loans to managers or relatives of managers may have occurred frequently. Operating systems, internal controls, and management information will also be degraded or outdated. Reforming the banking sector should begin with the development of a central bank. It will also involve transforming systems of insolvent and poorly managed banks into a structure capable of mobilizing resources and evaluating loans. Making the transition has posed many problems. The goal is to ensure that banks are able to provide effective intermediation between lenders and customers.

**9.7.24 Seek to rebuild trust in the banking system.** After violent conflict, most people have lost trust in the banking system and will be reluctant to convert their savings into the local currency. The majority of the population will likely rely on informal credit networks during the conflict. But without deposits, the banking system will have trouble playing a greater role in financing economic recovery. The central bank will have to regulate the banking system effectively to build confidence in the banking system once again.[598]

**9.7.25 Understand that microfinance can contribute to growth, but alone it is not a substitute for reconstituting the core banking capacity of the country.** Microfinance institutions usually form only a small part of the financial sector in relation to the commercial banking system, but they are valuable tools for creating jobs and promoting growth after violent conflict. While they are not substitutes for rebuilding the banking system, these institutions are useful socioeconomic development tools for poor populations without access to the formal banking sector. Microcredit programs are also positive ways to generate income for women and other marginalized groups and can build social capital by promoting interaction and exchange. These programs allow small groups, not individuals, to be collectively responsible for loan repayment and.[599] Microfinance projects should be undertaken within the context of a wider strategy for the broader financial sector.

---

596. USAID, "Economic Governance in War Torn Economies," 2004.
597. USAID, "Guide to Economic Growth," 2009.
598. Haughton, "Reconstruction of War-Torn Economies," 2002.
599. UNDP/USAID, "First Steps," 2007.

## 9.8 Necessary Condition: Employment Generation

### 9.8.1 What is employment generation? Why is it a necessary condition?

Creating jobs is a keystone of any economic recovery program. Many activities can fall under the rubric of job creation, including immediate short-term opportunities that yield quick impact, or the development of more enduring livelihoods in the civil service or private sector. It is important to distinguish between these different activities, recognizing that sustainability and long-term impact should be duly considered in implementing any employment generation program. Providing jobs is vital on many levels. Politically, employment opportunities give the population a stake in the peace process by providing young men and women with alternatives to violence. Economically, employment provides income to poor families, revives domestic demand for goods and services, and stimulates overall growth. Socially, employment can also promote social healing, encourage the return of displaced persons, and improve social welfare in the long run.

### 9.8.2 Guidance for Employment Generation

#### 9.8.3 Approach: Quick Impact

Developing enduring livelihoods is vital for long-term peace and economic growth, but getting concrete results can take many years. In the emergency phases of economic recovery, the most immediate imperative is getting people back to work and getting money flowing, even if it the work is only temporary. The point of emergency phase economic recovery is to get labor and capital back to work quickly to show visible benefits of peace.[600]

#### 9.8.4 Generate positive results by focusing on public works projects.[601] Public works projects are effective ways to generate a lot of employment quickly while demonstrating progress that benefits communities. Job opportunities can include small-scale food- or cash-for-work projects, such as cleaning up public places, repairing roads and facilities, or installing generators. Be sure to consult with the host nation population on these efforts and to communicate to the population that this is a partnership effort between international actors and the host nation population.

#### 9.8.5 Keep sustainability in mind, but avoid placing undue emphasis on it in the very early stages of recovery.[602] Jobs that favor quick impact cannot substitute for long-term livelihood creation and should be viewed as much as possible through a lens of long-term sustainability.[603] Any short-term job creation program should be established in parallel with sustainable employment programs. However, focusing too heavily on the sustainability of economic activities while ignoring short-term imperatives is a mistake. When implemented well, quick impact projects can be effective in employing large numbers of people in the immediate aftermath of violent conflict.

---

600. UNDPKO, *Principles and Guidelines,* 2008. United Kingdom Stabilisation Unit, "Helping Countries Recover," 2008. Hereafter: UK Stabilisation Unit, "Helping Countries Recover," 2008. USAID, "Guide to Economic Growth," 2009.

601. Mendelson Forman/Mashatt, "Employment Generation," 2007.

602. Mendelson Forman, "Achieving Socioeconomic Well-Being," 2002. Robert Perito, *The U.S. Experience with Provincial Reconstruction Teams in Afghanistan: Lessons Identified* (Washington, D.C.: U.S. Institute of Peace, 2005).

603. Mendelson Forman/Mashatt, "Employment Generation," 2007.

*See Trade-off: Section 9.9.7, Meeting urgent needs for jobs vs. focusing on sustainable employment.*

**9.8.6 Recognize the potential impact of the international presence on economic distortions.**[604] One distortion often occurs in the domestic labor, housing, and retail markets in the early recovery phases. International actors often pay high salaries for expatriates, international civil servants, domestic translators, and drivers, while increasing the demand for local housing and services attuned to foreign tastes and salaries. This creates tough competition for the host nation government to attract skilled professionals for public service.[605] The resulting disparity between the wealth of international actors and the economic hardships of the host nation population risks increasing friction, particularly between the country's urban centers and the rest of the country. To mitigate these effects, international actors should determine appropriate wage rates for local staff, making them comparable to local government pay scales. Progressive income taxes are another way to reduce the attractiveness of working for the international community versus the host nation government.[606]

**9.8.7 Approach: Agricultural Rehabilitation**
In most societies emerging from conflict, the agricultural sector provides the primary source of employment. Rehabilitating the agricultural sector and enabling landowners to grow the right crops, process them, and get them to market are key steps in economic recovery. During violent conflict, many farmers will have reduced their production of export crops, while increasing subsistence production. Governments may sometimes resort to heavy taxes on agricultural exports to finance their military spending.

**9.8.8 Provide broad assistance in rehabilitating the agricultural sector.** While most of the focus will be in rural farming, sometimes rehabilitation will include food processing and distribution, which would also involve work in urban areas. Assistance providers should understand what crops and livestock are staples for local diets and cash crops, and also when the crop cycles are in order to design employment programs that do not disrupt planting or harvests.[607] Public sector capacity is also necessary to regulate agricultural policy, including the establishment of a ministry of agriculture and development of farmers organizations. Immediate rehabilitation tasks should include the following:

- Mine clearance of farmlands
- Provision of seeds, tools and livestock
- Repair of infrastructure, including processing and transport equipment, irrigation and drainage facilities, construction of water supplies, and improvement of roads and local market facilities
- Development of trade relations to increase linkages among producers, processors, and markets
- Improvement of access to credit

604. IPA, "Economic Priorities," 2002. USAID, "Economic Governance in War Torn Economies," 2004.
605. JICA, "Handbook for Transition Assistance," 2006.
606. Dobbins/Jones/Crane/Cole DeGrasse, *Beginner's Guide*, 2007. USAID, "Guide to Economic Growth," 2009.
607. Dobbins/Jones/Crane/Cole DeGrasse, *Beginner's Guide*, 2007.

- Provision of training in livestock management and crop productivity
- Land reform.

***9.8.9 Avoid disincentivizing local farming through relief operations.*** In responding to humanitarian emergencies, governments and relief organizations flood supplies of food into the country. This drives down local food prices by decreasing demand for locally produced food. Donor assessments should identify potential effects of relief operations to ensure that food aid does not adversely impact domestic agriculture or marketing.[608]

### *9.8.10 Approach: Livelihood Development*

The development of sustainable livelihoods is critical to providing a predictable flow of income to families and build skills and capacity in the labor force. In these environments, most opportunities for long-term employment will be concentrated in the civil service, private sector, and agriculture.

***9.8.11 Recruit capable, accountable individuals for a lean and effective civil service.*** Running government operations will require individuals with the capacity to contribute managerial, technical, and administrative talent. The civil service can be a strong source for new employment if sustained over the long term by adequate revenue generation. There will be pressures to rapidly recruit people for the civil service, but be careful not to create a bloated force.[609] Place a premium on professionalism, accountability, political independence, and a public service ethos. There also may be pressure to introduce ex-combatants into the civil service as a long-term job, but doing so may jeopardize the integrity of the service if they support certain parties.[610]

***9.8.12 Focus on agriculture, construction and service sectors, which will often provide the bulk of job opportunities.***[611] After violent conflict, the labor force typically lacks workers with advanced education, training, or marketable skills, which were lost through flight of professionals, injury, or death. Because of this, the agriculture, construction, and service (hotels, transport, logistics) sectors will be enormous draws for the labor market, as they do not require highly specialized skills, and demand for these industries will likely be high. Focus on these areas in the employment generation strategy to maximize the number of jobs for the population.

***9.8.13 Pay special attention to women in micro-enterprise or vocational training.***[612] During violent conflict, many women may have become heads of large households. They will have acquired critical skills to adapt to food shortages and become micro-entrepreneurs in the informal economy. This reality is too often overlooked in livelihood development strategies. Women are left out of vocational training opportunities and face unequal access to credit, assets, and technologies, forcing them to find jobs in more traditional sectors with limited potential.[613] Supporting women economically, however, can help promote the welfare of their children. Women in this respect are major catalysts for peace.

---

608. Ibid.
609. WB, "Rebuilding the Civil Service," 2002.
610. Dobbins/Jones/Crane/Cole DeGrasse, *Beginner's Guide,* 2007.
611. USAID, "Guide to Economic Growth," 2009. IPA, "Economic Priorities," 2002. UNDP/USAID, "First Steps," 2007.
612. Mendelson Forman/Mashatt, "Employment Generation," 2007.
613. ILO, "Local Economic Development," 1997.

# 9.9 Trade-offs

*9.9.1 Economic efficiency vs. political stability.*[614] Because S&R missions are not development as usual, political considerations will typically trump economic ones. This means that the best approach may not be the most optimal or efficient from an economic perspective. It follows that the success of economic programming should be measured not purely by its economic criteria as it would be in a normal development scenario, but whether it supports peace and reconciliation.

*9.9.2 Sophistication vs. simplicity in the income tax system.* In the emergency phases, there will likely be weak capacity for administering tax policies. Rather than trying to create a sophisticated income tax system for the entire population, it may be wise to install an interim regime for simpler taxes, like excise or sales taxes, which are easier to raise.[615]

*9.9.3 Creating donor trust funds vs. strengthening the host nation budget process.* Many international actors prefer to manage their assistance funds, but doing so can create a bifurcation between host nation and donor-funded budget systems. Once accountability structures are functioning with adequate safeguards, spending should be integrated into a comprehensive state public investment program and capital budget to strengthen the government capacity and ensure host nation input in the budgetary process.[616]

*9.9.4 Macroeconomic reforms vs. political stability.*[617] While there may be an urge to quickly stabilize the economy, doing so too aggressively can have negative impacts on political stability. Cutting subsidies to public sector enterprises with bloated work forces, for example, can create a pool of unemployed and disgruntled recruits for groups seeking to disrupt the peace process. All economic stability measures must be accompanied by a careful assessment of the political situation in the country.[618] Ultimately, the solution is a matter of the degree to which macroeconomic stability is imposed.

*9.9.5 Employment opportunities for ex-combatants vs. women and minorities.* In war-torn economies, employment opportunities will be scarce. Prioritizing jobs for ex-combatants may mitigate violence, but it can also seem unjust to others who may be more qualified, particularly those who may have been systematically discriminated against before or during the conflict. This is a difficult trade-off, but the imperatives of maintaining a fragile peace may require prioritizing ex-combatants, at least in the near term.[619]

*9.9.6 Public vs. private sector in public utility services.* Having politicians manage local utilities may help build internal management and governance capacity. But doing so also risks preserving corrupt, pre-conflict arrangements that jeopardize quality service and perpetuate discriminatory practices. The private sector, on the other hand, would likely be more effective in reestablishing services and customer relationships. A careful balance

---

614. OECD, "Congo," 2003.
615. IPA, "Economic Priorities," 2002.
616. UNDP/USAID, "First Steps," 2007.
617. Scott Feil, "Building Better Foundations: Security in Post-Conflict Reconstruction," *The Washington Quarterly,* Autumn 2002.
618. IPA, "Economic Priorities," 2002.
619. Dobbins/Jones/Crane/Cole DeGrasse, *Beginner's Guide,* 2007.

must be struck between these two approaches. Some utilities may benefit from a hybrid public-private relationship, where a private concession is issued to operate a facility.[620]

*9.9.7 Meeting urgent needs for jobs vs. focusing on sustainable employment.* In the emergency phases, there is often an urgent need to put people to work. Doing so often involves jobs that may produce tangible results quickly, but do not necessarily develop sustainable incomes or livelihoods. Balancing these two imperatives has proven to be a critical challenge.

## 9.10 Gaps and Challenges

*9.10.1 Political-economic nexus.* Connections between those in power and ill-gotten wealth often develop during conflict and continue in its aftermath. This nexus can be detrimental to the legitimacy of the government and can undermine sustainable peace and development by diverting vital resources from the people. An integrated political-economic security strategy is an essential mechanism for dealing with this nexus.

*9.10.2 Monitoring diaspora remittances.* During violent conflict, diaspora remittances serve both positive and negative purposes, making them difficult to address. While they may constitute a major source of livelihood for many, remittances are also used to fuel conflict. Tracking the money is difficult because they often flow into the country through informal channels. Keeping remittances from fueling conflict is an unmet challenge.

*9.10.3 Managing the informal sector without hurting ordinary citizens.* Managing the informal economy is very difficult because its composition is often very diverse after lengthy periods of violent conflict. While it can include destabilizing criminal elements such as drug or human trafficking, the informal sector tends to comprise most of the economic activity that ordinary people resorted to as a means of survival in a war-torn economy.

*9.10.4 Microfinance and effective intermediation.* Loans are often readily available for large government reconstruction projects, while micro-entrepreneurs and small businesses find it difficult to access capital to finance smaller grassroots-level projects. Providing credit to these individuals and businesses is a challenge that can yield tremendous peace-building and social fabric-building effects in war-torn countries.

*9.10.5 Addressing economic factors in the peace agreement.* Peace negotiations typically focus on security and justice issues, while leaving out economic dimensions of conflict. Peace agreements are pivotal moments and should include provisions that establish clear benchmarks for sharing and managing resources, especially if there is a criminalized political economy where corruption or exploitation determines access to political power. When designed well, peace agreements can serve as a foundational roadmap for transforming conflict and providing a foundation for state building.

*9.10.6 Public finance management.* Transparent and accountable management of public resources is a problem that consistently plagues societies emerging from conflict. Corrupt financial management practices are a common feature in these governments and deprive the state of resources that are badly needed to fund major economic and social development projects. More attention must be paid to establishing proper means for oversight of finance management.

---

620. USAID, "Guide to Economic Growth," 2009.

# SECTION 10

# SOCIAL WELL-BEING

**Access to and Delivery of Basic Needs Services**
- Appropriate and Quality Assistance
- Minimum Standards for Water, Food, and Shelter
- Minimum Standards for Health Services

**Access to and Delivery of Education**
- System-Wide Development and Reform
- Equal Access
- Quality and Conflict-Sensitive Education

## SOCIAL WELL-BEING
Ability of the people to be free from want of basic necessities and to coexist peacefully in communities with opportunities for advancement.

**Social Reconstruction**
- Inter- and Intra-Group Reconciliation
- Community-Based Development

**Right of Return and Resettlement of Refugees and Internally Displaced Persons**
- Safe and Voluntary Return or Resettlement
- Property Dispute Resolution
- Reintegration and Rehabilitation

# Social Well-Being
*Ability of the people to be free from want of basic needs and to coexist peacefully in communities with opportunities for advancement.*

## 10.0 What is social well-being?
Social well-being is an end state in which basic human needs are met and people are able to coexist peacefully in communities with opportunities for advancement. This end state is characterized by equal access to and delivery of basic needs services (water, food, shelter, and health services), the provision of primary and secondary education, the return or resettlement of those displaced by violent conflict, and the restoration of social fabric and community life.

## 10.1 What are the key social well-being challenges in societies emerging from conflict?
Violent conflict may create humanitarian crises and inflict tremendous harm on civilian populations. These crises involve acute water, food, and shelter shortages; large-scale population displacement; and the absence of critical health services, among many other challenges. As families struggle to survive during and after violent conflict, social fabric may be torn apart within and among communities. Disputes about land, water, harvests, pasture rights, marriage, inheritance, and other inter- and intra-community issues typically arise and may threaten a fragile peace. Schools may be shut down or destroyed. Children may have missed years of education, and many may have been denied the chance to start primary school. Essential services infrastructure may be ruined, including ports, roads, and basic utilities.[621]

## 10.2 Why is social well-being a necessary end state?
Peace cannot be sustained over the long term without addressing the social well-being of a population. Without basic necessities such as food or shelter, large-scale social instability will persist because people will be unable to resume the functions of normal life—sustaining a livelihood, traveling safely, engaging in community activities, or attending school. Without helping people return to their homes or new communities of their choice or providing a means for peacefully resolving disputes, people may not move beyond violent conflict or rebuild their lives.

## 10.3 What are the necessary conditions to achieve social well-being?

- *Access To and Delivery of Basic Needs Services* is a condition in which the population has equal access to and can obtain adequate water, food, shelter, and health services to ensure survival and life with dignity. These services should be delivered in a manner that fosters reliability and sustainability.

- *Access To and Delivery of Education* is a condition in which the population has equal and continuous access to quality formal and nonformal education that provides the opportunity for advancement and promotes a peaceful society. This condition involves system-wide

---

621. UNDP/USAID, *First Steps*, 2007.

development and reform, and equal access to relevant, quality, and conflict-sensitive education.

- *Return and Resettlement of Refugees and Internally Displaced Persons* is a condition in which all individuals displaced from their homes by violent conflict have the option of a safe, voluntary, and dignified journey to their homes or to new resettlement communities; have recourse for property restitution or compensation; and receive reintegration and rehabilitation support to build their livelihoods and contribute to long-term development.

- *Social Reconstruction* is a condition in which the population is able to coexist peacefully through intra- and intergroup forms of reconciliation—including mechanisms that help to resolve disputes non-violently and address the legacy of past abuses—and through development of community institutions that bind society across divisions.

## 10.4 General Guidance for Social Well-Being

*10.4.1 Build host nation ownership and capacity.* Immediately after violent conflict, international assistance may be necessary to meet the basic needs of the population, address return and resettlement for refugees and IDPs, and promote community-based development and reconciliation, as the host nation may be unable to meet those challenges alone. Participation of the host nation population—particularly at the community level—in the assessment and design of basic services helps ensure that the services are responsive to actual needs and gives people a greater stake in the success of those services. All assistance activities should maximize the potential to build the capacity of the host nation population to sustain basic services. For example, one of the key components of humanitarian assistance can and should be to complement the work of nascent and often struggling ministries or bureaucracies. International actors should work within host nation government structures to help generate legitimacy for the host nation government.

*10.4.2 Act only with an understanding of the local context.* The key to improving the social well-being of the conflict-affected population is to understand the context of the conflict and the living conditions of the people. A thorough assessment might include the following questions:

- What role did the provision of basic needs play in the conflict?
- How has the host nation population met their basic needs in the past?
- What capacity do host nation institutions and actors have to deliver basic services?
- What is the relationship between the education system and the conflict?
- What is the scope of the displacement crisis?
- What host nation mechanisms already exist to promote dispute resolution and reconciliation?
- Where does popular support for dispute resolution and reconciliation programming lie?

*10.4.3 Prioritize to stabilize.* Social well-being is difficult to achieve even in the best of circumstances. In this environment, prioritize what is necessary for survival and for the resolution of disputes that could reignite violent conflict. Top priorities include preventing further loss of life and displacement, delivering aid and services to vulnerable populations, mitigating public health epidemics, and collecting evidence and witness statements to address the legacy of past abuses.[622] Focus on meeting the immediate needs of those most affected (typically women, children, the elderly, the disabled, IDPs, refugees, minorities, and those living with disease), while keeping in mind the impact of these actions on sustainability.[623] Once these priorities are addressed, focus on return and resettlement, education reform, and key aspects of social reconstruction.

*10.4.4 Use a conflict lens.* The provision of aid can never be entirely neutral. It inevitably involves a transfer of resources in countries where they are extremely scarce and where unequal distribution may have contributed to the conflict. With this in mind, recognize that every decision—where to locate an emergency medical facility, whether to empower a particular institution, how to deliver education in an IDP camp, or how to select an interim health minister—has implications for the conflict and a lasting political settlement.

*10.4.5 Recognize interdependence.* Addressing the social well-being of a population is critical for the success of broader recovery efforts. A broken social fabric will undermine progress made in the economic, governance, and rule of law arenas. Sustainability in these areas will be lost if the population has nothing to eat; if children cannot go to school; or if communities remain divided along ethnic, religious, or political lines. Progress in the economic, governance, or rule of law spheres provides the necessary infrastructure for the success of social well-being programs.

## 10.5 Necessary Condition: Access To and Delivery Of Basic Needs Services

### 10.5.1 What is access to and delivery of basic needs services? Why is it a necessary condition?

The Universal Declaration of Human Rights states that everyone has the right to adequate food, housing and medical care.[624] Access to and delivery of basic needs services is therefore a condition in which the population can obtain water, food, shelter and health services in adequate quantity and quality to ensure survival and satisfy their right to "life with dignity."[625] Normal systems for accessing these necessities will likely have been destroyed or incapacitated due to the conflict or may have failed to meet needs to begin with. Building or rebuilding physical infrastructure is necessary for the provision of services over the long term. Restoring access to these services is necessary to ensure the survival of conflict-affected populations, sustain livelihoods over the long-term, and to boost the legitimacy of the state.

### 10.5.2 Guidance for Access To and Delivery Of Basic Needs Services

*10.5.3 Approach: Appropriate and Quality Assistance*
Appropriate and quality assistance refers to how services are delivered. Appropriate means assistance that reflects conditions on the ground and is tailored to the cultural, social,

---

622. Dobbins, Jones, Crane, Cole DeGrasse, *The Beginner's Guide*, 2007). United Kingdom Stabilisation Unit, "Helping Countries Recover," 2008.

623. Sphere Project, *Humanitarian Charter and Minimum Standards in Disaster Response*, 2004. Hereafter: Sphere, *Humanitarian Charter*, 2004.

624. United Nations General Assembly, *Universal Declaration of Human Rights*, 1948.

625. Sphere, *Humanitarian Charter*, 2004.

and survival needs of the population. Quality assistance refers to providing equal access, coordinating assistance across the multiplicity of providers, and nesting the immediate methods of delivery in a locally driven plan for development and sustainability. It involves a required sensitivity to impartiality for service delivery and the recognition that inappropriate service delivery may actually do harm.

***10.5.4 Provide assistance based on the needs of conflict-affected populations to ensure equal access for all.*** Maximizing equal access requires the ability to recognize the vulnerabilities, needs, and capacities of conflict-affected groups. Age, gender, disability, and economic and HIV/AIDS status can create severe disadvantages for certain groups of people, who can be further marginalized as a result.[626] Provision should be enhanced for the most vulnerable to ensure that they are afforded the same access as the rest of the population. Providers should be trained to identify vulnerabilities.

***10.5.5 Tailor assistance to local culture.*** When delivering services, take care to avoid dishonoring local beliefs or traditions related to water, food, shelter, and health. Careful consideration of the local culture can help avoid sowing distrust in the population or exacerbating social cleavages.[627] Host nation actors know what systems the community will accept and how service programs can respect indigenous models and methods.[628] Incorporate women into planning and implementation processes and understand how the choice of host nation partners could impact stability in communities.

***10.5.6 Discourage the population from using coping strategies that arise from the inability to access basic services.*** Destructive coping strategies or "crisis strategies" include sale of land, distress migration of whole families, and deforestation. Some coping strategies employed by women and girls, such as prostitution or travel to unsafe areas, expose them to a higher risk of infection or sexual violence.[629] Understand which groups are employing coping strategies, why they are doing so, and use mitigation programs based on the context.

***10.5.7 Do no harm.*** In conflict-affected countries, assistance activities can never be completely neutral. Resources inevitably represent the distribution of power and wealth. Managing these resources can and will create tensions if careful attention is not given to how they are distributed and delivered. "Do no harm" is a principle that recognizes the potentially negative impacts of aid and seeks to prevent aid activity from harming the populations it is trying to help.[630] For more on nondiscrimination in providing service, see Section 8.6.11.

*See Trade-off: Section 8.9.3, Rapid service delivery and resource procurement vs. empowerment of spoilers or criminal elements.*

***10.5.8 Prioritize immediate relief, but do not neglect the impact on long-term development.*** One devastating impact of violent conflict may be an acute humanitarian crisis. While

626. Ibid.

627. Center for Stabilization and Reconstruction Studies, Assistant Secretary of Defense for Health Affairs, and International Medical Corps, *Healing the Wounds: Rebuilding Healthcare Systems in Post-Conflict Environments,* 2007. Hereafter: CSRS/ASDHA/IMC, *Healing the Wounds,* 2007.

628. CSRS/ASDHA/IMC, *Healing the Wounds,* 2007.

629. Sphere, *Humanitarian Charter,* 2004.

630. For further discussion, see Mary B. Anderson, *Do No Harm: How Aid Can Support Peace—or War* (Boulder, Colo.: Lynne Rienner Publishers, Inc., 1999). Hereafter: Anderson, *Do No Harm,* 1999.

this may require direct aid, always seek to maximize opportunities for building host nation capacity for the long-term and to minimize dependency. Understand the distortion of the host nation economy that can result from prolonged delivery of relief goods and services.[631] Risks to the host nation economy can be severe, including the creation of a "second civil service," the inevitable drawdown of international assistance, and the inability to sustain services.[632] Pay adequate attention to restoring or building basic service infrastructures that will allow host nation actors to provide necessities themselves after international actors leave.[633]

**10.5.9 Coordinate humanitarian assistance and development strategies to maximize coherence and sustainability.** Facilitating a smooth transition from relief activities to sustainable development is a major challenge in current practice. This transition refers to the shift from primarily life-saving measures to restoring livelihoods that contribute to long-term growth.[634] Activities in both areas of relief and development are often funded and managed as distinct programs. This may create gaps—both financial and institutional—in provision of basic needs when relief activities end and the development activities largely take over.[635] Coordinate assistance strategies closely with development strategies to ensure that relief activities are nested in and coherent with the longer-term objective of sustainability.[636]

*See Gap/Challenge: Section 10.10.3, Transition from relief to development activities.*

**10.5.10 Approach: Minimum Standards for Water, Food, and Shelter**
Meeting the minimum standards for water and food broadly involves ensuring the population has equal access to water and food, in adequate quantity and quality to survive, to contain the spread of waterborne diseases and to prevent malnutrition. The minimum standard for shelter involves ensuring access to housing to protect against environmental elements and ensure life with dignity.

**10.5.11 In the emergency phases of recovery, strive to meet the immediate survival needs of the population for water, food, and shelter.**

- *Clean water and proper sanitation.* At the minimum, the population should have safe and equal access to an adequate amount of clean water to prevent death from dehydration and to enable consumption, cooking, and good hygienic practices. The population should also have access to adequate sanitation systems to reduce the transmission of faeco-oral diseases and provide a means for excreta disposal, vector control, solid waste management, and drainage.[637]

- *Food security.* At the minimum, the population should have access to food in adequate quantity and quality, in a way that ensures their survival and upholds

---

631. United States Agency for International Development, *Fragile States Strategy,* 2005.

632. UNDP/USAID, "First Steps," 2007.

633. Ibid. CSRS/ASDHA/IMC, "Healing the Wounds," 2007.

634. United Nations Secretary-General, *Transition from Relief to Development: Key Issues Related to Humanitarian and Recovery/Transition Programmes,* 2006.

635. United Nations High Commissioner for Refugees, *Mind the Gap! UNHCR, Humanitarian Assistance and the Development Process,* 2001.

636. UNDP/USAID, "First Steps," 2007.

637. Sphere, "Humanitarian Charter," 2004.

their dignity.[638] Food security includes access to food, affordability of food, adequate quantity and availability of food, along with safety and cultural acceptability.

• *Shelter.* At the minimum, shelter should provide for personal safety against environmental elements and disease, provide a space for living and storage of personal belongings, and protect privacy to promote human dignity and emotional security.[639] The right to housing includes adequate space and protection from environmental elements and disease vectors. Strive for housing that is inhabitable, accessible, affordable, and culturally appropriate, and that enables access to goods and services such as safe drinking water, energy for household activities, sanitation and washing facilities, refuse disposal, drainage, and emergency health care services.[640]

***10.5.12 Provide quantity and quality of water to ensure survival, improve hygiene, and reduce health risks.*** People can survive longer without food than water.[641] Protecting clean water supplies from contamination is therefore a major priority. Water-related transmission of diseases results from both contaminated water supplies and insufficient quantities of water for personal and domestic hygiene. If it is impossible to meet both standards, focus first on providing access to sufficient quantities of water, even if the quality may be substandard.[642] HIV/AIDS-affected individuals will have a special requirement for water and personal hygiene. Water will also be in high demand for livestock and crops. Maximize storage capacity with containers, reservoirs, and tanks; storing untreated water undisturbed can considerably improve water quality.[643] Determining the number and location of water sources will depend on an assessment of the situation on the ground, including the climate, individual physiology, social and cultural norms, and types of food generally consumed.

***10.5.13 Impart important information to the public about the benefits of water and sanitation services and facilities.***[644] Providing clean water and sanitation facilities is not enough. Treated water sources have limited effects if the population does not understand its health benefits and the importance of using it. They may opt for water from rivers, lakes, wells, or other sources because of convenience, proximity, and taste. Focus on promotional messages that stress the importance of using protected water sources. Good personal and environmental hygiene is derived from knowledge and education about public health. Also consider creating water or sanitation committees to manage communal facilities such as water points, public toilets, or washing areas.

***10.5.14 Tailor water and food distribution and assistance according to local factors.***[645] The availability of supplies such as fuel, soap, clean water and cooking utensils will deter-

---

638. United Nations World Food Summit, *Rome Declaration on World Food Security and World Food Summit Plan of Action,* 1996.

639. United Nations High Commissioner for Refugees, *Handbook for Emergencies,* 2000. Hereafter: UNHCR, Handbook for Emergencies, 2000. Sphere, "Humanitarian Charter," 2004.

640. Sphere, "Humanitarian Charter," 2004.

641. United States Agency for International Development, *Field Operations Guide for Disaster Assessment and Response—Version 3.0,* 1998. Hereafter: USAID, *FOG,* 1998.

642. Sphere, "Humanitarian Charter," 2004. USAID, "FOG," 1998.

643. USAID, "FOG," 1998.

644. Sphere, "Humanitarian Charter," 2004.

645. Ibid. USAID, "FOG," 1998.

mine whether foods provided need to be ready to eat or if they can require some preparation. Also be sure to understand what foods may be culturally inappropriate. Assess the nutrition situation and tailor food programs based on nutritional conditions of the population.[646] Deciding the location of water sources will depend on population density and security requirements for women and others traveling to communal water sources.

***10.5.15 Use food assistance strategies that facilitate sustainability.*** Consider strategies to complement or replace direct food aid, such as bolstering the primary production capacities of the population, generating income and employment to improve purchasing power and livelihoods, and ensuring people's access to markets to acquire necessary food and other basic needs.[647] Other constructive options include subsidized food or food-for-work programs. These options are more desirable because they uphold dignity while promoting livelihood development and independence.

***10.5.16 Aim for equity in food and water distribution.***[648] Consult with local leaders on how to equitably distribute food and water resources and inform the population about the basis for determining food rations and water source location.[649] The population should perceive the provision of food and water to be fair and based on need, rather than on gender, disability, religion, or ethnic background. Local distribution agents for food and water should be selected based on their commitment to impartiality, capacity, and accountability. These agents can include local elders, elected relief committees, local institutions, host nation or international NGOs, or the government. Choose distribution points based on safe accessibility by the population rather than the convenience of the logistics agency. Registering individuals and households receiving food assistance will also boost effectiveness, especially when assistance will be needed over an extended period of time. Also be sure to evaluate the process to ensure that the food is reaching its intended recipients.

***10.5.17 Resort to providing free food aid only when the need is severe and there is no other alternative.*** Free distribution of food aid should be used only when absolutely necessary and should be stopped at the earliest possible moment to prevent dependency.[650] Direct food aid may be necessary to sustain life in some situations or to mitigate dangerous coping strategies of the population. This is the case if normal systems for food production, processing, and distribution have been disrupted, co-opted or destroyed by warring parties to the conflict. Any mass feeding or provision of cooked food that is ready to eat should only be provided on a short-term basis to those in greatest need who are unable to prepare food for themselves or if the distribution of dry food rations could endanger recipients. Avoid free distribution when food supplies are available in an area but people lack access to it, or if the absence of food in an area could be resolved by improving market systems.

***10.5.18 Develop tailored sanitation programs to best benefit the population.*** Sanitation programs involve many different areas: excreta disposal, control of disease

---

646. Sphere, "Humanitarian Charter," 2004. USAID, "FOG," 1998.
647. Sphere, "Humanitarian Charter," 2004.
648. United Nations World Food Programme, *Emergency Food Security Assessment Handbook*, 2005. USAID, *FOG*, 1998.
649. Sphere, "Humanitarian Charter," 2004.
650. Ibid.

vectors, solid waste management, and drainage systems.[651] In designing sanitation facilities, pay close attention to preferences and cultural habits. It may be difficult to accommodate the needs of every group—women, men, children, disabled—when building communal facilities intended to serve large numbers of people. In general, facilities should be located in safe places and have adequate lighting to better protect women and girls from attacks in communal sites. Vector control programs can mitigate the spread of disease, but simple steps such as hand-washing and other good hygienic practices can also go a long way. Reduce public health and environmental risks by setting up a means for managing solid waste and drainage to address standing water or water erosion from storms, floods, and medical waste.

**10.5.19 Provide shelter assistance to meet survival needs.** Everyone has a right to adequate housing that sustains life and dignity.[652] During and after violent conflict, many displaced people will require shelter assistance after being driven from their homes or while deciding whether or when to return to their homes.[653] Shelter assistance should strive to protect as many people as possible from environmental elements such as the cold, wind, rain, or heat. Locations of shelters should consider the presence of unexploded ordnance, availability of food and clean drinking water, proximity to toilets and other sanitation facilities, and accessibility of the site by relief agencies. Providing temporary transit housing for displaced persons can mitigate the problem of ad-hoc housing occupation.[654] Primary transitional shelter options for displaced populations include residing with host families, self-settling in rural or urban areas, or residing in mass shelters or camps.[655]

**10.5.20 When choosing a site for mass shelter, pay close attention to land rights.**[656] While the host nation often offers land for mass shelters, local communities frequently assert traditional or customary rights to the land.[657] Tensions and resentment may surface in local communities if the land depreciates as a result of a settlement, the settlement population refuses to leave, or if the camp population enjoys greater benefits and support than the local community. When choosing a site, clarify land ownership whenever possible. Any use of land should be grounded in formal legal arrangements in accordance with domestic law.[658] Occupants of the site should have full access and land use rights to graze animals and engage in agricultural activities.

**10.5.21 Tailor shelter designs and planning to local requirements.** In designing emergency shelters for survival, consider cultural norms for sleeping accommodations and subdivisions of living space to ensure safety and privacy for women, girls, and boys, who are most vulnerable to attack. When assisting with housing, other factors to consider include affordability; habitability; location; cultural appropriateness; access

---

651. Ibid.
652. Ibid.
653. Oxfam, *Transitional Settlement—Displaced Populations*, 2005.
654. Daniel Fitzpatrick, *Land Policy in Post-conflict Circumstances: Some Lessons from East Timor* (Geneva: United Nations High Commissioner for Refugees, 2002). Hereafter: Fitzpatrick, *Land Policy*, 2002.
655. Oxfam, *Transitional Settlement—Displaced Populations*, 2005.
656. Ibid. UNHCR, "Handbook for Emergencies," 2000.
657. USAID, *FOG*, 1998.
658. Ibid.

to natural resources; and the availability of services, facilities, materials, and infrastructure.[659] Build insulation or ventilation into the design as needed, depending on the climate.

**10.5.22 Use shelter construction processes as an opportunity to build host nation capacity and promote livelihood development.**[660] Host nation actors should partake in procuring building materials or contributing manual labor to build capacity and promote livelihood development. Develop skills training programs and apprenticeship schemes to maximize capacity building for host nation actors in housing construction processes. Those who are less physically able can assist in tracking inventory and other administrative responsibilities.

**10.5.23 In addition to housing, be prepared to provide nonfood items that may be necessary to maximize self-sufficiency and self-management.**[661] Most displaced people will have few possessions and may need everyday items such as changes of durable clothing; bedding materials that are culturally appropriate; bath and laundry soaps; and cooking facilities and utensils, including stoves, ovens, fuel, pots, pans, and silverware. Materials from damaged homes or buildings can also be used to enhance living spaces in improvised shelters.

### 10.5.24 Approach: Minimum Standards for Health Services

Minimum standards for health services involve the provision of care to prevent untimely death and illness. Careful thought should also be given to laying the foundations for a health care system built on sustainable infrastructure, services, and public health education.[662] After violent conflict, it is not uncommon to find that health care systems, if they even existed before the conflict, have collapsed, health information has disappeared, and communication systems have broken down. Other major health challenges include a lack of health-related information about the population, low absorption capacity, and persistent political and financial uncertainties.

*See Gap/Challenge: Section 10.10.8, Mental health needs of conflict-affected populations.*

**10.5.25 Treat those with the most immediate health risks while restoring basic health services for the broader population.**[663] Provide medical attention to those in greatest need. The immediate priorities of health care in this environment should be to prevent and reduce levels of death and illness.[664] The greatest vulnerabilities often involve women, children, the elderly or disabled, and people living with HIV/AIDS. Epidemics may be rampant, while other ailments common among war-torn populations may include mosquito-borne and gastrointestinal diseases.[665] In these environments, the most staggering health indicators are maternal mortality and under-five mortality from waterborne diseases, lack of immunization, malaria, and other infectious diseases. Standing up health clinics at the community level is critical to treat people with immediate

659. Sphere, "Humanitarian Charter," 2004.
660. Ibid.
661. Ibid.
662. UNDP/USAID, "First Steps," 2007.
663. Inter-Agency Standing Committee, *Guidelines for HIV/AIDS Interventions in Emergency Settings,* 2003. Hereafter: IASC, *Guidelines for HIV/AIDS,* 2003.
664. Sphere, "Humanitarian Charter," 2004.
665. UNDP/USAID, "First Steps," 2007. World Food Programme and World Bank (High-Level Forum on the Health Millennium Development Goals), "Health Service Delivery in Post-Conflict States," 2005. Hereafter: WFP/WB, "Health Service Delivery," 2005.

health needs and provide necessary attention to HIV/AIDS and other communicable diseases with the potential to adversely affect stability. Pay special attention to the possibility of public health epidemics and focus on strategies that deliver the most health benefits to the most people.[666]

***10.5.26 Support a sustainable health care system for the population.***[667] While service delivery is critical, address the development of health care infrastructure, education, and training that are the foundation for sustainable health care. This may begin with support for the ministry of health in developing a national health policy and plan. Developing an effective and efficient health care system will be an enormous undertaking, as it is a complex interaction of parts that may have been absent or severely dilapidated before and following the conflict.[668] In laying the foundation for this system, strive to provide equal access to the population by overcoming geographical or financial barriers. Building a health sector from scratch is very difficult, so refrain from throwing out what is there. Assess health care structures and build on them.

***10.5.27 Work closely with host nation health authorities and affected populations to ensure that critical needs are met.*** Consult closely with host nation health authorities to identify areas with the most need, where the population is not already being serviced by a local facility. Because women and children will be the primary users of health care, women should participate in the planning and design of health care services to maximize the effectiveness of those programs.[669] Consider infrastructure obstacles that may restrict certain populations from accessing these services. Mobile clinics may be necessary to fill gaps in service, but be careful not to duplicate existing efforts. The best entry points for emergency health care provision will be at the community level in the form of clinics and health posts. Many people will seek medical attention in these environments—community-level facilities can help to accommodate this influx, separating critical cases from those involving simple ailments.

***10.5.28 Mainstream multi-sectoral HIV/AIDS interventions into recovery programming.*** Recovery programs do not adequately account for HIV/AIDS challenges. Given its broad impacts across society, HIV/AIDS is an issue that should be "mainstreamed" or seriously accounted for in broader recovery programs.[670] Ensure that peacekeepers, humanitarian staff, and other military forces present in these environments are included in prevention strategies.[671] HIV/AIDS should be factored into food security programs, and shelter and site planning projects. Those handling HIV/AIDS programs should understand cultural stigmas and discrimination that hamper the effective provision of treatments. Use approaches that reduce the root causes of stigmas through awareness programs, mass media campaigns, public dialogue and interaction between HIV-affected people and target audiences, and participatory education to address common fears and misconceptions.[672]

---

666. Sphere, "Humanitarian Charter," 2004.
667. WFP/WB, "Health Service Delivery," 2005.
668. Ibid.
669. Sphere, "Humanitarian Charter," 2004.
670. IASC, "Guidelines for HIV/AIDS," 2003.
671. Ibid.
672. Joint United Nations Programme on HIV/AIDS (UNAIDS), *Reducing HIV Stigma and Discrimination: A Critical Part of National AIDS Programmes*, 2007. Hereafter: UNAIDS, *Reducing HIV Stigma and*

**10.5.29 Respond appropriately and adequately to victims of sexual and gender-based violence.** The lawlessness of war-torn countries often makes women particularly vulnerable to sexual violence and exploitation and more likely to assume high-risk sexual behavior in exchange for goods or services as a means for survival.[673] Common forms of assault against women include rape, sexual harassment, genital mutilation, domestic violence, forced marriages, and sexual exploitation.[674] Men can also suffer sexual and gender-based violence through rape or genital mutilation. Health care providers should be trained to respond appropriately and provide psychological services for these victims, taking into account cultural stigmas and discrimination that may be relevant. Be prepared to provide free voluntary and confidential counseling services, testing for HIV/AIDS and other communicable diseases, and necessary medical supplies to treat infections that occur. Health care providers should also be sensitized to medical confidentiality and should be trained on international standards for handling victims of sexual violence. Sometimes health care providers will have to fill out police forms or testify in court in cases involving sexual violence, which is difficult to balance against principles of confidentiality and respect for the victim.

**10.5.30 Restore information systems to promote public health.**[675] Information systems will likely be broken down after violent conflict, making it difficult to communicate important public health messages to the population and collect critical data that informs the delivery of health care services. Without a means for communication, it will also be difficult to identify or access victims of sexual and gender-based violence to determine the prevalence of HIV/AIDS and to provide necessary treatments. Restore public information systems as quickly as possible and develop education and prevention strategies.[676] Collecting accurate information on the prevalence and spread of diseases is also a serious gap that should be improved to enhance responses to those in most need.[677]

## 10.6 Necessary Condition: Access To and Delivery Of Education

**10.6.1 What is access to and delivery of education? Why is it a necessary condition?** Education is a basic right, recognized by many international conventions including the Universal Declaration of Human Rights (1948), the UN Convention on the Rights of the Child (1989) and the Geneva Convention (IV) Relative to the Protection of Civilian Persons in Time of War.[678] Access to and delivery of education is a condition in which every child receives primary education, even in times of war and without regard to ethnicity, gender, or location. This condition also includes access to higher education for advanced learning, development of professional skills, and nonformal education for youth

---

*Discrimination*, 2007.

673. Timothy Docking, *AIDS and Violent Conflict in Africa* (Washington, D.C.: U.S. Institute of Peace, 2001). Hereafter: Docking, "AIDS and Violent Conflict," 2001.

674. IASC, "Guidelines for HIV/AIDS," 2003.

675. USAID, "FOG," 1998.

676. UNAIDS, "Reducing HIV Stigma and Discrimination," 2007.

677. Docking, "AIDS and Violent Conflict," 2001. Sphere, "Humanitarian Charter," 2004.

678. Inter-Agency Network for Education in Emergencies (INEE), *Minimum Standards for Education in Emergencies, Chronic Crises and Early Reconstruction*, 2004. Hereafter: INEE, "Minimum Standards for Education," 2004.

and adults who may have never received or completed formal education.[679] The continued delivery of education during and following violent conflict is particularly critical. There is a movement to include education as a "fourth pillar" of humanitarian response, along with food, health, and shelter.[680] Education can help prevent the renewal of conflict by offering children and their families a source of stability and normalcy that can help them cope with conflict and its aftermath. It can provide children with a safe space and be the means for identifying affected children who need specific services. It can also inspire cultural and moral changes that transform sources of conflict and encourage peaceful coexistence, play a crucial role in promoting human and social capital, foster a sense of national identity, and fuel sustainable development and peace.[681]

**10.6.2 Guidance for Access To and Delivery Of Education**

*10.6.3 Approach: System-Wide Development and Reform*
System-wide development and reform of education involves meeting emergency needs for primary education while laying the foundations for a comprehensive and sustainable education system. Education development begins with bringing local and state authorities and civil society actors together to encourage dialogue; to empower and bestow legitimacy on local and national institutions; and to determine common goals in which education promotes peace, stability, and prosperity.[682] Common effects of violent conflict on the education system include lower enrollment rates, destroyed facilities, shortages of teachers, lack of funding, sub-par standards and quality of education services, loss of state legitimacy and presence, and corruption.[683] While needs assessments and emergency response come first,[684] there may be no sharp distinction between the humanitarian phase and the reconstruction phase since they are undertaken at the same time.[685]

*10.6.4 Use a "community-based participatory approach."*[686] To develop a quality and long-lasting education system, it is crucial that the community participates in every stage of the reforms, from assessment and planning to implementation, monitoring, and evaluation.[687] Community participation in educational reforms can help build social cohesion and host nation ownership and ensure the education system's long-term sustainability. Educational reform programs should use community members as teachers, establish community school boards, and train youth leaders. Often community members have already developed ways to continue education during conflict,

679. Yolande Miller-Grandvaux, "DRAFT Context Paper: What is the role of education as it relates to reducing fragility?" (Washington, D.C.: U.S. Agency for International Development, 2009). Hereafter: Miller-Grandvaux, "DRAFT Context Paper," 2009.

680. Miller-Grandvaux, "DRAFT Context Paper," 2009.

681. United Kingdom Department for International Development, *Education, Conflict, and International Development*, 2003. Hereafter: UK DfID, *Education, Conflict and International Development*, 2003.

682. United Nations Educational, Scientific, and Cultural Organization, *Education in Situations of Emergency, Crisis and Reconstruction: UNESCO Strategy Working Paper*, 2003. Hereafter: UNESCO, *Education in Situations of Emergency*, 2003.

683. USAID, "DRAFT Context Paper," 2009.

684. Margaret Sinclair, *Planning Education in and After Emergencies* (Paris: United Nations Educational, Scientific, and Cultural Organization, 2002). Hereafter: Sinclair, *Planning Education in and After Emergencies*, 2002.

685. World Bank, *Reshaping the Future: Education and Post-Conflict Reconstruction*, 2005. Hereafter: WB, *Reshaping the Future*, 2005.

686. Sinclair, *Planning Education in and After Emergencies*, 2002.

687. INEE, "Minimum Standards for Education," 2004.

including designing their own educational activities. This can be a basis for reform. Be aware, though, of the danger of local power politics hijacking the process and using it to increase the power of one group over the other.[688]

**10.6.5 Assess the context-specific relationship between education and conflict.** Education reform and development should be based on a complete overview and conflict analysis of the education system.[689] Conflict analysis should be present in every aspect of planning, from emergency education to education system reform. It should provide a thorough understanding of the relationship, both positive and negative, between the education system and the conflict, focusing particularly on the role played by government involvement, curriculum, language, religion, and teachers and teaching methods. It should also evaluate the impact of the conflict on the education system, which is often devastating.[690] Finally, conflict analysis should identify conflict reduction measures that can be included in a long-term, sustainable plan for education reform.[691]

**10.6.6 Develop both a short-term plan for emergency action and a long-term plan for education reconstruction and development.**[692] While emergency education programs will likely be necessary, these programs should be embedded in a long-term strategy of systematic development and reform. The period following violent conflict offers a society the opportunity to reform its entire education system. Since this system can drive—and already may have driven—conflict, it is crucial to rebuild both the physical and human educational infrastructure in ways that promote peace.[693] Prioritize the reconstruction of basic education,[694] but also pay attention to the development of higher education, including secondary and tertiary education, and nonformal education, such as accelerated education (which condenses essential primary school classes into fewer years than the formal primary school system, thus allowing accelerated reentry), life skills training, and workforce development.[695] See Section 9.7.17 for a discussion on human capital development. If programs are externally driven, plan for a transition to host nation authorities when capacities are sufficient; this is a critical step in developing government accountability and public perception of legitimacy.[696]

**10.6.7 Insulate the education system from politics.** Education systems can be manipulated to spread hatred and serve political agendas. For example, curriculum can be used to distort history and promote division. Education systems are particularly susceptible to political influence through intrusion into decision-making. The decentralization of education without appropriate safeguards—often used as a means to increase ownership, citizen participation, and accountability—can also increase the danger of political

688. UK DfID, "Education, Conflict and International Development," 2003.
689. Ibid.
690. Miller-Grandvaux, "DRAFT Context Paper," 2009.
691. UK DfID, "Education, Conflict and International Development," 2003.
692. Sinclair, "Planning Education in and After Emergencies," 2002.
693. Robert C. Orr, *Winning the Peace: An American Strategy for Post-Conflict Reconstruction* (Washington, D.C.: Center for Strategic & International Studies, 2004). UK DfID, "Education, Conflict and International Development," 2003.
694. WB, "Reshaping the Future," 2005.
695. Miller-Grandvaux, "DRAFT Context Paper," 2009. Sinclair, "Planning Education In and After Emergencies," 2002.
696. Organisation for Economic Co-operation and Development, *Education in Fragile States*, 2006.

influence by devolving powers of enforcement to the local level.[697] Education reformers should recognize these dangers and protect the education system through system-wide development and reform.[698]

***10.6.8 Reduce systemic corruption in the education system.***[699] Systemic corruption in the delivery and management of education is closely tied to weak or nonfunctioning governments. Corruption may include collection of unapproved fees or bribes, administration fraud, and favoritism during teacher recruitment or certification.[700] Corruption can be reduced and prevented through proper governance, mechanisms for transparency and accountability, and host nation capacity building and training.[701]

***10.6.9 Approach: Equal Access***

Equal access to education means that all children receive relevant, quality education and that the population as a whole has means of accessing higher or nonformal education. Following violent conflict, the affected population places a high priority on returning to school.[702] Access to education can provide children with protection and the community with a feeling of return to normalcy and stability. For more on access to and delivery essential services, including education, see Section 8.5.11.

***10.6.10 Ensure equal access as a mitigator of conflict.*** Access to education can be used as a tool for dominance and oppression. Vulnerable groups may be refused access to education during and after conflict. Security concerns may keep students—girls in particular—from attending school. Inequality of access based on identity issues—such as race, ethnicity, gender, and religion—can be a factor in social unrest.[703] Likewise, equal access for all identity groups to education at all levels can be a stabilizing force. Transparency in education management and accurate monitoring can help assure the population that everyone will have access to and receive the same education.[704]

***10.6.11 Provide interim emergency education for children.*** In the emergency phase, access to the formal education system may be very limited, particularly for vulnerable groups. These groups must be identified and special care taken to provide them with relevant, quality education.[705] It may be necessary to provide interim emergency education to ensure the continuation of schooling. This requires educational programming, materials, a safe gathering space, and teachers.[706] Education providers may have to find creative ways to ensure the continuation of education for IDPs and refugees.[707] Other alternative emergency education programs may include accelerated learning

---

697. UK DfID, "Education, Conflict and International Development," 2003.
698. Ibid.
699. Miller-Grandvaux, "DRAFT Context Paper," 2009.
700. Ibid.
701. UK DfID, "Education, Conflict and International Development," 2003.
702. Sinclair, "Planning Education In and After Emergencies," 2002.
703. Miller-Grandvaux, "DRAFT Context Paper," 2009.
704. UK DfID, "Education, Conflict and International Development," 2003.
705. INEE, "Minimum Standards for Education," 2004.
706. Save the Children UK defines emergency education as "a set of linked project activities that enable structured learning to continue in times of acute crisis or long-term instability." (UK DfID, "Education, Conflict and International Development," 2003.)
707. UK DfID, "Education, Conflict and International Development," 2003.

and distance education programs, skills training, and other nonformal education."[708] As capacity develops, however, education development will increasingly involve more activities.[709]

*See Gap/Challenge: Section 10.10.4, Emergency education.*

**10.6.12 Incorporate higher and nonformal education.** There are often large numbers of demobilized young soldiers and war-affected youths and adults who never received basic education. These populations can be a major destabilizing force. Access to and delivery of nonformal education such as skills training or accelerated learning programs can help reintegrate them into society. Secondary and tertiary education can help provide qualified teachers for the education system and legal, economic, and other professionals, who are typically in short supply, and offer the population greater opportunities for advancement.[710]

**10.6.13 Pay attention to refugees and IDPs.** The Convention on the Rights of the Child states that a government may not deny access to education to any child on its territory. This means that governments must provide access to education to children in the refugee and IDP population. Take care that education policies do not prevent these children from enrolling by requiring permanent addresses, identity cards, or other documents which they may not have. In addition to formal education, refugees and IDPs may need access to nonformal education such as accelerated learning to help them reach their appropriate class level. Keep in mind that IDPs may face different challenges to accessing education than refugees, including continued fighting or remaining internal intergroup tensions.[711]

**10.6.14 View education as a tool for child protection and welfare.** Many in the affected population will experience trauma after violent conflict. Returning to school can be both a sign of stability to the community and a means of identifying the children and young people who need psychosocial services.[712] Combining nutrition and health assistance in schools can enhance the welfare of children.[713] Schools also provide a protected space for children, enabling their parents or caretakers to focus on work.

**10.6.15 Construct appropriate educational facilities.**[714] In building school structures, consider their long-term use, available resources, community participation, and whether the local community can afford them. Schools should be physically accessible to all, provide separate sanitation facilities for males and females, and ensure that water is readily available.

**10.6.16 Develop appropriate resource standards and monitor resource use.**[715] Set clear standards for the acquisition of equipment, shelter, and materials; develop plans for meeting these standards; and monitor their implementation. These standards should

---

708. Miller-Grandvaux, "DRAFT Context Paper," 2009.
709. WB, "Reshaping the Future," 2005.
710. Miller-Grandvaux, "DRAFT Context Paper," 2009.
711. Sinclair, "Planning Education In and After Emergencies," 2002.
712. Ibid.
713. INEE, "Minimum Standards for Education," 2004. UK DfID, "Education, Conflict, and International Development," 2003. Miller-Grandvaux, "DRAFT Context Paper," 2009.
714. INEE, "Minimum Standards for Education," 2004.
715. Sinclair, "Planning Education In and After Emergencies," 2002.

take into account the need for sustainability. Peg standards to those used by the best of the public schools, but understand that standards will vary according to each situation.

### 10.6.17 Approach: Quality and Conflict-Sensitive Education

Depending on what is taught and how it is taught, education in these environments has the power to either spark renewed conflict or aid in its resolution. This approach is about the quality of education and the teaching and learning environment that is created for this conflict-sensitive situation. Quality education should not seek to be neutral but to actively support the peace process. Quality curriculum includes course materials and instruction that do not exacerbate tensions from the conflict but promote a shared future of peaceful coexistence. Quality teaching and administration involves appropriate training in creating a conflict-sensitive, learner-centered, participatory school environment.[716]

**10.6.18 Ensure that curricula promote peace and long-term development.**[717] Educational reforms should identify the role curriculum may have played in aggravating the conflict. Textbooks that use biased histories and hateful language may have inflamed tensions. Pay particular attention to the curriculum's approach to identity issues (including religion, culture, and language) and subject areas such as history, geography, and literature.[718] Promote the most inclusive language of instruction as possible in order not to exacerbate conflicts and differences nor alienate any social groups. This environment may offer an opportunity to help create a modern education program that unifies the population behind a common vision for the future.[719] When modernizing curricula, be aware of conflict with local traditions. Working with local traditional and religious leaders can help ensure that the new curriculum respects the local culture.[720] See Section 9.7.17 for more on the development of human capital.

**10.6.19 Enrich curricula with education on life skills.**[721] Curriculum in these situations should deliver information vital for the peace process on topics such as health, human rights, safety, multiculturalism, democracy, conflict resolution, and environmental awareness. When combined with quality curricula on standard subjects, this information can help bring about behavior change in children, youth, and adults that enables them to live more healthy and peaceful lives.[722]

**10.6.20 Develop and support quality teachers and administrators.** The number of teachers and administrators in a country emerging from violent conflict may be greatly decreased. This can be due to violence directed at teachers, the imprisonment of teachers who engaged in the violence, the emigration of the educated class, or the spread of disease. Programs and reforms may be needed to recruit and train new teachers and administrators. Ensure that different ethnic groups and languages, as appropriate, are represented among them. The quality of training that teachers and administrators

---

716. INEE, "Minimum Standards for Education," 2004.

717. Sinclair, "Planning Education In and After Emergencies," 2002.

718. Elizabeth A. Cole and Judy Barsalou, *Unite or Divide? The Challenges of Teaching History in Societies Emerging from Violent Conflict* (Washington, D.C.: U.S. Institute of Peace, 2006). UK DfID, "Education, Conflict and International Development," 2003.

719. Sinclair, "Planning Education In and After Emergencies," 2002.

720. UK DfID, "Education, Conflict and International Development," 2003. OECD, "Education in Fragile States," 2006.

721. Sinclair, "Planning Education In and After Emergencies," 2002.

722. UK DfID, "Education, Conflict and International Development," 2003.

receive will be critical to the success of educational reforms. Good teacher training should begin in refugee camps so that capacity is in place once violent conflict ends, and good teachers can migrate back home during the repatriation process. Teachers have the moral responsibility of teaching peacebuilding values and messages and may face additional challenges such as ethnic tensions or psychological trauma.[723] Administrators must understand how to run comprehensive assessments, to plan and implement appropriate programs, and to monitor progress.

***10.6.21 Promote a student-centered, participatory learning environment.***[724] Without the proper classroom and school environment, quality curriculum will be of little use. In a society emerging from conflict, a student-centered learning environment is even more significant. This includes student participation, active learning, respect (for each other and for the teacher), cooperation, teamwork, and student interaction. Teacher training should emphasize pedagogy, understanding of content, emphasis on values and attitudes, conflict resolution skills, classroom management, and the development of student-centered learning approaches. Schools should be managed in ways that welcome teacher input, ensure that student voices are heard, and encourage community input and parental involvement, particularly in determining goals, needs, and rules.

## 10.7 Necessary Condition: Return and Resettlement of Refugees and Interally Displaced Populations

### 10.7.1 What is return and resettlement of refugees and IDPs?[725] Why is it a necessary condition?

Return and resettlement of refugees and IDPs is a condition in which all individuals displaced from their homes during conflict are assured the option for a voluntary, safe, and dignified return to their homes or resettlement into new homes and communities. Once they reach their destinations, returnees should have recourse for property restitution or compensation, and should receive strong reintegration and rehabilitation support to build their livelihoods and contribute to long-term economic and political development.[726] With proper support, displaced persons can serve as critical and essential human resources toward the rebuilding of the host nation.[727] Return and resettlement can represent a visible end to violent conflict, legitimize the new political

723. Ibid. OECD, "Education in Fragile States," 2006.

724. INEE, "Minimum Standards for Education," 2004.

725. In the context of this chapter, refugees are defined as individuals who are outside the country of their nationality due to well-founded fear of being persecuted for reasons of race, religion, nationality, or membership of a social group or political opinion. This definition is derived from the 1951 Convention Relating to the Status of Refugees. IDPs are defined as "persons or groups of persons who have been forced or obliged to flee or to leave their homes or places of habitual residence, in particular as a result of or in order to avoid the effects of armed conflict, situations of generalized violence, violations of human rights or natural or human-made disasters, and who have not crossed an internationally recognized State border." This definition is derived from the United Nations Office for the Coordination of Humanitarian Affairs, "Guiding Principles on Internal Displacement," 2004.

726. United Nations High Commissioner for Refugees, *Framework for Durable Solutions for Refugees and Persons of Concern*, 2003. Hereafter: UNHCR, *Framework for Durable Solutions*, 2003.

727. Sarah Petrin, *Refugee Return and State Reconstruction: A Comparative Analysis* (Geneva: United Nations High Commissioner for Refugees, 2002). Hereafter: Petrin, *Refugee Return*, 2002.

order, and restore normal life for the conflict-affected population.[728] Resolving rights to nationality, residency, and property will contribute to an effective, trustworthy, and durable state-citizen relationship.

## 10.7.2 Guidance for Return and Resettlement of Refugees and IDPs[729]

### 10.7.3 Approach: Safe and Voluntary Return or Resettlement

Safe and voluntary return or resettlement involves a guarantee of choice for return and one of safety for those who choose to return. These processes include reuniting families and support systems separated because of violent conflict and ensuring a safe and voluntary journey for refugees returning to their country of origin, IDPs returning to their hometowns, or any displaced individuals or groups resettling in new communities.

**10.7.4 Understand the situation on the ground in order to plan effectively.**[730] Planning requires reliable information about the areas where displaced people seek to return or resettle, to minimize the challenges they face upon arrival. While it is important to gather credible information on the numbers and conditions of IDPs and refugees, it is also key not to jeopardize the security and freedom of movement of displaced populations. Collecting data for such an assessment will not be easy, as displaced populations are not always easily accessible. They may not be in camps where they can be registered, but may have assimilated into local communities or urban areas. Others may be in hiding or may fear being identified. Before initiating any strategy for the return of refugees and IDPs, be sure to assess and understand the scope of the problem by considering the following:

- How many people have been displaced? Is the government understating or inflating numbers of IDPs or refugees in order to influence outside response?
- To where have people been displaced?
- Are the displaced refugees, IDPs, or both?
- Does the host nation have the capacity to reintegrate the displaced?
- What are the needs of the displaced population?
- What are conditions in the host nation or local communities?
- Are conditions at places of origin or resettlement communities less dangerous than conditions in the camps for the displaced?
- Do viable resettlement options exist for the displaced?

**10.7.5 Ensure voluntary return for refugees and IDPs.** Voluntary return or resettlement is the cornerstone of any assistance related to refugees and IDPs. All displaced persons should be permitted to make their own decision without coercion or harassment of any

---

728. Walter Kalin, *Durable Solutions for Internally Displaced Persons: An Essential Dimension of Peacebuilding* (Washington, D.C.: Brookings Institution, 2008). Hereafter: Kalin, *Durable Solutions for IDPs, 2008.*

729. An integrated approach for the return of refugees known as the "4R's" (repatriation, reintegration, rehabilitation, and reconstruction) has been proposed by the word's leading agency, the UN High Commissioner for Refugees. The approach aims to ensure linkages between the four processes by bringing together humanitarian and development actors and funds to ensure durable solutions for those who have returned, poverty reduction, and the creation of good local governance. This requires dedicating greater resources to creating a conducive environment inside the countries of origin in order to facilitate sustainable repatriation and prevent further displacement of the population. For more, see UNHCR, "Framework for Durable Solutions," 2003.

730. Petrin, "Refugee Return," 2002.

kind, and they should be able to freely choose their place of residence.[731] In keeping with the principle of non-refoulement for refugees, no person should be forced into a situation in which they may face persecution or death.[732] This applies to IDPs as well. While "right of return" has traditionally referred to the right of refugees to return to their countries at any time, the concept is increasingly applied to IDPs returning to their homes. When the prospect of returning causes great fear, however, displaced populations should always have the option of a safe and assisted resettlement in their home country, or in the case of refugees, in the present country through asylum or a third-party country that is able and willing to take them.

**10.7.6 Ensure safety of return for refugees and IDPs.** Return and resettlement processes should focus on providing safe passage for displaced populations as they return to their homes or country of origin. Upon return or relocation, displaced persons should still receive protection from continued threats of violence, harassment, intimidation, or persecution. While it is the responsibility of the host nation government to provide this protection, international actors may have to help maximize equal access for returnees to security, health, and other public services, along with providing judicial or legal recourse when needed. The following activities can help improve protection for returning populations:[733]

- *Disarm and demobilize armed groups.* The presence of armed groups will likely deter potential returnees and prevent them from successfully rebuilding their lives in old or new communities, especially in cases where these armed groups triggered the initial displacement. Disarming and demobilizing such groups sends a message to the displaced that violent conflict is over and that they can return safely. See Section 6.7.3 for a discussion about the disarmament and demobilization of ex-combatants.

- *De-mine the paths and communities of returnees.* Land mines and unexploded ordnance could prevent the displaced from making it to their homes and could deter those who have yet to begin their journey home. In rural areas, where people depend on the land for subsistence and livelihood, de-mining farmlands is necessary for returnees to rebuild their livelihood.[734] For more on freedom of movement, see Section 6.9.3.

- *Protect vulnerable groups from abuse.* During the return phase, women, children, and other groups are susceptible to criminal and sexual abuse from those around them, including other returnees.[735] Ensure special protection for these populations through targeted public security and law enforcement programs. See Section 6.8.3 for more on the security of vulnerable populations.

*See Trade-off: Section 10.9.3, Responsibility to protect vs. safety of relief workers.*

731. UNHCR, "Framework for Durable Solutions," 2003.

732. Kalin, *Durable Solutions for IDPs,* 2008.

733. United Nations High Commissioner for Refugees, *Guiding Principles on Internal Displacement,* 1998. http:// www.unhcr.ch/html/menu2/7/b/principles.htm, accessed June 22, 2009. International Peace Academy, Housing, Land, Property and Conflict Management: Identifying Policy Options for Rule of Law Programming, 2005. Hereafter: IPA, *Housing, Land, Property and Conflict Management,* 2005.

734. Brookings Institution and University of Bern, *Addressing Internal Displacement in Peace Processes. Peace Agreements and Peace-Building,* 2007. Hereafter: Brookings/Bern, *Addressing Internal Displacement,* 2007.

735. UNHCR, "Framework for Durable Solutions," 2003.

**10.7.7 Provide refugees and IDPs with full access to the information they need to decide whether or not to return.** One means for doing this is to arrange visits for IDP or refugee representatives to assess the conditions of the potential destination. Women and members of different ethnic, racial, religious, and political groups should be included as much as possible on these trips.[736] Important information should be available in a language understood by the population and should include the following:[737]

- The political and security situation of intended destinations, including freedom of movement; amnesties; and the availability of assistance and protection for women, children, minorities, and other vulnerable groups.

- A realistic assessment about whether the causes of displacement have been resolved and about the availability of reintegration assistance. If the situation remains dangerous, keep displaced populations informed and be careful about offering return assistance.[738]

- Procedures for returning or resettling, including details on what items can be brought for the journey, required documentation, available modes of transportation, and other administrative requirements.

- Information about landmine risks, potential housing disputes, opportunities for employment, and availability of public services and facilities.

**10.7.8 Develop internal resettlement alternatives for those who decide not to return to their original homes.** Some of the displaced may choose not to return to their previous homes for fear of discrimination or violence. Others may return to find their homes destroyed or land unusable as a result of landmines or ongoing occupation by militias. In these cases, resettlement should remain a viable option with appropriate compensation. In certain cases, the restitution of property to some returnees will result in the eviction of other displaced persons who have moved in since the displacement. Measures need to be taken to ensure that upon eviction, these persons will be able to find adequate shelter and compensation if they cannot have access to their own properties.[739]

**10.7.9 Manage refugee returns as far from the border as possible.** The best strategy for managing refugee returns and reducing the risk of chaos and violence is to do so as far from the border as possible. This allows for the proper preparation of refugees and border officials (and security officials) so all know what to expect. Those who pose security risks can be dealt with or screened before entry rather than after entry. Strong pre-entry and entry controls enhance security, reassure refugees, and reduce unauthorized movements of people, particularly reducing the exploitation of refugees by human smugglers.

---

736. Kalin, "Durable Solutions for IDPs," 2008.

737. Ibid.

738. Barry N. Stein, "Refugee Repatriation, Return, and Refoulement During Conflict," presented at the United States Agency for International Development Conference Promoting Democracy, Human Rights, and Reintegration in Post-conflict Societies (October 30–31, 1997). Hereafter: Stein, "Refugee Repatriation," 1997.

739. Brookings/Bern, "Addressing Internal Displacement," 2007.

### 10.7.10 Approach: Property Dispute Resolution

Efficient and effective property dispute resolution is a major gap in many S&R missions and poses serious challenges to political stability.[740] During violent conflict, many homes and properties are destroyed, along with property titles and records. Disputes arise when displaced persons return, seeking to reclaim their houses, land, or property. The situation is further complicated by massive population displacement, illegal occupation of houses and buildings, conflicting claims to property, absence of documentation to determine resolution, and discrimination against women in accessing land.[741] Common means for dispute resolution include restitution of property and compensation for resettlement.

**10.7.11 Address property disputes to encourage the return of displaced populations.** Without a level of confidence that they will have homes to return to, many displaced populations may opt not to return, or may simply occupy homes that belong to other displaced persons, further complicating the situation. To mitigate this problem, establish a transparent process for handling property claims/disputes and for addressing land policy, along with a plan for constructing shelters as needed.[742]

**10.7.12 Base resolution processes in a legal framework to ensure consistency and enforceability.** In defining the kinds of homes, land, and property that should be subject to restitution or compensation, consider both formal property and tenure laws, as well as informal practices.[743] A formal land law should also be established to govern land rights, the status of registered land titles, the recognition of traditional rights to land, and the regulation of land rental markets or land transfers.[744] In the midst of conflict, land records are often destroyed or misplaced. Where possible, it is necessary to collect, restore, or reestablish records quickly to prevent and resolve property disputes.[745] Mechanisms for resolution should be linked to local reconciliation and transitional justice mechanisms, since they can also be the source of further conflict if badly managed.[746] Don't rule out local informal mechanisms for resolving disputes, particularly in countries with complex legal frameworks, disputed records, and weak enforcement. See also Section 7.8.15. To ensure that decisions are binding and to limit corruption and other illicit property activities, legal means of enforcement will be necessary.[747] For more on legal reform and property rights, see Section 7.5.9.

*See Gap/Challenge: Section 10.10.7, Effective property laws.*

**10.7.13 Return property lost during conflict to its original owners where possible and offer compensation for those who must resettle.** Where clear ownership can be proven, property should be restored to the owners who lost it as a result of the conflict. This may require evicting other displaced persons who have been using the abandoned property for shelter and finding alternative solutions for those evicted. This may also involve dealing with those who have seized abandoned properties and brought

---

740. IPA, "Housing, Land, Property and Conflict Management," 2005.
741. Ibid.
742. Brookings/Bern, "Addressing Internal Displacement," 2007.
743. IPA, "Housing, Land, Property and Conflict Management," 2005.
744. Fitzpatrick, "Land Policy," 2002.
745. Ibid.
746. Brookings/Bern, "Addressing Internal Displacement," 2007.
747. Fitzpatrick, "Land Policy," 2002.

them into the illicit property market by either renting or selling them. In some cases, displaced persons may have forcibly lost claim to their properties before the conflict on a discriminatory basis by the last administration.[748] Efforts need to be taken to restore these properties to their original owners. Additional compensation for those who are forced to move or resettle may also be appropriate.

*See Trade-off: Section 10.9.5, Giving property to their original owners vs. existing occupants.*

**10.7.14 Ensure property rights of women, orphans, and other vulnerable populations.** Without a male head of the household, female heads of households or parentless children often run into obstacles upon return. In the case of divorce, abandonment, or death of the male, women or children often hold no formal claim to property. These problems prevent them from submitting claims for repossession or reconstruction of their houses. Procedures should be put in place to ensure that these vulnerable groups are given proper compensation and shelter and to address inequalities and discrimination.[749] In certain cases, people may hold traditional, informal claims to property, which are typical for minorities or indigenous people who have been residents of the land and lack recognition by formal authorities. Recognize these traditional claims and provide the property owners with formal titles to the property so that they may return to their lands without fear of further conflict.[750]

**10.7.15 Allocate properties for community and commercial uses as needed.** Even while property is being fought over for purposes of shelter, putting property aside for community and commercial purposes remains vital to the reintegration and rehabilitation of a community.[751] Homes are not the only forms of property lost amidst conflict. Farmers and fisherman may return to find their equipment and livestock destroyed. Try to provide compensation support to those who have lost infrastructure or other forms of property that serve as the means for livelihoods.[752] International players in a reconstruction zone will also need buildings or headquarters from which to operate.[753]

**10.7.16 Approach: Reintegration and Rehabilitation**
Upon arrival at their new destinations, those who return or resettle will need reintegration and rehabilitation support to promote long-term economic and social development. A major gap exists in transitioning seamlessly from the return or resettlement processes to sustainable development activities. The latter activities are vital to ensure that people who return or resettle are not abandoned but are given the support needed to rebuild their lives over the long term.

*See Gap/Challenge: Section 10.10.6, Long-term development needs of returnees.*

**10.7.17 Promote self-reliance and empowerment of refugees and IDPs to prevent dependency on aid.**[754] Displaced people need to be given opportunities to be pro-

---

748. Ibid.
749. Brookings/Bern, "Addressing Internal Displacement," 2007.
750. Ibid.
751. Fitzpatrick, "Land Policy," 2002.
752. Ibid.
753. Ibid.
754. UNHCR, "Framework for Durable Solutions," 2003.

ductive and self-reliant, as opposed to being passive recipients of aid. This requires that the host nation government treat displaced populations as contributors to local development and that these groups have access to socioeconomic activity. This will involve gradually integrating education, health, agriculture, and livelihood-promoting activities that link up with longer-term development programs.

***10.7.18 Recognize that displaced populations represent a rich body of potential human and material assets and resources.***[755] Refugees and IDPs bear characteristics of resilience, courage, and determination to thrive and employ a rich set of skills to survive. To develop their human potential, it is important to provide this group of people with opportunities for education, skills training, and income-generating initiatives. If they are not provided such opportunities, displaced populations can become sources of instability. Male refugees, in particular, sometimes turn to violence, exploitation, and other criminal activities when they are disempowered by their experience as refugees or displaced people. Communicate to communities the benefits of welcoming returnees and new settlers, including the influx of new skills, resources, higher education, health and gender equality, which they may have gained during the period of displacement. Try to preserve these gains when people reintegrate back into more traditional social structures.[756]

***10.7.19 Create an environment that sustains return.***[757] Physically helping displaced people return or resettle is only the first step of many. The environment to which the displaced return should be comfortable enough for them to remain and rebuild their lives. If the host nation or community cannot properly absorb them, a new wave of displacement can occur.[758] Good local governance, protection of the rights of communities, social services, economic revival, livelihood creation, and improved access to services help prevent further displacement of the population.[759] Plans should include programs to reunite families and offer support systems for those who were separated during the repatriation process.

- *Access to essential services and livelihood opportunities.* Return and resettlement populations should be assured access to essential services. In addition to shelter, water, food, sanitation, and health services, infrastructure and education should be readily available in the local community in order to sustain its population at the most basic level and serve as a platform for further reconstruction and development.[760] Providing these populations with access to livelihoods will enable them to rebuild their lives and give them a sense of ownership in the reconstruction of the country.

- *Reunification of families.* Reuniting family and friends helps returnees to feel comfortable in their new communities. Intimate and familiar relationships are key to a person's psychological support system. When families are unable to reunite in their own communities, secondary migration is common.[761]

---

755. Ibid.
756. UNHCR, Handbook for Emergencies, 2000.
757. Brookings/Bern, "Addressing Internal Displacement," 2007.
758. Petrin, "Refugee Return," 2002.
759. UNHCR, "Framework for Durable Solutions," 2003.
760. Fitzpatrick, "Land Policy," 2002.
761. Petrin, "Refugee Return," 2002.

- *Redevelopment of local communities through processes to promote peaceful coexistence.* Processes to promote reconciliation among members of a community should be implemented to build a new support system and preventing new or old tensions from arising.[762]

- *Revitalization of civil society.* A functioning civil society at a grassroots level is critical to the reconstruction of community identity. By giving a voice to those who were most likely silenced during conflict, civil society is an important element to the reintegration process.[763] See Section 8.8.3 for more on civil society development.

- *Host nation presence at the local level.* The national government will not be perceived as legitimate by rural populations if it is seen merely as a distant power. Once the government has assisted in repatriation it should maintain visibility at the local level, assisting and supporting the local population, and enabling them to feel like part of the new state. Lack of assistance and support at a local level will encourage some returnees to move to larger cities, where prospects for assistance from the national government are higher.[764] See Section 8.6.11 for a discussion on strengthening subnational governance institutions.

- *Adequate rights for returnees in old and new communities.* Steps aimed at ensuring transitional justice are necessary, taking into account displaced persons' rights to restitution, compensation, rehabilitation, reparation, and guarantees of non-repetition. If justice is not assured, further inter- and intra-communal tensions over access to land, water, and other resources are likely.[765] Protections against discrimination based on ethnicity, background, or the basis of having been displaced should be enforced. See Section 7.7.3 for a discussion on transitional justice.

### 10.7.20 Through conflict-sensitive development, strive to build the following characteristics in the returning or resettling populations:[766]

- *Economic characteristics.* Displaced people become less reliant on aid, attaining self-reliance and are able to pursue sustainable livelihoods. Economic integration allows refugees to better interact with the local population, as they are viewed as contributors rather than as a burden.

- *Social and cultural characteristics.* Interactions between displaced populations and local communities enable peaceful relations and encourage returnees and new settlers to live amongst or alongside the host population. Displaced populations can live without discrimination or exploitation and can contribute to the development of their host communities.

- *Legal characteristics.* Displaced groups are granted a progressively wider range of rights by the government, which are equal to those of citizens. These include

---

762. Stein, "Refugee Repatriation," 1997.
763. Ibid.
764. Petrin, "Refugee Return," 2002.
765. Brookings/Bern, "Addressing Internal Displacement," 2007.
766. UNHCR, "Framework for Durable Solutions," 2003.

freedom of movement; access to education, employment, and public services; the possibility of acquiring and disposing of property; and the capacity to travel with valid travel and identity documents. Eventually, refugees and IDPs should receive permanent residence rights and perhaps citizenship in the country of settlement.

## 10.8 Necessary Condition: Social Reconstruction

### 10.8.1 What is social reconstruction? Why is it a necessary condition?

Social reconstruction is a condition in which the population achieves a level of tolerance and peaceful co-existence; gains social cohesion through acceptance of a national identity that transcends individual, sectarian, and communal differences; has the mechanisms and will to resolve disputes nonviolently; has community institutions that bind society across divisions; and addresses the legacy of past abuses. For the social well-being of a society, social reconstruction includes twin approaches: directly addressing the legacy of violent conflict through inter- and intra-group reconciliation[767] and indirectly building societal links[768] by promoting reconciliation through community-based development and cooperative action.[769] Following violent conflict, social cohesion may be almost nonexistent. Returnees, combatants, and victims of the conflict often have great difficulty finding their place in the community again. Disputes over land, water, pasture rights, inheritance, marriage, and other community issues may arise, further affecting already traumatized communities. Local institutions—both formal and informal—that helped bind the population before the conflict may be shattered. Spoiler narratives and impromptu war memorials that reinforce societal cleavages may be present. Without the tolerance and cohesion that enables peaceful coexistence, individuals and communities may resort to violence to address their grievances and resolve disputes.

### 10.8.2 Guidance for Social Reconstruction

#### 10.8.3 Approach: Inter- and Intra-Group Reconciliation

Reconciliation is a contentious term. The controversy derives from its meaning as both a goal and a process.[770] While reconciliation may not be a realistic end goal within the time constraints of a typical S&R mission, reconciliation processes are still crucial to the social recovery and development of the population. Simply put, reconciliation is a process through which people move from a divided past to a shared future, the ultimate goal being the peaceful coexistence of all individuals in a society. Reconciliation programs seek to promote tolerance and mutual respect, reduce anger and prejudice from the conflict, foster intergroup understanding, strengthen nonviolent conflict resolution mechanisms, and heal the wounds of conflict. As well as address the causes of conflict, reconciliation can deter future violence and violations of human rights.

#### 10.8.4 Assess existing sources of conflict to restore social capital and promote reconciliation.

---

767. "Reconciliation" is a term widely used but rarely defined in this context and with few literal translations in other languages. For the purposes of this manual, reconciliation will be treated as a process that occurs on many levels at once—personal and societal, legal, political, and economic.

768. Organisation for Economic Co-operation and Development, *Reconciliation: Development Assistance Committee Issues Brief*, 2005. Hereafter: OECD, *Reconciliation*, 2005.

769. United States Agency for International Development, *Community-Based Development in Conflict-Affected Areas: An Introductory Guide for Programming*, 2007. Hereafter: USAID, *Community-Based Development*, 2007.

770. Judy Barsalou and Victoria Baxter, *The Urge to Remember* (Washington, D.C.: U.S. Institute of Peace, 2007). Hereafter: Barsalou/Baxter, *The Urge to Remember*, 2007.

While many definitions exist, social capital is widely understood to be the resources that create a strong network of institutionalized relationships.[771] To restore social capital in a war-torn country, be sure to understand underlying social cleavages that create conflict and tension. Assess the distribution of resources across society and the opportunities for individuals and groups to access those resources. Reliable delivery of and access to essential services builds vertical capital. For more on delivery of services, see Section 8.5.11. Community and intergroup reconciliation builds horizontal capital. In a society emerging from conflict, resolving the status of marginalized groups—including minorities, refugees, and IDPs—is necessary to build social capital. Individual human capital, such as skills and dignity, should also be preserved and supported.[772]

***10.8.5 Understand the cultural context to shape strategies for promoting reconciliation.*** Reconciliation processes are delicate and highly political in nature and should be grounded in the culture.[773] To mitigate potential skepticism and fear about biases and intentions, reconciliation programs should involve all of society, including everyone from high-level politicians down to the ordinary survivor.[774] Creating effective reconciliation programs requires assessing the social, political, economic, and cultural context before determining the best methods. Restoring social relationships successfully involves paying close attention to cultural or traditional mechanisms that exist for dealing with crises. It also entails assessing popular support for these processes to ensure that programs will be effective and that victims do not feel pressured into participating.[775]

***10.8.6 Build on indigenous practices for healing and acknowledging wrongdoing.*** To ensure effective social recovery, be sure to assess the traditional or cultural means a society may have for acknowledging past misdeeds.[776] Rather than displacing these mechanisms, build on them and use them in ways that can be constructive toward the reconciliation process.[777]

***10.8.7 Ensure host nation ownership over the reconciliation process.*** Host nation ownership is vital to success; reconciliation cannot be imported. Reconciliation processes should be led and implemented by the host nation population, not international actors. Consulting with the population on the design and implementation of the programs is essential to ensure that the efforts are locally driven.[778] On the other hand, the role of international third parties can also be helpful as an honest broker. Leaders of these processes need to understand that they require political will from host nation leaders, a

---

771. The definitions of vertical social capital ("relations between state, market, and civil society") and horizontal social capital ("the nurturing of trust and civic engagement among like and diverse groups") can be found in World Bank, *Violent Conflict and the Transformation of Social Capital: Lessons from Cambodia, Rwanda, Guatemala, and Somalia,* 2000. Hereafter: WB, *Violent Conflict,* 2000.

772. Brookings Institution, Rethinking "Relief" and "Development" in Transitions from Conflict, 1999. Hereafter: Brookings, *Rethinking Relief and Development,* 1999.

773. OECD, "Reconciliation," 2005. United States Agency for International Development, Promoting Social Reconciliation in Post-Conflict Societies, 1999. Hereafter: USAID, *Promoting Social Reconciliation,* 1999.

774. OECD, "Reconciliation," 2005.

775. Ibid. USAID, "Promoting Social Reconciliation in Post-Conflict Societies," 1999.

776. Rosalind Shaw, *Rethinking Truth and Reconciliation Commissions. Lessons from Sierra Leone* (Washington, D.C.: U.S. Institute of Peace, 2005. Hereafter: Shaw, *Rethinking Truth and Reconciliation,* 2005.

777. USAID, "Promoting Social Reconciliation," 1999.

778. Ibid.

degree of buy-in from the local community, and dedicated resources.

***10.8.8 Recognize that reconciliation is an ongoing process—not an end goal—that may last for generations.*** Reconciliation is an extremely complex and multifaceted process that can be strongly impacted by political, economic, and cultural variables that are not always easy to measure or manage. Forgiveness and healing are very personal processes that may require time and nuanced approaches to promote. Because the process may take a very long time, it is absolutely critical to be explicit about the time frame and expectations of the process.[779] The host nation government and civil society, therefore, should be prepared to continue promoting reconciliation processes from many different angles and over an extended period of time.[780]

***10.8.9 Pay attention to sequencing.***[781] In undertaking reconciliation processes, timing and sequencing is crucial. Immediately after violent conflict ends, collection of evidence and witness statements should occur as soon as possible, when memories are still fresh and the destruction of critical war crimes evidence can be avoided. However, other processes, such as truth telling, may be best implemented after people have had time to absorb their experiences, resources have been secured, and a sound program has been developed through broad consultation with various groups. Rushing into reconciliation processes too quickly, when wounds are still raw and resources are scarce, can be a risky move.

*See Trade-off: Section 10.9.6, Pursuing reconciliation vs. stability.*

***10.8.10 Consider the many different strategies that exist to promote reconciliation processes.*** No single effort can solve all of the problems of a society emerging from conflict, but collectively, they can contribute greatly to social reconciliation.[782] See Section 7.7.3 for a discussion of transitional justice.

- *Truth telling.* While there are many variations, this strategy generally involves the public recounting of memories of violence and is one of the most common techniques for confronting the past. Truth telling is founded on the idea that a comprehensive understanding of the conflict can help to restore social relationships. Truth telling is sometimes described as historical justice or means of setting the record straight. This strategy is often pursued through the establishment of truth commissions, which seek to uncover the past and bring to light the violations that occurred on all sides of the conflict.[783] Truth commissions are generally understood to be:[784]

  - Temporary bodies, usually in operation for one to two years
  - Nonjudicial bodies with some degree of independence
  - Officially sanctioned, authorized, or empowered by the host nation government

---

779. Ibid.

780. Judy Barsalou, *Trauma and Transitional Justice in Divided Societies* (Washington, D.C.: U.S. Institute of Peace, 2005). Hereafter: Barsalou, "Trauma and Transitional Justice," 2005.

781. Barsalou/Baxter, "The Urge to Remember," 2007.

782. Barsalou, "Trauma and Transitional Justice," 2005.

783. USAID, "Promoting Social Reconciliation," 1999. Institute for Democracy and Electoral Assistance (IDEA), *Reconciliation After Violent Conflict: A Handbook,* 2003. Hereafter: IDEA, *Reconciliation After Violent Conflict,* 2003.

784. IDEA, "Reconciliation After Violent Conflict," 2003.

- Created at a point of political transition.

Truth commissions typically:

- Investigate patterns of past abuses and specific violations committed over a period of time, not just a single specific event
- Focus on violations of human rights and sometimes of humanitarian norms
- Complete their work with the submission of a final report that contains conclusions and recommendations.

- *Peace commissions.* Peace commissions play a role in fostering tolerance, promoting dialogue, and preventing violence.[785] Means for doing this include mediating among groups, offering peace education and training through community programs, and countering rumors that may contribute to instability. Peace commissions typically comprise local leaders and representatives of the broader community.

- *Retributive justice and dispute resolution mechanisms.* The prosecution of war crimes is an important aspect of the reconciliation process, as it holds war criminals and human rights violators accountable for their actions. But just as important are the other forms of justice, such as the issuance of reparations to victims, the documentation of truth, and mediation of ongoing disputes through traditional mechanisms. Retributive justice also entails strengthening the rule of law system to combat impunity and ensure the protection of human rights. Retributive justice contributes to reconciliation by:[786]

- Discouraging revenge
- Protecting against the return to power of perpetrators
- Fulfilling an obligation to the victims
- Individualizing guilt
- Strengthening legitimacy and process of democratization
- Breaking the cycle of impunity.

- *Restorative justice.*[787] Restorative justice mechanisms are often employed as an alternative or a complement to retributive justice efforts. While retributive justice focuses primarily on the perpetrator, restorative justice engages the victim, the perpetrator, and the broader community in an effort to restore relationships destroyed as a result of violent conflict. Rather than focusing on punishment of the perpetrator, restorative justice mechanisms emphasize getting perpetrators to accept responsibility for their actions. One model for restorative justice involves a mediation process where willing victims meet with willing perpetrators to explore and express their feelings about the facts surrounding an offense and seek to mend relationships.

- *Lustration.* Lustration is the administrative step of barring a whole class of individuals from public employment, political participation, and the enjoyment of other civil rights based on involvement with a prior regime. Many variables to consider when using lustration include to what extent the group being barred

---

785. USAID, "Promoting Social Reconciliation," 1999.
786. IDEA, "Reconciliation After Violent Conflict," 2003.
787. Ibid.

has been defeated or discredited, its social influence, and its potential for mounting resistance.

- *Reparations.* Reparations are a form of justice that seeks to compensate victims for their losses and to acknowledge the violations they suffered. Many terms exist to describe similar concepts as the idea has evolved over time: restitution, compensation, rehabilitation, or satisfaction and redress. Reparations may be an important element of the reconciliation process for vulnerable populations that suffered from the conflict, such as youth, women, torture victims, and ethnic minorities. When considering using reparations, be aware that victims may feel that they are simply being paid off. Reparations processes can be expensive and typically employ direct financial transfers, but can also include grants for victims' children or targeted programs for groups or regions that suffered greatly.[788]

- *Mass media.* Radio, television, and art are all media through which peace messages and peace education can be promulgated in an effective way. UN missions, for example, often establish UN radio through which peace messages are communicated, including providing information on disarmament and demobilization sites, dispelling rumors, countering hate speech, and providing a forum for dialogue.

- *Healing.* Healing is broadly defined as any strategy or activity that seeks to promote the psychological health of individuals after they have experienced trauma. Healing processes are lengthy, intensive, and are often linked with the rehabilitation of national and local communities to restore a sense of normalcy and belonging.[789]

- *Memorialization.* Memorialization is a process that, when properly constructed, can honor victims and serve as a tool to address the past and promote a peaceful future. By educating and reminding people about the past, memorialization aims to prevent the renewal of conflict and to aid in social reconstruction by creating a "never again" mentality.[790] Experience shows that memorials that prompt survivors to examine contested recollections of the past and facilitate exchange across ethnic, cultural, and religious groups can advance social reconstruction. It also shows, however, that impromptu memorials run the risk of reigniting old tensions. Build memorialization initiatives with intensive, deliberate, and locally led consultation and design, based on a thorough understanding of the following local context; beliefs about death and burial, grieving, revenge, and justice; and important cultural, historic, and other symbolic sites and document collections.[791] Explore how transitional justice processes can relate to memorialization.

**10.8.11 Be prepared to provide necessary security.**[792] Some reconciliation processes can stir strong reactions from victims and perpetrators, which can result in violence from those

---

788. Grossmann, Georg and Hildegard Lingnau, *Addressing the Past—Fostering Reconciliation* (Berlin: Deutsche Gesellschaft fur Technische Zusammenarbeit, 2003). Hereafter: Grossmann/Lingnau, *Addressing the Past,* 2003.

789. IDEA, "Reconciliation After Violent Conflict," 2003.

790. Barsalou/Baxter, "The Urge to Remember, 2007. Ibid.

791. Ibid.

792. Shaw, "Rethinking Truth and Reconciliation," 2005. IDEA, "Reconciliation After Violent Conflict," 2003.

who seek to undermine those processes. Because of the political volatilities, a credible guarantee of security is vital to the success of these processes and to ensure public participation in them, particularly in truth telling processes and in administering retributive justice. Common fears include victims' fear of retaliation by perpetrators, perpetratorsí fear for their own lives after testifying, fear of government reprisals, and fear that testimonies given in truth commissions will be used in legal prosecutions.

### 10.8.12 Approach: Community-Based Development

Community-based development, long separated in official guidance from governance, humanitarian assistance, reconstruction, and reconciliation, is now understood to unite all of these fundamental activities in conflict-affected societies through community-driven processes that have stood the test of time and been applied in dozens of missions.[793] Development that brings representatives of divided societies together helps them learn to govern and reconcile while rebuilding their shattered communities. This approach can rebuild social capital and trust within and between communities.[794]

**10.8.13 Build relationships and trust through collaborative development processes.**[795] This collaborative approach should be considered the heart of any strategy to promote peaceful coexistence and eventual reconciliation.[796] The features of development processes that aid in reconciliation and promote governance include the following:

- Democratically selected community bodies reflecting the diverse make-up of localities with a special focus on inclusion of gender and minority representation
- Joint community decision-making to assess and prioritize needs
- Community selection of projects (e.g., schools, community centers, health clinics)
- Community receipt of aid money and management of the allocation of resources
- Contribution of labor to reconstruction projects
- Accountability and transparency mechanisms to ensure integrity of the process.

**10.8.14 Understand that the development process is as important as the projects.** The process outlined above, and the cooperation and solidarity it can instill, enables social reconstruction. Do not rush the process because doing so can exacerbate community tensions by unleashing a new contest for power. Be patient because building democratic processes in this manner may mean that projects take longer to complete.[797]

**10.8.15 Provide resources to ensure sustainability.** In every S&R mission for the past two decades, community-based development programs have been launched to promote reconstruction and reconciliation. Many of these programs suffer from a lack of sustained resources, which can undermine the legitimacy of the peace process and

---

793. USAID, "Community-Based Development," 2007.

794 115 Ibid.

795. USAID, "Promoting Social Reconciliation," 1999.

796. Models for this approach include the Municipal Development and Citizen Participation Project (in El Salvador), the Community Assistance Program (in Iraq), Community Improvement Councils (in Kosovo), and the National Solidarity Program (in Afghanistan).

797. United States Agency for International Development, Office of Transition Initiatives, *Guide to Program Options in Conflict-Prone Settings*, 2001.

reconciliation prospects. This requires a commitment of aid money to the community-based development program, as well as capacity-building and technical support for the process.[798]

**10.8.16 Ensure inclusion and transparency to promote reconciliation and healing.** Include all stakeholders in community-based development decision-making structures, particularly marginalized groups that have been excluded in the past. These often include women, minorities, youth, and the disabled. Transparent and participatory approaches include access to project records, routine reporting to the community on the progress of development programs, and monitoring by media and civil society organizations.[799]

# 10.9 Trade-offs

**10.9.1 Delivering assistance through host nation vs. international capacity.**[800] In the emergency phase, conflict-affected populations may need immediate survival assistance (water, food, shelter, and health services) that only international actors are equipped to deliver. Delivering aid through international organizations, however, can promote a culture of dependency and thwart the development of host nation capacity if sustained for an extended period of time. To minimize this impact, balance the demand to meet emergency survival needs with opportunities to promote host nation capacity.

**10.9.2 Meeting immediate survival needs vs. instability.**[801] While there may be an urgency to meet immediate survival needs, humanitarian assistance can be captured by insurgents or rebel groups and redirected to support those engaged in the conflict. Also, relief, if directed more toward families of combatants, can create perceptions of inequity from victims of the conflict and create tensions.[802] Plan relief efforts carefully and monitor delivery to mitigate potential negative consequences.

**10.9.3 Responsibility to protect vs. safety of relief workers.** The humanitarian crisis in a war-torn country may be severe, demanding urgent delivery of basic needs for survival. But the severity of a crisis can also mean that the security situation in the country or region is very untenable and unpredictable, placing relief workers at great risk.[803] Ensure adequate security for staff workers who must go into danger zones to provide relief.

**10.9.4 Rapid return of displaced populations vs. instability.**[804] Having displaced populations return to their homes creates a positive sign for the prospects of peace. However, encouraging large populations to return without proper groundwork can simply create greater problems, including further internal displacement. Prepare receiving communities for the influx, provide security guarantees, establish property dispute mechanisms, and offer economic and humanitarian assistance to prevent instability.

**10.9.5 Giving property to their original owners vs. existing occupants.** Returning prop-

---

798. WB, "Violent Conflict," 2000.
799. Ibid.
800. United States Agency for International Development, *U.S. Foreign Aid: Meeting the Challenges of the Twenty-First Century*, 2004.
801. Fiona Terry, *Condemned to Repeat* (Ithaca and London: Cornell University Press, 2002).
802. Brookings, "Rethinking Relief and Development," 1999.
803. Ibid. UN WFP, Emergency Food Security Assessment Handbook, 2005.
804. Petrin, "Refugee Return," 2002.

erty back to pre-conflict owners may be ideal and just, but doing so may simply displace existing occupants who sought shelter in the property during the conflict. Evicting large numbers of tenants, particularly in a country where property ownership laws are ambiguous, can be very destabilizing. Property dispute mechanisms, compensation arrangements, and other means to address this recurring trade-off should be planned for in advance.

***10.9.6 Pursuing reconciliation vs. stability.*** In a society emerging from violent conflict, it can be tempting to forget the past, as remembering runs the risk of reigniting old tensions. But depending on the society, sustainable resolution of the conflict may require that the population actively seek reconciliation.[805] Plan efforts carefully and with great sensitivity to timing, broad participation, and the need for resourcing and sustainability of these complex reconciliation processes.

***10.9.7 Restorative vs. retributive justice.*** Restorative justice programs focus on restoring relations between the victim and the perpetrator, but they may fall short of punishing war criminals and human rights violators. Retributive justice programs hold these criminals accountable for their actions, but do not necessarily strengthen the community's social bonds, which can cause problems down the road. Balance these approaches based on the local environment and their potential for supporting long-term stability.

# 10.10 Gaps and Challenges

***10.10.1 Protection of humanitarian space.*** In today's environments, humanitarian actors often find themselves operating in the same space with intervening military forces conducting S&R activities. This can place relief workers in jeopardy when their actions are no longer perceived to be independent from the military or impartial with regard to assistance. Pay close attention to guidelines to help mitigate the negative consequences of this recurring challenge affecting humanitarian space.[806]

***10.10.2 Aid effectiveness.*** While development aid to peaceful countries is frequently monitored and evaluated, similar mechanisms to assess the effectiveness of aid in societies emerging from violent conflict are lacking.[807] A massive waste of resources, inappropriate aid programs, and a failure to achieve timely results are hallmarks of many S&R missions. Monitoring and evaluation must be part of planning and should be resourced adequately to ensure that aid is benefiting stabilization and reconstruction.

***10.10.3 Transition from relief to development activities.*** A major S&R challenge involves facilitating a smooth transition from relief activities focused on short-term survival needs to development activities that promote long-term growth. Better coherence, coordination, and collaboration, between relief and development strategies can ensure a seamless transition between the communities of practice. This is particularly true in the education sector, where a variety of humanitarian and development programs occurs simultaneously.[808]

805. Parliament of Burundi, Inter-Parliamentary Union, and the International Institute for Democracy and Electoral Assistance, "Summary and Recommendations Presented by the Rapporteur of the Seminar, Regional Seminar on the Role of Parliaments in the National Reconciliation Process in Africa," 2005.
806. United States Institute of Peace, InterAction, United States Armed Forces, *Guidelines for Relations Between the U.S. Armed Forces and Nongovernmental Humanitarian Organizations,* 2007.
807. Brookings, "Rethinking Relief and Development, 1999.
808. WB, *Reshaping the Future,* 2005. UK DfID, "Education, Conflict, and International Development," 2003.

*10.10.4 Emergency education.* Education is still most commonly viewed as a development or reconstruction issue, which can prevent children in emergency situations from receiving education for extended periods of time.[809] If emergency education is not provided early on, the delay can cause irreparable damage to the rebuilding of lives and livelihoods. Emergency international standby capacity, already inadequate, needs to be developed as a priority.[810] Plans for secondary and tertiary education, which are critical for long-term social and economic development, should be included as part of an emergency education strategy.

*10.10.5 Youth in recovery efforts.* While there is recognition that youth should be engaged rapidly and early on in these environments, few programs properly address their needs. Neglecting youth populations can also have negative consequences for stability when youth who are unemployed or not in school join criminal gangs or militias, turn to prostitution and trafficking, or engage in other illicit activities. Develop practical programs that harness and develop the potential of this population and include them in efforts to rebuild their country.[811]

*10.10.6 Long-term development needs of returnees.* The host nation and the international community often consider the return of the displaced the end goal. The systematic failure to incorporate the needs of the returnees in any strategic development plan leaves them in deprived conditions for long periods of time and undermines recovery.[812] Programs to address the need of returnees to have productive livelihoods and receive essential services are needed.

*10.10.7 Effective property laws.* Individuals may not have formal land titles or documentation, but may assert customary or traditional rights to certain properties. Property resolution processes raise complex questions that bring with them risks of increased instability.[813] Figuring out how to create, reform, and/or enforce property laws quickly and legitimately is a key S&R job.

*10.10.8 Mental health needs of conflict-affected populations.* The predominant focus of health care services for refugees, IDPs, and other conflict-affected populations has been nutrition, disease prevention, maternal and child health, or the management of infectious diseases. Resources and attention for mental health and psychological support, however, are still severely lacking.[814]

---

809. UNESCO, "Education in Situations of Emergency," 2003.
810. Ibid. UK DfID, "Education, Conflict, and International Development," 2003.
811. WB, *Reshaping the Future*, 2005. UK DfID, "Education, Conflict, and International Development," 2003.
812. UNHCR, "Framework for Durable Solutions," 2003.
813. Fitzpatrick, "Land Policy," 2002.
814. World Health Organization, *Rapid Assessment of Mental Health Needs of Refugees, Displaced and Other Populations Affected by Conflict and Post-Conflict Situations*, 2001.

# SECTION 11
# APPENDICES

# Appendix A. Resource List[815]

### Overarching

African Union and New Partnership for Africa's Development. "African Post-Conflict Reconstruction Policy Framework." 2005.

Call, Charles. "Institutionalizing Peace: A Review of Post-Conflict Peacebuilding, Concepts and Issues for DPA." 2005.

Center for Strategic and International Studies and Association of the United States Army. "Post-Conflict Reconstruction: Task Framework." 2002.

Cohen, Craig. "Measuring Progress in Stabilization and Reconstruction." Washington, DC: U.S. Institute of Peace, 2006.

Covey, Jack, Michael J. Dziedzic, and Leonard R. Hawley, eds. *The Quest for Viable Peace: International Intervention and Strategies for Conflict Transformation.* Washington, DC: United States Institute of Peace Press, 2005.

Defense Science Board. "Study on Transition to and from Hostilities." 2004.

Dobbins, James, Seth G. Jones, Keith Crane, and Beth Cole DeGrasse. *The Beginner's Guide to Nation-Building.* Santa Monica: RAND Corporation, 2007.

Dziedzic, Mike, Barbara Sotirin, and John Agoglia, eds. "Measuring Progress in Conflict Environments (MPICE)—A Metrics Framework for Assessing Conflict Transformation and Stabilization." Washington, DC: Defense Technical Information Catalog, 2008.

European Union. "A Secure Europe in a Better World." 2003.

Federal Republic of Germany. "Action Plan—Civilian Crisis Prevention, Conflict Resolution and Post-Conflict Peacebuilding." 2004.

France (Interministerial Committee on International Cooperation and Development). "Fragile States and Situations of Fragility: France's Policy Paper." 2007.

Ghani, Ashraf, and Clare Lockhart. *Fixing Failed States: A Framework for Rebuilding a Fractured World.* Oxford: Oxford University Press, 2008.

Human Rights Web. "A Summary of United Nations Agreements on Human Rights." http://www.hrweb.org/legal/undocs.html (accessed September 9, 2008).

International Forum for the Challenges of Peace Operations. "A Comparative Study on Doctrine and Principles for Multinational Peace Operations: A Case for Harmonization and Enhanced Interoperability." 2007.

International Forum for the Challenges of Peace Operations. "Challenges of Peace Operations: Into the 21st Century. Concluding Report, 1997–2002." 2002.

International Forum for the Challenges of Peace Operations. "Meeting the Challenges of Peace Operations: Cooperation and Coordination." 2005.

International Monetary Fund (Policy Development and Review Department). "The

---

815. These resources were reviewed to inform the writing of this manual and primarily come from institutional actors.

Fund's Engagement in Fragile States and Post-Conflict Countries—A Review of Experience—Issues and Options." 2008.

International Monetary Fund and the World Bank. "Assistance to Post-Conflict Countries and the HIPC Framework." 2001.

Japan International Cooperation Agency. *Handbook for Transition Assistance*. 2006.

Joint Utstein Study of Peacebuilding (Royal Norwegian Ministry of Foreign Affairs, German Federal Ministry for Economic Cooperation and Development, the Netherlands Ministry of Foreign Affairs, and the Department for International Development, United Kingdom). "Towards a Strategic Framework for Peacebuilding: Getting Their Act Together." 2004.

North Atlantic Treaty Organisation. "Allied Joint Publication 3.4.1, Peace Support Operations." 2001.

Organisation for Economic Co-operation and Development (Development Co-operation Directorate and Development Assistance Committee). "Fragile States: Policy Commitment and Principles for Good International Engagement in Fragile States and Situations." 2007.

Organisation for Economic Co-operation and Development (Development Assistance Committee). "Helping Prevent Violent Conflict." 2001.

Organisation for Economic Co-operation and Development (Development Assistance Committee). "Whole of Government Approaches to Fragile States." 2006.

Organisation for Security Co-operation in Europe. "OSCE Handbook." 2007.

Perito, Robert, ed. *Guide for Participants in Peace, Stability, and Relief Operations: Guidelines for Relations Between U.S. Armed Forces and Nongovernmental Humanitarian Organizations in Hostile or Potentially Hostile Environments*. Washington, DC: United States Institute of Peace Press, 2007.

Sphere Project. "Humanitarian Charter and Minimum Standards in Disaster Response." 2004.

United Kingdom Comprehensive Approach Working Group, "DRAFT: Inter-Departmental Glossary of Planning Terminology," version 1.1. 2007.

United Kingdom Department for International Development, "Review of the United Kingdom Government Approach to Peacebuilding." 2004.

United Kingdom Ministry of Defence. "Joint Doctrine Publication 3-40, Security and Stabilisation: The Military Contribution." 2009.

United Kingdom Stabilisation Unit. "The United Kingdom Approach to Stabilisation—A Stabilisation Unit Guidance Note." 2008.

United Nations Department of Peacekeeping Operations. "Handbook on United Nations Multidimensional Peacekeeping Operations." 2003.

United Nations Department of Peacekeeping Operations and Department of Field Support. "Peacekeeping Operations Principles and Guidelines." 2008.

United Nations Development Group, United Nations Development Programme, and World Bank. "Practical Guide to Multilateral Needs Assessments in Post-Conflict Situations." 2004.

United Nations Development Group and United Nations Executive Committee for Humanitarian Affairs. "Interagency Framework for Conflict Analysis in Transition Situations." 2004.

United Nations Development Group and World Bank. "WORKING DRAFT FOR CIRCULATION: Joint Guidance Note on Integrated Recovery Planning Using Post Conflict Needs Assessments and Transitional Results Frameworks." 2007.

United Nations Development Programme and United States Agency for International Development. "First Steps in Post-Conflict State-Building: A UNDP-USAID Study." 2007.

United Nations Office of the High Commissioner for Human Rights. "Frequently Asked Questions on a Human Rights-Based Approach to Development Cooperation." 2006.

United Nations Peacebuilding Commission. "Sierra Leone Compact." 2007.

United Nations Peacebuilding Commission. "Strategic Framework for Peacebuilding in Burundi." 2007.

United Nations Security Council. "Comprehensive Review of the Whole Question of Peacekeeping Operations in All Their Aspects." 2000. http://www.un.org/documents/ga/res/51/ares51-136.htm (accessed July 2009).

United Nations Security Council. "United Nations Security Council Resolution 1325." October 31, 2000. www.un.org/events/res_1325e.pdf (accessed July 2009).

United States Agency for International Development (Conflict Management and Mitigation Office). "Conducting a Conflict Assessment: A Framework for Strategy and Program Development." 2005.

United States Agency for International Development. "Fragile States Strategy." 2005.

United States Agency for International Development (Office of Transition Initiatives). "Guide to Program Options in Conflict-Prone Settings." 2001.

United States Agency for International Development. "Nine Principles of Reconstruction and Development." 2005.

United States Army. *Field Manual 3-07: Stability Operations.* 2008.

United States Department of State (Office of the Coordinator for Reconstruction and Stabilization). "Post-Conflict Reconstruction Essential Tasks." 2005.

United States Department of State (Office of the Coordinator for Reconstruction and Stabilization). "Principles for Stabilization, Reconstruction, and Conflict Transformation." 2008.

United States Department of State and United States Joint Forces Command. "United States Joint Forces Command J-7 Pamphlet, version 1.0. United States Government

Draft Planning Framework for Reconstruction, Stabilization and Conflict Transformation." 2005.

United States Government. "Counterinsurgency Guide." 2009.

United States Government. "Principles of the Interagency Conflict Assessment Framework." 2008.

United States Institute of Peace (Center for Post-Conflict Peace and Stability Operations). "Strategic Framework: Fragile States and Societies Emerging from Conflict." 2007.

United States President. National Security Presidential Directive 44. "Management of Interagency Efforts Concerning Reconstruction and Stabilization." 2005.

United States President. Presidential Decision Directive 56. "Managing Complex Contingency Operations." 1997.

World Bank (Conflict Prevention and Reconstruction Team). "DRAFT: Conflict Analysis Framework." 2005.

**Safe and Secure Environment**

African Union and New Partnership for Africa's Development. "African Post-Conflict Reconstruction Policy Framework." 2005.

Andrews, Katherine, Brandon Hunt, and William Durch. "Post-Conflict Borders and UN Peace Operations." Stimson Center Report, no. 62 (2007): 1–60.

Australian Federal Police. "International Deployment Group." http://www.afp.gov.au/international/IDG.html (accessed August 19, 2009)

Ball, Nicole. "Democratic Governance and the Security Sector in Conflict-Affected Countries," in Derick W. Brinkerhoff, ed., *Governance in Post-Conflict Societies: Rebuilding Fragile States*. New York: Routledge, 2007.

Bayley, David H. *Changing the Guard: Developing Democratic Police Abroad*. Oxford: University Press Oxford, 2006.

Boscawen, Col. Hugh, Col. Mike Redmond, and Bertram Welsing. "Intelligence to Evidence Operations." Presented at the United Nations Department of Peacekeeping Operations Command Development Seminar, Center of Excellence for Stability Police Units (COESPU). 2006.

Center for Army Lessons Learned. "Provincial Reconstruction Team Playbook." 2007.

Center for Peace Research and Strategic Studies. "Building Local Ownership in Security Sector Reform: Challenges for Local and External Actors in Post-conflict States." 2007.

Cole, Beth, Michael Dziedzic, and Robert Perito. "Building Civilian Capacity for U.S. Stability Operations: The Rule of Law Component." 2004.

Conference of American Armies. "Peace Operations Manual." 2007.

Conflict Research Consortium (International Online Training Program on Intractable Conflict, University of Colorado). "Principled Negotiation." http://www.colorado.edu/conflict/peace/ treatment/pricneg.htm (accessed September 3, 2008).

Covey, Jack, Michael J. Dziedzic, and Leonard R. Hawley, eds. *The Quest for Viable Peace: International Intervention and Strategies for Conflict Transformation.* Washington, DC: United States Institute of Peace Press, 2005.

Darby, John. *The Effects of Violence on Peace Processes.* Washington, DC: United States Institute of Peace Press, 2001.

Deutsche Gesellschaft für Technische Zusammenarbeit GmbH (GTZ). *DDR: A Practical Field and Classroom Guide,* 2004.

Dobbins, James, Seth G. Jones, Keith Crane, and Beth Cole DeGrasse. *The Beginner's Guide to Nation-Building.* Santa Monica: RAND Corporation, 2007.

Dziedzic, Mike, Barbara Sotirin, and John Agoglia, eds. "Measuring Progress in Conflict Environments (MPICE)—A Metrics Framework for Assessing Conflict Transformation and Stabilization." Washington, DC: Defense Technical Information Catalog, 2008.

European Union. "European Union Concept for Support to Disarmament, Demobilisation, and Reintegration (DDR)." 2006.

Feil, Scott. "Building Better Foundations: Security in Post-Conflict Reconstruction." *The Washington Quarterly,* vol. 24, no. 4 (2002): 97–109.

Flournoy, Michèle and Michael Pan. "Dealing with Demons: Justice and Reconciliation." *The Washington Quarterly* vol. 25, no. 4 (2002): 111–23.

French Land Forces. "FT-01. Winning the Battle, Building Peace: Land Forces in Present and Future Conflicts." 2007.

Geneva Centre for the Democratic Control of Armed Forces. "Border Control Services and Security Sector Reform." 2002.

Geneva Centre for the Democratic Control of Armed Forces. "The Post-Conflict Security Sector." 2006.

Geneva Centre for the Democratic Control of Armed Forces. "Shaping a Security Governance Agenda in Post-Conflict Peacebuilding." 2005.

Gleichmann, Colin, Michael Odenwald, Kees Steenken, and Adrian Wilkinson. "Disarmament, Demobilisation, and Reintegration: A Practical Field Guide and Classroom Guide." German Technical Co-operation, The Norwegian Defence International Centre, Pearson Peacekeeping Centre, and the Swedish National Defence College. 2004.

International Commission on Intervention and Sovereignty. "The Responsibility to Protect." 2001.

International Committee of the Red Cross. "The Fundamental Principles of the Red Cross." 1996.

International Peace Academy and United Nations Development Programme. "A Framework for Lasting Disarmament, Demobilization, and Reintegration of Former Combatants in Crisis Situations." International Peace Academy Workshop Report. 2002.

International Security Assistance Force. "Provincial Reconstruction Team Handbook," vols. I and II. 2007.

Italy (Carabinieri General Headquarters). "Doctrine and Procedures for the Employment of the Multinational Specialised Units (MSU)." 2003.

Japan International Cooperation Agency. "Handbook for Transition Assistance." 2006.

Jones, Seth G., Jeremy M. Wilson, Andrew Rathmell, and K. Jack Riley. *Establishing Law and Order After Conflict*. Santa Monica: RAND Corporation, 2005.

Malan, Mark. "Physical Protection in Practice: International and Regional Peacekeeping in Africa." http://www.issafrica.org/Pubs/ASR/9No2/Malan.html (accessed September 17, 2008).

McFate, Sean. "Securing the Future. A Primer on Security Sector Reform in Conflict Countries." United States Institute of Peace Special Report, no. 209 (2008): 1–20.

Nordic Coordinated Arrangement for Military Peace Support. "Peace Support Operations Tactical Manual." 2007.

North Atlantic Treaty Organization. "Allied Joint Publication 3.4.1, Peace Support Operations."

Oakley, Robert, Michael Dziedzic, and Eliot M. Goldberg, eds. *Policing the New World Disorder*. Honolulu: University Press of the Pacific, 2002.

Organisation for Economic Co-operation and Development (Development Co-operation Directorate and Development Assistance Committee). "Designing, Implementing, and Monitoring Armed Violence Reduction." Development Assistance Committee Network on Conflict, Peace, and Development Co-operation Framing Paper. 2007.

Organisation for Economic Co-operation and Development. "Economic Reconstruction in Post-Conflict Transitions: Lessons for the Democratic Republic of Congo (DRC)." 2003

Organisation for Economic Co-operation and Development (Development Assistance Committee). *Handbook on Security Sector Reform: Supporting Security and Justice*. 2007.

Organisation for Economic Co-operation and Development (Development Assistance Committee). "Helping Prevent Violent Conflict." 2001.

Organisation for Economic Co-operation and Development (Development Assistance Committee). "Introduction to Security System Reform." 2005.

Orr, Robert, ed. *Winning the Peace: An American Strategy for Post-Conflict Reconstruction*. Washington, DC: The Center for Strategic and International Studies Press, 2004.

Pearson Peacekeeping Center. "Reintegration of Ex-Combatants through Micro-Enterprise: An Operational Framework." 2005.

Perito, Robert. *Where's the Lone Ranger When You Need Him? America's Search for a Post-Conflict Stability Force*. Washington, DC: United States Institute of Peace Press, 2004.

Rausch, Colette, ed. *Combating Serious Crimes in Post-Conflict Societies: A Handbook for Policymakers and Practitioners.* Washington, DC: United States Institute of Peace Press, 2006.

Stedman, Stephen. "Spoiler Problems in Peace Processes." *International Security,* vol. 22, no 2 (1997): 5–53.

United Kingdom Department for International Development. "Fighting Poverty to Build a Safer World: A Strategy for Security and Development." 2005.

United Kingdom Department for International Development. "Security and Justice Sector Reform Programming in Africa." Evaluation Working Paper, no. 23 (2007): 1–98.

United Kingdom Department for International Development. "Why We Need to Work More Effectively in Fragile States." 2005.

United Kingdom Foreign and Commonwealth Office. *Peace Support Operations: Information and Guidance for UK Police Personnel.* 2007.

United Kingdom Ministry of Defence. "Joint Doctrine Publication 3-40, Security and Stabilisation: The Military Contribution." 2009.

United Kingdom Ministry of Defence. "Joint Warfare Publication 3-50: The Military Contribution to Peace Support Operations," 2nd ed. 2004.

United Kingdom Stabilisation Unit. "Helping Countries Recover From Violent Conflict." 2008.

United Kingdom Stabilisation Unit. "Quick Guide to Stabilisation Planning." 2007.

United Kingdom Stabilisation Unit. "The United Kingdom Approach to Stabilisation—A Stabilisation Unit Guidance Note." 2008.

United Nations. "Handbook on United Nations Multidimensional Peacekeeping Operations." 2003.

United Nations. *Integrated Disarmament, Demobilization and Reintegration Standards.* http://www.unddr.org/iddrs/framework.php (accessed September 2, 2008).

United Nations. "Peacekeeping Operations Principles and Guidelines." 2008.

United Nations. "UN Security Council Resolution 1373, Threats to International Peace and Security Caused by Terrorist Acts," September 28, 2001. http://www.undemocracy.com/S-RES-1373(2001).pdf (accessed September 17, 2008).

United Nations. "UN Security Council Resolution 1540, Non-proliferation of Weapons of Mass Destruction," April 28, 2004. http://www.nti.org/db/1540/pdfs/UNSCR_1540.pdf (accessed September 17, 2008).

United Nations Department of Peacekeeping Operations. "Disarmament, Demobilization, and Reintegration of Ex-Combatants in a Peacekeeping Environment: Principles & Guidelines." 1999.

United Nations Department of Peacekeeping Operations. *Prison Support Guidance Manual.* 2006.

United Nations Department of Peacekeeping Operations. "Security Sector Reform and Peace Operations: 'Improvisation and Confusion' from the Field." 2006.

United Nations Development Programme. "Enhancing Security Sector Governance: A Conceptual Framework for the United Nations Development Programme." 2002.

United Nations Development Programme and United States Agency for International Development. "First Steps in Post-Conflict State-Building: A UNDP-USAID Study." 2007.

United Nations Office of the High Commissioner for Human Rights. "Human Rights and Law Enforcement: A Manual on Human Rights Training for the Police." Professional Training Series, no. 5 (1997): 1–211. http://www.unhchr.ch/html/menu6/2/training.htm (accessed September 12, 2008).

United Nations Secretary-General. "Note to the General Assembly. A/C.5/59/31." 2005.

United States Agency for International Development (Office of Transition Initiatives). "Guide to Program Options in Conflict-Prone Settings." 2001.

United States Army. *Field Manual 3-0: Full Spectrum Operations.* 2008.

United States Army. *Field Manual 3-07: Stability Operations.* 2008.

United States Army and Marine Corps. *Field Manual 3-24: Counterinsurgency.* 2007.

United States Department of State (Office of the Coordinator for Reconstruction and Stabilization). "Lessons-Learned: Demobilization, Disarmament, and Reintegration (DDR) in Stabilization and Reconstruction Operations. A Guide for United States Government Planners." 2006.

U.S. Department of State, U.S. Department of Defense, and U.S. Agency for International Development, "Security Sector Reform," 2008.

United States Institute of Peace, InterAction, and United States Department of Defense. *Guidelines for Relations Between the U.S. Armed Forces and Non Governmental Humanitarian Organizations.* 2007.

Woodrow Wilson School of Public and International Affairs, Princeton University (Graduate Student Working Group). "The Missing Priority: Post-Conflict Security and the Rule of Law." 2003.

## Rule of Law

Alemika, Etannibe E.O., and Innocent C. Chukwuma. "The Poor and Informal Policing in Nigeria: A Report on the Poor's Perceptions and Priorities on Safety, Security and Policing in Access to Justice Focal States in Nigeria." Lagos: Center for Law Enforcement Education, 2004.

Amnesty International. "Afghanistan: Police Reconstruction Essential for the Protection of Human Rights." 2003.

Barsalou, Judy, and Victoria Baxter. "The Urge to Remember. The Role of Memorials in Social Reconstruction and Transitional Justice." United States Institute of Peace Stabilization and Reconstruction Series, no. 5 (2007): 1–22.

Baskin, Mark. "Lessons Learned on UNMIK Judiciary." Ottawa: Government of

Canada, Department of Foreign Affairs and International Trade, 2001.

Bayley, David H. *Changing the Guard: Developing Democratic Police Abroad.* Oxford: University Press Oxford, 2006.

Belton, Rachel Kleinfeld. "Competing Definitions of the Rule of Law: Implications for Practitioners." Carnegie Papers, Rule of Law Series, no. 55 (2005): 1–38.

Berkowitz, David, Katharina Pistor, and Jean-François Richard. *The Transplant Effect.* Cambridge, Mass.: Harvard University, Center for International Development, 2000.

Berling, Per, Lars Bejstam, Jenny Ederlöv, Erik Wennerström, and Richard Zajac Sannerholm. "Rule of Law in Public Administration: Problems and Ways Ahead in Peace Building and Development." Sweden: Folke Bernadotte Academy, 2008.

Blackman, Lani. "Products of Law Reform Agencies," in *The Promise of Law Reform.* Sydney, Australia: The Federation Press, 2005.

Call, Charles T., ed. *Constructing Justice and Security After War.* Washington, DC: United States Institute of Peace Press, 2007.

Carlson, Scott N. "Legal and Judicial Rule of Law Work in Multidimensional Peacekeeping Operations: Lessons-Learned Study." United Nations Department of Peacekeeping Operations. 2006.

Center for Strategic and International Studies and Association of the United States Army. "Post-Conflict Reconstruction: Task Framework." 2002.

Colletta, Nat, and Michelle Cullen. *Violent Conflict and the Transformation of Social Capital. Lessons from Cambodia, Rwanda, Guatemala, and Somalia.* Washington, DC: World Bank, 2000.

Covey, Jack, Michael J. Dziedzic, and Leonard R. Hawley, eds. *The Quest for Viable Peace: International Intervention and Strategies for Conflict Transformation.* Washington DC: United States Institute of Peace Press, 2005.

Dobbins, James, Seth G. Jones, Keith Crane, and Beth Cole DeGrasse. *The Beginner's Guide to Nation-Building.* Santa Monica: RAND Corporation, 2007.

European Union (European Commission Conflict Prevention and Crisis Management Unit). "Civilian Instruments for European Union Crisis Management." 2003.

Glendon, Mary Ann, Michael Gordon, and Christopher Osakwe. *Comparative Legal Traditions: Text, Materials, and Cases on the Civil and Common Law Traditions, with Special Reference to French, German, and English.* Eagan: West Group, 1999.

Godson, Roy. "A Guide to Developing a Culture of Lawfulness." Presented at the Symposium on the Role of Civil Society in Countering Organized Crime: Global Implications of the Palermo, Sicily Renaissance. 2000.

Golub, Stephen. "Beyond Rule of Law Orthodoxy: Legal Empowerment Initiative." Washington, DC: Carnegie Endowment for International Peace, 2003.

Hague Institute of the Internationalisation of Law. "Rule of Law Inventory Report." 2007.

Hurwitz, Agnes, and Kaysie Studdard, "Rule of Law Programs in Peace Operations." New York: International Peace Academy (Security-Development Nexus Program), 2005.

Inter-American Development Bank, "Resource Book on Participation." www.iadb.org/aboutus/VI/resource_book/table_of_contents.cfm?language=english (accessed July 8, 2009).

International Monetary Fund Legal Department. "Plain English Tax Law Drafting." 2008.

International Network to Promote the Rule of Law. "Prison Security in Societies Emerging from Conflict." Consolidated Response (07-007), 2007.

International Peace Academy (Security-Development Nexus Program). "Securing the Rule of Law: Assessing International Strategies for Post-Conflict Criminal Justice." 2005.

Jones, Seth G., Jeremy M. Wilson, Andrew Rathmell, and K. Jack Riley. *Establishing Law and Order After Conflict*. Santa Monica: RAND Corporation, 2005.

Leckie, Scott, ed. *Housing Land and Property Rights in Post-Conflict United Nations and Other Peace Operations: A Comparative Survey and Proposal for Reform*. London: Cambridge University Press, 2008.

Meierhenrich, Jens. "The Ethics of Lustration." *Ethics and International Affairs*, vol. 20, no. 1 (2006): 99–120.

Narayan, Deepa, Robert Chambers, Meera K. Shah, Patti Petesch. *Voices of the Poor: Crying Out for Change*. Oxford: Oxford University Press, 2000.

Oakley, Robert, Michael Dziedzic, and Eliot M. Goldberg, eds. *Policing the New World Disorder*. Honolulu: University Press of the Pacific, 2002.

O'Connor, Vivienne, and Colette Rausch, eds. *Model Codes for Post-Conflict Criminal Justice: Volume I, Model Criminal Code*. Washington, DC: United States Institute of Peace Press, 2007.

O'Connor, Vivienne and Colette Rausch, eds. *Model Codes for Post-Conflict Criminal Justice: Volume II: Model Code of Criminal Procedure*. Washington, DC: United States Institute of Peace Press, 2008.

Organisation of Economic Co-operation and Development (Development Assistance Committee). *Handbook on Security Sector Reform*. Paris, France: OECD Publishing, 2007.

Organisation for Economic Co-operation and Development (Development Assistance Committee). "The Development Assistance Committee Guidelines: Helping Prevent Violent Conflict." 2001.

Penal Reform International. "Making Standards Work: An International Handbook on Good Prison Practice." 2001.

Rausch, Colette, ed. *Combating Serious Crimes in Post-Conflict Societies: A Handbook for Policymakers and Practitioners*. Washington, DC: U.S. Institute of Peace Press, 2006.

Rose-Ackerman, Susan. "Establishing the Rule of Law," in Robert Rotberg ed., *When States Fail: Causes and Consequences*. Princeton: Princeton University Press, 2003.

Scheye, Eric. "Pragmatic Realism in Justice and Security Development: Supporting Improvement in the Performance of Non-State/Local Justice and Security Networks." The Hague: Clingendael Institute, 2009.

SIGMA (A Joint Initiative of the OECD and the European Union). "Improving Policy Instruments Through Impact Assessment." Sigma Paper no. 31, 2001.

Stromseth, Jane. *Can Might Make Rights?: Building the Rule of Law after Military Interventions*. Cambridge: Cambridge University Press, 2006.

Tolbert, David, and Andrew Solomon. "United Nations Reform and Supporting the Rule of Law in Post-Conflict Societies." *Harvard Human Rights Journal*, no. 19 (2006): 29–62.

United Kingdom Department for International Development, "Briefing: Justice and Accountability." 2008.

United Kingdom Department for International Development. "Education, Conflict, and International Development." 2003.

United Kingdom Department for International Development. "Explanatory Note on Security and Access to Justice for the Poor." 2007.

United Kingdom Department for International Development. "Non-State Justice and Security Systems." 2004.

United Kingdom Department for International Development. "Safety, Security, and Accessible Justice: Putting Policy into Practice." 2002.

United Kingdom Department for International Development and United Kingdom House of Commons International Development Committee. "Conflict and Development: Peacebuilding and Post-Conflict Reconstruction. Sixth Report of the Session. Volume I." 2006.

United Kingdom Foreign and Commonwealth Office. *Peace Support Operations. Information and Guidance for UK Police Personnel.* 2007.

United Kingdom Justice Assistance Network. "Principles of Engagement." 2005.

United Kingdom Stabilisation Unit. "Stabilisation Issues Notes: Rule of Law and Stabilisation." 2008.

United Kingdom Stabilisation Unit. "The United Kingdom Approach to Stabilisation —A Stabilisation Unit Guidance Note." 2008.

United Nations. "Basic Principles on the Use of Force and Firearms by Law Enforcement Officials." 1990.

United Nations. "Guidance Note of the Secretary-General: United Nations Approach to Rule of Law Assistance." 2008.

United Nations. "Law Overruled: Strengthening the Rule of Law in Postconflict States." 2008.

United Nations. "Protocol to Prevent, Suppress and Punish Trafficking in Persons, Especially Women, Supplementing the United Nations Convention against Transnational Organized Crime." 2000.

United Nations. "Report of the Secretary-General on the Rule of Law and Transitional Justice in Conflict and Post-Conflict Societies." 2004.

United Nations. "Uniting Our Strengths: Enhancing United Nations Support for the Rule of Law. Report of the Secretary-General." 2006.

United Nations. "Universal Declaration of Human Rights." December 10, 1948.

United Nations Commission on the Legal Empowerment of the Poor. "Concept to Action." 2006.

United Nations Committee on Human Rights. "Equality Before the Courts and the Right to a Fair and Public Hearing by an Independent Court Established by Law." 1984.

United Nations Committee on Human Rights. "International Standards of Elections: The Right to Participate in Public Affairs, Voting Rights and the Right of Equal Access to Public Service." 1996.

United Nations Department of Peacekeeping Operations. "Primer for Justice Components in Multidimensional Peace Operations: Strengthening the Rule of Law." 2006.

United Nations Department of Peacekeeping Operations. *Prison Support Guidance Manual.* 2006.

United Nations Development Programme. "Access to Justice Practice Note." 2004.

United Nations Development Programme. "Gender Equality and Justice Programming: Equitable Access to Justice for Women." 2007.

United Nations Development Programme. "Programming for Justice: Access for All: A Practitioner's Guide to Human Rights-Based Approach to Access to Justice." 2005.

United Nations Development Programme and United States Agency for International Development. "First Steps in Post-Conflict State-Building: A UNDP-USAID Study." 2007.

United Nations Office of the High Commissioner for Human Rights. "Basic Principles on the Independence of the Judiciary." December 13, 1985.

United Nations Office of the High Commissioner for Human Rights. "Basic Principles on the Role of Lawyers." September 7, 1990.

United Nations Office of the High Commissioner for Human Rights. "Basic Principles on the Use of Force and Firearms by Law Enforcement Officials." September 7, 1990.

United Nations Office of the High Commissioner for Human Rights. "Code of Conduct for Law Enforcement Officials." December 17, 1979.

United Nations Office of the High Commissioner for Human Rights. "Convention Against Torture and Other Cruel, Inhuman or Degrading Treatment or Punishment." June 26, 1987.

United Nations Office of the High Commissioner for Human Rights. "Convention on the Elimination of All Forms of Discrimination against Women." September 3, 1981.

United Nations Office of the High Commissioner for Human Rights. "Convention on the Rights of the Child." September 2, 1990.

United Nations Office of the High Commissioner for Human Rights. "Declaration of Basic Principles of Justice for Victims of Crime and Abuse of Power." November 29, 1985.

United Nations Office of the High Commissioner for Human Rights. "Guidelines on the Role of Prosecutors." September 7, 1990.

United Nations Office of the High Commisioner for Human Rights and the International Bar Association. "Human Rights in the Administration of Justice: A Manual on Human Rights for Judges, Prosecutors and Lawyers." 2002.

United Nations Office of the High Commissioner for Human Rights. "International Covenant on Civil and Political Rights." March 23, 1976.

United Nations Office of the High Commissioner for Human Rights. "International Covenant on Economic, Social and Cultural Rights." January 3, 1976.

United Nations Office of the High Commissioner for Human Rights. "Principles Relating to the Status of National Institutions." 1993.

United Nations Office of the High Commissioner for Human Rights. "Rule-of-Law Tools for Post-Conflict States: Mapping the Justice Sector." 2006.

United Nations Office of the High Commissioner for Human Rights. "Rule-of-Law Tools for Post-Conflict States: Reparations Programs." 2008.

United Nations Office of the High Commissioner for Human Rights. "Rule-of-Law Tools for Post-Conflict States: Truth Commissions." 2006.

United Nations Office of the High Commissioner for Human Rights. "Rule-of-Law Tools for Post-Conflict States: Vetting." 2006.

United Nations Office of the High Commissioner for Human Rights. "Standard Minimum Rules for the Administration of Juvenile Justice." November 29, 1985.

United Nations Office of the High Commissioner for Human Rights. "Standard Minimum Rules for the Treatment of Prisoners." May 13, 1977.

United Nations Office on Drugs and Crime. *Handbook on Restorative Justice Programs. Criminal Justice Handbook Series.* 2006.

United Nations Secretary-General." In Larger Freedom: Towards Development, Security and Human Rights for All (UN Doc A/59/2005)." 2005.

United Nations Security Council. "The Rule of Law and Transitional Justice in Conflict and Post-Conflict Societies. Report of the Secretary-General." 2004.

United States Agency for International Development (Office of Transition Initiatives). "Guide to Program Options in Conflict-Prone Settings." 2001.

United States Agency for International Development. "Guide to Rule of Law Country Analysis: The Rule of Law Strategic Framework." 2008.

Watson, Alan. "Legal Transplants: An Approach to Comparative Law," (2nd ed.) London: The University of Georgia Press, 1993.

Samuels, Kirsti. "Rule of Law Reform in Post-conflict Countries: Operational Initiatives and Lessons Learnt." Washington, DC: World Bank, 2006.

**Stable Governance**

Anten, Louise. "Strengthening Governance in Post-Conflict Fragile States." The Hague, The Netherlands: Clingendael Institute, 2009.

Bajraktari, Yll, and Emily Hsu. "Developing Media in Stabilization and Reconstruction Operations." United States Institute of Peace Stabilization and Reconstruction Series, no. 7 (2007): 1–19.

Ball, Nicole. "Democratic Governance and the Security Sector in Conflict-Affected Countries," in *Governance in Post-Conflict Societies: Rebuilding Fragile States*. New York: Routledge, 2007.

Ballentine, Karen and Heiko Nitzschke. "The Political Economy of Civil War and Conflict Transformation." Berghof Research Center for Constructive Conflict Management. Final Version April 2005.

Beasley, Kenneth W. "Job Creation in Post-Conflict Societies." United States Agency for International Development (Center for Development Information and Evaluation). Issue Paper, no. 9 (2006): 1–43.

Bjornlund, Eric, Glenn Cowan, and William Gallery. "Election Systems and Political Parties in Post-Conflict and Fragile States," in *Governance in Post-Conflict Societies: Rebuilding Fragile States*. New York: Routledge, 2007.

Bolongaita, Emil. "Controlling Corruption in Post-Conflict Countries." Kroc Institute Occasional Paper vol. 2, no. 26 (2005): 1–18.

Brahimi, Lakhdar. "State Building in Crisis and Post-Conflict Countries." 7th Global Forum on Reinventing Government and Rebuilding Trust in Government. 2007.

Brinkerhoff, Derick, ed. *Governance in Post-Conflict Societies: Rebuilding Fragile States*. New York: Routledge, 2007.

Brinkerhoff, Derick, Ronald Johnson, Richard Hill and Susan Merrill, eds. "Guide to Rebuilding Public Sector Services in Stability Operations: A Role for the Military." 2009.

Bryan, Shari. "Engaging Political Parties in Post-Conflict Parliaments." International Conference on Parliaments, Crisis Prevention, and Recovery. 2006.

Bryden, Alan, Timothy Donais, and Heiner Hanggi. "Shaping a Security Governance Agenda in Post-Conflict Peacebuilding." Geneva Centre for the Democratic Control of Armed Forces Policy Paper, no. 11 (2005): 1–29.

Center for Strategic and International Studies and the Association of the United States Army. "Post-Conflict Reconstruction: Task Framework." 2002.

Cliffe, Sarah, Scott Guggenheim, and Markus Kostner. "Community-Driven Reconstruction as an Instrument in War-to-Peace Transitions." World Bank Conflict Prevention and Reconstruction Unit Working Papers, no 7 (2003): 1–21.

Clingendael Institute (Conflict Research Unit). "DRAFT: Rebuilding Governance/Statebuilding in Fragile States, Part 1." 2009.

Cole DeGrasse, Beth, and Christina Caan. "Transitional Governance: From Bullets to Ballots." Washington, DC: United States Institute of Peace, 2006.

Collier, Paul, ed. *Breaking the Conflict Trap: Civil War and Development Policy.* Washington, DC: The International Bank for Reconstruction and Development and The World Bank, 2003.

Conaway, Camille Pampell. *The Role of Women in Stabilization and Reconstruction.* United States Institute of Peace Stabilization and Reconstruction Series, no. 3 (2006): 1–22.

Covey, Jack, Michael J. Dziedzic, and Leonard R. Hawley, eds. *The Quest for Viable Peace: International Intervention and Strategies for Conflict Transformation.* Washington, DC: United States Institute of Peace Press, 2005.

Debiel, Tobias, and Ulf Terlinden. "Promoting Good Governance in Post-Conflict Societies." Federal Ministry for Economic Cooperation and Development, Division State and Democracy, Project on Democracy and the Rule of Law. 2004.

Department for International Development, United Kingdom. "Eliminating World Poverty: Making Governance Work for the Poor." 2006.

Dobbins, James, Seth G. Jones, Keith Crane, and Beth Cole DeGrasse. *The Beginner's Guide to Nation-Building.* Santa Monica: RAND Corporation, 2007.

Feldman, Noah. "Agreeing to Disagree in Iraq." *New York Times.* August 30, 2005. http://www.nyt imes.com/2005/08/30/opinion/30feldman.html (accessed September 18, 2008).

Fraenkel, Eran and Sheldon Himelfarb. "DRAFT Purpose and Possibility: A Formative Media Assessment Template." United States Institute of Peace Peacebrief (2009).

Ghani, Ashraf, and Clare Lockhart. *Fixing Failed States: A Framework for Rebuilding a Fractured World.* Oxford: Oxford University Press, 2008.

Governance and Economic Management Assistance Program. "Overview." http://www.gemapliberia. org/pages/overview (accessed September 18, 2008).

Guttieri, Karen, and Jessica Piombo, eds. *Interim Governments: Institutional Bridges to Peace and Democracy?* Washington, DC: United States Institute of Peace Press, 2007.

Hart, Vivien. "Democratic Constitution Making." United States Institute of Peace Special Report, no. 107 (2003): 1–12.

Inbal, A.B., and H. Lerner. "Constitutional Design, Identity, and Legitimacy in Post-Conflict Reconstruction," in *Governance in Post-Conflict Societies: Rebuilding Fragile States.* New York: Routledge, 2007.

International Center for Not-for-Profit Law. "Enabling Organizational Development: NGO Legal Reform in Post-Conflict Settings." *The International Journal of Not-for-Profit Law,* vol. 9, no. 4 (2007): 1–87.

Jackson, Paul, and Zoe Scott. "Local Government in Post-Conflict Environments."

United Nations Development Programme, Oslo Governance Centre, and Democratic Governance Group. 2008.

Lamptey, Comfort. "Engaging Civil Society in Peacekeeping: Strengthening Strategic Partnerships between United Nations Peacekeeping Missions and Local Civil Society Organizations during Post-conflict Transition." United Nations Department of Peacekeeping Operations. 2007.

London School of Economics. "Center for Civil Society." http://www.lse.ac.uk/collections/CCS/ (accessed July 2009).

Lund, Michael, Peter Uvin, and Sarah Cohen. "Building Civil Society in Post-Conflict Environments: From the Micro to the Macro." Woodrow Wilson International Center for Scholars Occasional Paper Series, no. 1 (2006): 1–15.

MacDonald, Mott. "Provision of Infrastructure in Post-Conflict Situations." Department for International Development, United Kingdom. 2005.

National Academy of Public Administration (Institutions for Fragile States Initiative). "Civil Service Reforms and International Assistance: An Initial Framework of Lessons Learned." 2007.

Organisation for Economic Co-operation and Development (Development Co-operation Directorate and Development Assistance Committee). "Fragile States: Policy Commitment and Principles for Good International Engagement in Fragile States and Situations." 2007.

Organisation for Economic Co-operation and Development. "From Fragility to Resilience: Concepts and Dilemmas of Statebuilding in Fragile States." 2007.

Organisation of Economic Co-operation and Development (Development Assistance Committee). *Handbook on Security Sector Reform.* Paris, France: OECD Publishing, 2007.

Orr, Robert. "Governing When Chaos Rules: Enhancing Governance and Participation," in Robert Orr. ed., *Winning the Peace: An American Strategy for Post-Conflict Reconstruction.* Washington, DC: The Center for Strategic and International Studies Press, 2004.

Pouligny, Beatrice. "Civil Society and Post-Conflict Peacebuilding: Ambiguities of International Programmes Aimed at Building 'New' Societies." *Security Dialogue*, vol. 26, no. 4 (2005): 495–510.

RAND. *Guidebook for Economic Development in Stability Operations.* Santa Monica, Calif: RAND Corporation, 2009.

Shankleman, Jill. "Managing Natural Resource Wealth." United States Institute of Peace Stabilization and Reconstruction Series, no. 4 (2006): 1–12.

South African Defense and Security Management Network. "SADSEM: The South African Defense and Security Management Network." http://sadsem.org (accessed June 17, 2009).

Transparency International. "Transparency International Anti-Corruption Handbook

(ACH): National Integrity System in Practice." http://www.transparency.org/policy_research/ach (accessed September 2, 2008).

United Kingdom Stabilisation Unit. "The United Kingdom Approach to Stabilisation—A Stabilisation Unit Guidance Note." 2008.

United Nations. "Universal Declaration of Human Rights." December 10, 1948. http://www.un.org/ Overview/rights.html (accessed March 17, 2009).

United Nations. "International Covenant on Civil and Political Rights." March 23, 1976. http://www.unhchr.ch/html /menu3/b/a_ccpr.htm (accessed September 2, 2008).

United Nations. "United Nations Security Council Resolution 1325." October 31, 2000. http://www.un. org/events/res_1325e.pdf (accessed September 17, 2008).

United Nations Department of Economic and Social Affairs and United Nations Development Programme. "The Challenges of Restoring Governance in Crisis and Post-Conflict Countries." 2007.

United Nations Department of Economic and Social Affairs (Governance and Public Administration Branch and Reconstruction of Governance and Public Administration Cluster). "Governance Strategies for Post-Conflict Reconstruction, Sustainable Peace, and Development." 2007.

United Nations Department of Economic and Social Affairs. *Reconstructing Governance and Public Administration for Peaceful, Sustainable Development.* New York: United Nations, 2003.

United Nations Development Programme. "Access to Information Practice Note." 2003.

United Nations Development Programme. "Access to Justice Practice Note." 2004.

United Nations Development Programme. "Anti-Corruption Practice Note." 2004.

United Nations Development Programme. "Decentralized Governance for Development: A Combined Practice Note on Decentralization, Local Governance, and Urban/Rural Development." 2004.

United Nations Development Programme. "Democratic Governance Group Annual Report." 2007.

United Nations Development Programme. "Electoral Systems and Processes Practice Note." 2004.

United Nations Development Programme. "Parliamentary Development Practice Note." 2003.

United Nations Development Programme. "Parliaments, Crisis Prevention, and Recovery: Guidelines for the International Community." 2006.

United Nations Development Programme (Institutional Development Group, Bureau for Development Policy). "United Nations Development Programme Lessons Learned in Parliamentary Development." 2002.

United Nations Development Programme and Christian Michelsen Institute. "Governance in Post-Conflict Situations." 2004.

United Nations Development Programme and United States Agency for International Development. "First Steps in Post-Conflict State-Building: A UNDP-USAID Study." 2007.

United Nations Economic Commission for Africa. "2005 African Governance Report." 2005.

United States Agency for International Development. "Community-Based Development in Conflict-Affected Areas: An Introductory Guide for Programming." 2007

United States Agency for International Development (Office of Democracy and Governance, Bureau for Global Programs, Field Support, and Research). "Decentralization and Democratic Local Governance Programming Handbook." 2000.

United States Agency for International Development. "Economic Governance in War Torn Economies: Lessons Learned from the Marshall Plan to the Reconstruction of Iraq." 2004.

United States Agency for International Development. "DRAFT: Guidance for Democracy and Governance Programming in Post-Conflict Countries." 2009.

United States Agency for International Development. "Political Party Assistance Policy." 2003.

United States Agency for International Development (Economic Growth Office, Bureau for Economic Growth, Agriculture and Trade). "A Guide to Economic Growth Program Planning in Rebuilding Countries." 2007.

United States Agency for International Development (Office of Democracy and Governance, Bureau for Democracy, Conflict and Humanitarian Assistance). "Money in Politics Handbook: A Guide to Increasing Transparency in Emerging Democracies." 2003.

United States Army. *Field Manual 3-07: Stability Operations*. 2008.

United States Department of State (Office of the Coordinator for Reconstruction and Stabilization). "Transition Elections and Political Processes in Reconstruction and Stabilization Operations: Lessons Learned." 2007.

Whaites, Alan. "States in Development: Understanding State-building." Department for International Development, United Kingdom (Governance and Social Development Group, Policy and Research Division). *DFID Working Paper* (2008): 1–24.

World Bank (Conflict Prevention and Reconstruction Unit). "Rebuilding the Civil Service in a Post-Conflict Setting: Key Issues and Lessons of Experience." Dissemination Notes, no. 1 (2002): 1–4.

World Bank (Social Development Department). "Civil Society and Peacebuilding: Potential, Limitations and Critical Factors." 2006.

World Bank. "Strengthening Local Governance and Promoting Community Based Development in Afghanistan." 2008.

World Bank Institute. "Governance: A Participatory, Action-Oriented Program." 2001.

**Sustainable Economy**

Ballentine, Karen, and Heiko Nitzschke. "The Political Economy of Civil War and Conflict Transformation." Berghof Research Center for Constructive Conflict Management. Final Version April 2005.

Bhatia, Michael and Jonathan Goodhand. "Profit and Poverty: Aid, Livelihoods and Conflict in Afghanistan." *Humanitarian Policy Group Background Paper.* London: Overseas Development Institute, 2003.

Carvalho, Antonio, and Samia Melhem. *Attracting Investment in Post-Conflict Countries: The Importance of Telecommunications.* Washington, DC: World Bank, 2005.

Christian Michelsen Institute. "Peace Processes and Statebuilding—Economic and Institutional Provisions of Peace Agreements." 2007.

"Coffee Rwanda." http://www.coffeerwanda.com/coffee.html (accessed September 26, 2008).

Collier, Paul. "Introduction," in Jean-Paul Azam et al., "Demobilization and Insecurity—A Study in the Economics of the Transition from War to Peace," *Journal of International Development*, vol. 6, issue 3 (1994).

Collier, Paul. "Post-Conflict Economic Recovery." International Peace Academy. 2006.

Collier, Paul. "Post-Conflict Recovery: How Should Policies Be Distinctive?" Centre for the Study of African Economies. 2007.

Covey, Jock, Michael J. Dziedzic, and Leonard R. Hawley, eds. *The Quest for Viable Peace: International Intervention and Strategies for Conflict Transformation.* Washington, DC: United States Institute of Peace Press, 2005.

"Deardorff's Glossary of International Economics." http://www-personal.umich. edu/~alandear /glossary/h.html (accessed March 4, 2009).

Department for International Development, United Kingdom. "Fighting Poverty to Build a Safer World: A Strategy for Security and Development." 2005.

Department for International Development, United Kingdom. "Why We Need to Work More Effectively in Fragile States." 2005.

DeSoto, Hernando. *The Other Path: The Invisible Revolution in the Third World.* New York: Harper & Row, 1989.

Dobbins, James, Seth G. Jones, Keith Crane, and Beth Cole DeGrasse. *The Beginner's Guide to Nation-Building.* Santa Monica: RAND Corporation, 2007.

Dougherty, Carter. "Rwanda Savors the Rewards of Coffee." *The New York Times.* July 27, 2004. http://www.nytimes.com/2004/07/27/business/rwanda-savors-the-rewards-of-coffee-production.html?n=Top/News/Business/Companies/Starbucks%20Corporation (accessed March 4, 2009).

Ducci, Maria. "Guidelines for Employment and Skills Training in Conflict-Affected Countries." ILO Action Programme on Skills and Entrepreneurship Training for

Countries Emerging from Armed Conflict. http://www.ilo.org/public/english/employment/skills/training/publ/pub21.htm (accessed July 2009).

European Union. "Concept for DDR." 2006.

Feil, Scott. "Building Better Foundations: Security in Post-Conflict Reconstruction." *The Washington Quarterly*, Autumn 2002: 97–109.

Forman, Johanna Mendelson. "Achieving Socioeconomic Well-Being in Postconflict Settings." *The Washington Quarterly*, Autumn 2002: 125–38.

Forman, Johanna Mendelson and Merriam Mashatt. "Employment Generation and Economic Development in Stabilization and Reconstruction Operations." Washington, DC: U.S. Institute of Peace, 2007.

Frasier, Susan, and Majda Bne Saad. "Microfinance in Postconflict Situations: A Case Study of Mozambique." CDS Research Briefings, Development Research Briefings. 2003.

Ghani, Ashraf, and Clare Lockhart. *Fixing Failed States: A Framework for Rebuilding a Fractured World*. New York: Oxford University Press, 2008.

Gilpin, Raymond. "Debt Relief in Fragile States." Presented at "Debt Relief and Beyond: A World Bank Conference on Debt and Development." The World Bank. Washington, DC: April/May 2009.

Gilpin, Raymond. "Toward Conflict-Sensitive Macroeconomic Growth: Unraveling Challenges for Practitioners." Presented at "Building Capacity in Stability Operations: Security Sector Reform, Governance and Economics." United States Army Peacekeeping and Stability Operations Institute and Center for Naval Analysis. Washington, DC: April 2009.

Haughton, Jonathan. "The Reconstruction of War-Torn Economies and Peace-Building Operations." 2002.

International Labour Organization. "Local Economic Development Operational Guidelines in Post-Crisis Situations."

International Labour Organization and United Nations High Commissioner on Refugees. "Micro-finance in Post-Conflict Situations: Towards Guiding Principles for Action." 1999.

International Monetary Fund. "Rebuilding Fiscal Institutions in Post-Conflict Countries." 2004.

International Monetary Fund (Monetary and Exchange Affairs Department). "Restoring and Transforming Payments and Banking Systems in Post-Conflict Economies." 2002.

International Peace Academy and the Center for International Security and Cooperation, Stanford University. "Economic Priorities for Peace Implementation." *International Peace Academy Policy on Peace Implementation Paper Series* (2002): 1–15.

Japan International Cooperation Agency. "Handbook for Transition Assistance." 2006.

Kuehnast, Kathleen. "Innovative Approaches to Microfinance in Post-Conflict Situations: Bosnia Local Initiatives Project." *Social Development Notes*, no. 50 (2001): 1–4.

MacDonald, Mott. "Provision of Infrastructure in Post-Conflict Situations." Department for International Development, United Kingdom. 2005.

Measuring Progress in Conflict Environments (MPICE). *Metrics Framework for Assessing Conflict Transformation and Stabilization*. 2007.

Mendelson Forman, Johanna. "Achieving Socioeconomic Well-Being in Postconflict Settings." *The Washington Quarterly*, vol. 25, no. 4 (2002): 125–38.

Mendelson Forman, Johanna and Merriam Mashatt. "Employment Generation and Economic Development in Stabilization and Reconstruction Operations." United States Institute of Peace Stabilization and Reconstruction Series, no. 6 (2007): 1–21.

Organisation for Economic Co-operation and Development. "Economic Reconstruction in Post-Conflict Transitions: Lessons from the Democratic Republic of Congo." 2003.

Pearson Peacekeeping Centre. "Reintegration of Ex-Combatants Through Micro-Enterprise: An Operational Framework." 2005.

Perito, Robert. "The U.S. Experience with Provincial Reconstruction Teams in Afghanistan: Lessons Identified." United States Institute of Peace Special Report, no. 152 (2005): 1–16.

RAND. *Guidebook for Economic Development in Stability Operations*. Santa Monica, Calif: RAND Corporation, 2009.

Shankleman, Jill. "Managing Natural Resource Wealth." United States Institute of Peace Stabilization and Reconstruction Series, no. 4 (2006): 1–12.

United Kingdom Stabilisation Unit. "Helping Countries Recover." 2008.

United Nations. "Integrated Disarmament, Demobilization and Reintegration Standards." http://www.und dr.org/iddrs/framework.php (accessed September 2, 2008).

United Nations (Expert Group Meeting on Natural Resources and Conflict in Africa). "Transforming a Peace Liability into a Peace Asset." 2006.

United Nations Department of Peacekeeping Operations. "Peacekeeping Operations Principles and Guidelines." 2008.

United Nations Development Programme. "The Role of Private Sector Development in Post-Conflict Economic Recovery." 2007.

United Nations Development Programme. "Sustaining Post-Conflict Economic Recovery: Lessons and Challenges." 2005.

United Nations Development Programme and United States Agency for International Development. "First Steps in Post-Conflict State-Building: A UNDP-USAID Study." 2007.

United Nations Environment Programme. "From Conflict to Peacebuilding. The Role of Natural Resources and the Environment." 2009.

United Nations Secretary-General. *Note to the General Assembly*, A/C.5/59/31. 2005.

United Nations University. "Strategy for Rebuilding Fiscal Institutions." 2007.

United States Agency for International Development. "Accelerating the Transition from Conflict to Sustainable Growth." 2008.

United States Agency for International Development. "Economic Governance in War Torn Economies: Lessons Learned from the Marshall Plan to the Reconstruction of Iraq." 2004.

United States Agency for International Development. "A Guide to Economic Growth Program Planning in Rebuilding Countries." 2007.

United States Agency for International Development. "Market Development in Crisis-Affected Environments: Emerging Lessons for Achieving Pro-Poor Economic Reconstruction." 2007.

United States Agency for International Development. "Micronote #34. Tools for Economic Recovery: A Brief Literature Review." 2007.

United States Army. *Field Manual 3-07: Stability Operations*. 2008.

Winer, Jonathan. "Illicit Finance and Global Conflict." Fafo Report, no. 380 (2002): 1–59.

World Bank. "Contracting and Procurement Guidelines." 2004. http://web.worldbank.org/WBSITE/EXTERNAL/TOPICS/CSO/0,,contentMDK:20094613~menuPK:220448~pagePK:220503~piPK:220476~theSitePK:228717,00.html, accessed June 22, 2009.

World Bank. "Natural Resources and Violent Conflict: Options and Actions." 2003.

World Bank (Conflict Prevention and Reconstruction Unit). "Rebuilding the Civil Service in a Post-Conflict Setting." Dissemination Notes. 2002.

United States Agency for International Development. "Livelihoods and Conflict. A Toolkit for Intervention. Key Issues, Lessons Learned, Program Options, Resources." 2005.

## Social Well-Being

Anderson, Mary B. *Do No Harm: How Aid Can Support Peace—or War.* Boulder: Lynne Rienner Publishers, Inc., 1999.

Barsalou, Judy. "Trauma and Transitional Justice in Divided Societies." United States Institute of Peace Special Report, no. 135 (2005): 1-11.

Barsalou, Judy and Victoria Baxter. "The Urge to Remember. The Role of Memorials in Social Reconstruction and Transitional Justice." United States Institute of Peace Stabilization and Reconstruction Series, no. 5 (2007): 1–22.

Brookings Institution. "Durable Solutions for IPDs: An Essential Dimension of Peacebuilding," 2009.

Brookings Institution (Project on Internal Displacement). "Rethinking 'Relief' and 'Development' in Transitions from Conflict." 1999.

Brookings Institution (Project on Internal Displacement) and the University of Bern. "Addressing Internal Displacement in Peace Processes, Peace Agreements and Peace-Building." 2007.

Center for Stabilization and Reconstruction Studies. "Humanitarian Roles in Insecure Environments." 2005.

Center for Stabilization and Reconstruction Studies, Assistant Secretary of Defense for Health Affairs, and International Medical Corps. "Healing the Wounds: Rebuilding Healthcare Systems in Post-Conflict Environments." 2007.

Cole, Elizabeth A., and Judy Barsalou. "Unite or Divide? The Challenges of Teaching History in Societies Emerging from Violent Conflict." Washington, DC: U.S. Institute of Peace, 2006.

Colletta, Nat, and Michelle Cullen. *Violent Conflict and the Transformation of Social Capital. Lessons from Cambodia, Rwanda, Guatemala, and Somalia.* Washington, DC: World Bank, 2000.

Collier, Paul, and Anke Hoeffler. "Aid, Policy, and Growth in Post-Conflict Societies." World Bank Policy Research Working Paper, no. 2902 (2002): 1–24.

Conflictsensitivity.org "Chapter 1: An Introduction to Conflict-Sensitive Approaches to Development. Humanitarian Assistance and Peacebuilding," in *Conflict-Sensitive Approaches to Development, Humanitarian Assistance and Peacebuilding: A Resource Pack.* http://conflictsensitivity.org/node/51 (accessed April 9, 2009).

Covey, Jack, Michael J. Dziedzic, and Leonard R. Hawley, eds. *The Quest for Viable Peace: International Intervention and Strategies for Conflict Transformation.* Washington, DC: United States Institute of Peace Press, 2005.

Dobbins, James, Seth G. Jones, Keith Crane, and Beth Cole DeGrasse. *The Beginner's Guide to Nation-Building.* Santa Monica: RAND Corporation, 2007.

Docking, Timothy. "AIDS and Violent Conflict in Africa." Washington, DC: U.S. Institute of Peace, 2001.

Fitzpatrick, Daniel. "Land Policy in Post-conflict Circumstances: Some Lessons from East Timor." New Issues in Refugee Research, United Nations High Commissioner for Refugees Working Paper, no. 58 (2002): 1–27.

Flournoy, Michèle, and Michael Pan. "Dealing with Demons: Justice and Reconciliation." *The Washington Quarterly* vol. 25, no. 4 (2002): 111–23.

Gallagher, Dennis. "Challenges to Voluntary Repatriation." United States Agency for International Development Conference. October 30–31, 1997.

Grossmann, Georg, and Hildegard Lingnau. "Addressing the Past—Fostering Reconciliation." Deutsche Gesellschaft fur Technische Zusammenarbeit (GTZ). 2003.

Institute for Democracy and Electoral Assistance. "Reconciliation after Violent Conflict: A Handbook." 2003.

Institute for Resource and Security Studies. "Social Reconstruction in Afghanistan through the Lens of Health and Human Security." 2003.

Inter-Agency Network for Education in Emergencies (INEE). "Minimum Standards for Education in Emergencies, Chronic Crises and Early Reconstruction." 2004.

Inter-Agency Standing Committee. "Guidelines for HIV/AIDS Interventions in Emergency Settings." 2004.

International Committee of the Red Cross. " International Committee of the Red Cross Position on Internally Displaced Persons (IDPs)." 2006.

International Peace Academy. "Housing, Land, Property and Conflict Management: Identifying Policy Options for Rule of Law Programming." 2005.

International Peace Academy. "International Assistance to Countries Emerging from Conflict: A Review of Fifteen Years of Interventions and the Future of Peacebuilding." The Security-Development Nexus Program Policy Paper (2006): 1–67.

International Peace Academy. "The Role of Civil Society in National Reconciliation and Peacebuilding in Liberia." 2002.

Joint United Nations Programme on HIV/AIDS (UNAIDS). "Reducing HIV Stigma and Discrimination: A Critical Part of National AIDS Programmes." 2007.

Kalin, Walter. "Durable Solutions for Internally Displaced Persons: An Essential Dimension of Peacebuilding." Washington, DC: Brookings Institution, 2008. http://www. brookings.edu/papers/2008/0313_peacebuilding_kalin.aspx, accessed June 22, 2009.

Miller-Grandvaux, Yolande. "DRAFT Context Paper: What is the role of education as it relates to reducing fragility?" United States Agency for International Development. 2009.

Newbrander, William. "Rebuilding Health Systems and Providing Health Services in Fragile States." *Management Sciences for Health,* no. 7 (2007).

Nicolai, Susan. "Learning independence: Education in emergency and transition in Timor-Leste since 1999." International Institute for Educational Planning, United Nations Educational, Scientific and Cultural Organization. 2004.

Organisation for Economic Co-operation and Development (Development Assistance Committee). "Education in Fragile States: Capturing Lessons and Identifying Good Practice." 2006.

Organisation for Economic Co-operation and Development. "High-Level Forum on the Health MDGs: Health in Fragile States: An Overview Note." Development Co-operation Directorate, DCD (2005) 8/REV2. 7 April 2005.

Organisation for Economic Co-operation and Development. "Reconciliation." Development Assistance Committee Issues Brief. 2005.

Organisation for Economic Co-operation and Development. "Service Delivery in Fragile States: Advancing Donor Practice." 2005.

Orr, Robert, ed. *Winning the Peace: An American Strategy for Post-Conflict Reconstruction.* Washington, DC: The Center for Strategic and International Studies Press, 2004.

Oxfam. "Transitional Settlement—Displaced Populations." 2005.

Parliament of Burundi, Inter-Parliamentary Union, and the International Institute for

Democracy and Electoral Assistance. "Summary and Recommendations Presented by the Rapporteur of the Seminar, Regional Seminar on the Role of Parliaments in the National Reconciliation Process in Africa." 2005.

Petrin, Sarah. "Refugee Return and State Reconstruction: A Comparative Analysis." United Nations High Commissioner for Refugees Working Paper, no. 66 (2002).

Ranson, Kent, Tim Poletti, Olga Bornemisza, and Egbert Sondorp. "Promoting Health Equity in Conflict-Affected Fragile States." World Health Organization, Health Systems Knowledge Network. February 3, 2007.

Refugee Studies Centre and Norwegian Refugee Council. "Education in Emergencies: Learning for a peaceful future." *Forced Migration Review*, no. 22, January 2005.

Rose, Pauline and Martin Greeley. *Education in Fragile States: Capturing Lessons and Identifying Good Practice.* DAC Fragile States Group, May 2006.

Seitz, Klaus. "Education and Conflict: The role of education in the creation, prevention and resolution of societal crises—Consequences for development cooperation." Deutsche Gesellschaft fur Technische Zusammenarbeit for Federal Ministry for Economic Cooperation and Development. December 2004.

Shaw, Rosalind. "Rethinking Truth and Reconciliation Commissions. Lessons from Sierra Leone." United States Institute of Peace Special Report, no.130 (2005): 1–12.

Sinclair, Margaret. "Planning education in and after emergencies." Fundamentals of Educations Planning vol. 73. Paris: United Nations Educational, Scientific and Cultural Organization, 2002.

Smith, Alan, and Tony Vaux. "Education, Conflict and International Development." London: United Kingdom Department for International Development, 2003.

Sphere Project. "Humanitarian Charter and Minimum Standards in Disaster Response." 2004.

Stein, Barry, N. "Refugee Repatriation, Return, and Refoulement During Conflict." United States Agency for International Development Conference, October 30–31, 1997.

Swiss Peace Foundation. "Dealing with the Past in Post-Conflict Societies: Ten Years after the Peace Accords in Guatemala and Bosnia-Herzegovina." 2007.

Terry, Fiona. *Condemned to Repeat.* Ithaca and London: Cornell University Press, 2002.

Theissen, Gunnar. "Supporting Justice, Co-existence, and Reconciliation after Armed Conflict: Strategies for Dealing with the Past." http://www.berghof-handbook.net/uploads/download/theissen _handbook.pdf (accessed April 10, 2009).

United Kingdom Department for International Development. "Education, Conflict, and International Development." 2003.

United Nations. "Transition From Relief to Development: Key Issues Related to Humanitarian and Recovery/Transition Programmes." 2006.

United Nations. "Universal Declaration of Human Rights," December 10, 1948.

Joint United Nations Programme on HIV/AIDS (UNAIDS). "Reducing HIV Stigma and Discrimination: A Critical Part of National AIDS Programmes." 2007.

United Nations Development Programme and Inter-Agency Standing Committee. "Guidelines for Field Staff for Promoting Reintegration in Transition Situations." 2001.

United Nations Development Programme and Tokyo International Conference on African Development. "Post-Conflict Reconstruction of Communities and Socio-Economic Development." 2006.

United Nations Development Programme and United States Agency for International Development. "First Steps in Post-Conflict State-Building: A UNDP-USAID Study." 2007.

United Nations Educational, Scientific, and Cultural Organization. "Education in Situations of Emergency, Crisis, and Reconstruction." 2003.

United Nations High Commissioner for Refugees (Core Group on Durable Solutions, United Nations High Commissioner for Refugees Geneva). "Framework for Durable Solutions for Refugees and Persons of Concern." 2003.

United Nations High Commissioner for Refugees. "Handbook for Emergencies." 2000.

United Nations High Commissioner for Refugees. "Mind the Gap! UNHCR, Humanitarian Assistance and the Development Process." New Issues in Refugee Research Working Paper, no. 43 (2001).

United Nations Office for the Coordination of Humanitarian Affairs. "Guiding Principles on Internal Displacement." 2004.

United Nations Office of the High Commissioner for Human Rights. "Convention on the Rights of the Child." September 2, 1990.

United Nations Office for the High Commissioner for Human Rights. "Guiding Principles on Internal Displacement." 1998.

United Nations World Food Programme (Emergency Needs Assessment Branch). "Emergency Food Security Assessment Handbook." 2005.

United Nations World Food Programme and World Bank (High-Level Forum on the Health Millennium Development Goals). "Health Service Delivery in Post-Conflict States." 2005.

United Nations World Food Summit. "Rome Declaration on World Food Security and World Food Summit Plan of Action." 1996.

United States Agency for International Development. "Community-Based Development in Conflict-Affected Areas." 2007.

United States Agency for International Development (Bureau for Humanitarian Response, Office of Foreign Disaster Assistance). "Field Operations Guide for Disaster Assessment and Response. Version 3.0." 1998.

United States Agency for International Development. *Fragile States Strategy*. 2005.

United States Agency for International Development (Office of Transition Initiatives).

"Guide to Program Options in Conflict-Prone Settings." 2001.

United States Agency for International Development. "Promoting Social Reconciliation in Post-Conflict Societies: Selected Lessons from USAID's Experience." USAID Program and Operations Assessment Report, no. 24. 1999.

United States Agency for International Development (Bureau for Policy and Program Coordination). "United States Foreign Aid: Meeting the Challenges of the Twenty-first Century." United States Agency for International Development White Paper (2004): 1–34.

United States Institute of Peace, InterAction, and United States Department of Defense. Guidelines for Relations Between the U.S. Armed Forces and Nongovernmental Humanitarian Organizations. 2007.

Waldman, Ron. "Health in Fragile States, Country Case Study: Democratic Republic of the Congo." Arlington, Va.: Basic Support for Institutionalizing Child Survival (BASICS) for U.S. Agency for International Development. 2006.

Waldman, Ron. "Health Programming for Rebuilding States: A Briefing Paper." Arlington, Va.: Basic Support for Institutionalizing Child Survival (BASICS) for U.S. Agency for International Development. 2007.

World Bank. "Financing and Aid Management Arrangements in Post-Conflict Settings." *Social Development Notes, Conflict Prevention & Reconstruction*, no. 12 (2003): 1–4.

World Bank. "Reshaping the Future. Education and Postconflict Reconstruction." 2005.

World Bank. "Violent Conflict and the Transformation of Social Capital: Lessons from Cambodia, Rwanda, Guatemala, and Somalia." 2000.

World Bank (World Bank Operations Evaluation Department). "The World Bank's Experience with Post-Conflict Reconstruction." 1998.

World Health Organization. "Rapid Assessment of Mental Health Needs of Refugees: Displaced and Other Populations Affected by Conflict and Post-Conflict Situations. A Community-Oriented Assessment." 2001.

# Appendix B. Participants in Review Process[816]

## United States Government

U.S. Department of State (DOS)
U.S. Agency for International Development (USAID)
U.S. Department of Defense (DOD)
U.S. Department of Health and Human Services (HHS)
U.S. Department of Justice (DOJ)

## United Nations

Department of Peacekeeping Operations (DPKO)
Department of Political Affairs (DPA)
Development Programme (UNDP)
High Commissioner for Refugees (UNHCR)
Institute for Disarmament Research (UNIDIR)
International Labour Organisation (ILO)
Office for the Coordination of Humanitarian Affairs (OCHA)
Peacebuilding Support Office (PBSO)

## United Kingdom

Cabinet Office
Department for International Development (DFID)
Foreign and Commonwealth Office (FCO)
Ministry of Defence (MOD)
Stabilisation Unit

## France

Ministry of Foreign Affairs (MFA)
Ministry of Defence (MOD)
Unit for Conflict Prevention and Reconstruction (CPRU)

## Germany

Zentrum fur Internationale Friedenseinsatze (ZIF)
Ministry of Foreign Affairs (MFA)
Ministry of Defence (MOD)

## Netherlands

Ministry of Foreign Affairs (MFA)
Ministry of Defence (MOD)

---

816. The agencies on this list were consulted and involved at various points in the development of this manual.

## Intergovernmental Organizations

European Union (EU)
  European Council
  European Commission
International Committee of the Red Cross (ICRC)
North Atlantic Treaty Organisation (NATO)


## Nongovernmental Organizations

Environmental Law Institute
European Council of Foreign Relations (ECFR)
Geneva Centre for Security Policy
Geneva Democratic Control of Armed Forces (DCAF)
Geneva Peacebuilding Platform (GPP)
German Agency for Technical Cooperation (GTZ)
International Council of Voluntary Agencies (ICVA)
International Crisis Group (ICG)
Netherlands Institute of International Relations–Clingendael
World Vision

# Appendix C. Summary of Strategic Frameworks Surveyed

| International | Regional | State | Nongovernmental |
|---|---|---|---|
| Challenges Project | African Union | Japanese International Cooperation Agency | Center for Strategic and International Studies |
| Organisation for Economic Co-operation and Development | North Atlantic Treaty Organization | UK Department for International Development | Association of the U.S. Army |
| UN Department of Political Affairs | Organization for Security and Co-operation in Europe | UK Stabilisation Unit | National Defense University |
| UN Department of Economic and Social Affairs | European Union | U.S. Agency for International Development | RAND Corporation |
| UN Department of Peacekeeping Operations | | U.S. State Department | Sphere Project |
| World Bank | | U.S. Defense Science Board | State Effectiveness Institute |
| UN Development Programme | | U.S. Army | Atlantic Council |
| International Monetary Fund | | U.S. Joint Forces Command | U.S. Institute of Peace |
| | | Utstein Study: Germany, Norway, United Kingdom | |
| | | France | |
| | | Germany | |
| | | Norwegian Institute of International Affairs | |

# Appendix D. Snapshot of Components from Overarching Resources

| CSIS-AUSA | RAND | UNDP-USAID | US Army | OECD | UNDP/World Bank | US S/CRS | AU NEPAD |
|---|---|---|---|---|---|---|---|
| Security | Security | Civil security | Security | Security | Security | Security | Security |
| Justice and reconciliation | Democratization | Judicial governance | Civil control | | | Justice and reconciliation | Human rights, justice, and reconciliation |
| Governance and participation | Governance | Political governance | Support to governance | Political | Political | Governance and participation | Political transition, governance |
| | Economic stabilization | Economic | Support to economic/ infrastructure development | Economic | Economic | Economic stabilization and infrastructure | Socioeconomic development |
| Social and economic well-being | Humanitarian relief | | Restore essential services | Social | Social | | |
| | Development | Administrative | | | | | Coordination and management |

**Acronyms:**

AU NEPAD  African Union New Partnership for Africa's Development
AUSA  Association of the U.S. Army
CSIS  Center for Strategic and International Studies
OECD  Organisation for Economic Co-Operation and Development
UNDP  United Nations Development Programme
USAID  U.S. Agency for International Development
US S/CRS  U.S. Department of State Coordinator for Reconstruction and Stabilization

# Appendix E. Acronyms and Glossary of Selected Key Terms

**Acronyms**

| | |
|---|---|
| ADR | Alternative dispute resolution |
| APM | Antipersonnel mines |
| ATM | Antitank mines |
| CSO | Civil society organization |
| DD | Disarmament and demobilization |
| DDR | Disarmament, demobilization, and reintegration |
| ICRC | International Committee of the Red Cross |
| IDP | Internally displaced person |
| IMF | International Monetary Fund |
| FDI | Foreign direct investment |
| MPICE | Measuring Progress in Conflict Environments |
| NATO | North Atlantic Treaty Organization |
| NGO | Nongovernmental organization |
| NSJS | Non-state justice system |
| NSPD 44 | National Security Presidential Directive 44 |
| OECD | Organisation for Economic Co-Operation and Development |
| OSCE | Organization for Security and Co-operation in Europe |
| PEM | Public expenditure management |
| S&R | Stabilization and reconstruction |
| S/CRS | Office of the Coordinator for Reconstruction and Stabilization at the U.S. Department of State |
| SPEC | Sectoral Practices and Experience in Coordination |
| SSR | Security sector reform |
| UK DFID | United Kingdom Department for International Development |
| UN | United Nations |
| UNDG | United Nations Development Group |
| UNDP | United Nations Development Programme |
| UNDPKO | United Nations Development of Peacekeeping Operations |
| USAID | United States Agency for International Development |
| UXO | Unexploded ordnance |

# Terms

*This glossary lists selected terms. An asterisk appears in cases where this manual presents an original definition. All other definitions are cited to resources that can be found in Appendix A, Resource List.*

**Accountability**
Holding individuals and organizations responsible for performance measured as objectively as possible. Accountability stands on three key pillars: financial, political, and administrative. (Transparency International & UN Human Settlements Programme, "Tools to Support Transparency in Local Governance.")

**Basic Human Needs**
The needs required by human beings for survival with dignity, such as food security and nutrition, water and sanitation, primary health care, family planning and reproductive health, shelter and education. All of these needs are enshrined in international legal instruments and can also be understood as human rights. (JICA, *Handbook for Transition Assistance.*)

**Capacity Building\***
The transfer of technical knowledge and skills to host nation individuals and institutions to help them develop effective policies and administer state services across the economic, social, political, and security realms.

**Civil-Military Cooperation\***
The resources and arrangements that support three relationships: between civilian and military actors of official government and intergovernmental institutions; between the military and nongovernmental organizations; and between the military and the host nation government and its population.

**Civil Society**
The arena of uncoerced collective action around shared interests, purposes and values. In theory, its institutional forms are distinct from those of the state, family, and market, though in practice, the boundaries among state, civil society, family, and market are often complex, blurred, and negotiated. Civil society organizations can include a wide array of nongovernmental and not-for-profit organizations that have a presence in public life, expressing the interests and values of their members or others, based on ethical, cultural, political, scientific, religious, or philanthropic considerations. (World Bank, "Civil Society and Peacebuilding" and London School of Economics, Centre for Civil Society.)

**Coherence\***
Close cooperation and consistency in policy across agencies working toward a shared goal in a stabilization and reconstruction environment. (Derived from DRAFT United Kingdom Comprehensive Approach Working Group, Inter-Departmental Glossary of Planning Terminology [CAWG].)

**Comprehensive Approach\***
An approach that brings together the efforts of the departments and agencies of the U.S. government, intergovernmental and nongovernmental organizations, multinational partners, and private sector entities based on commonly understood principles and collaborative processes, toward a shared goal.

## Conflict Transformation

The process of diminishing the motivations and means for destructive forms of conflict while developing local institutions so they can take the lead role in national governance, economic development, and enforcing the rule of law. Success in this process permits an evolution from internationally imposed stability to a peace that is sustainable by local actors, with the international community providing continued support at a greatly reduced costs. (U.S. Government, "Draft Planning Framework for Reconstruction, Stabilization, and Conflict Transformation.")

## Cooperation*

The sharing of information and the deconfliction of activities as much as possible among independent individuals or institutions so as not to undermine a shared goal.

## Coordination*

A deliberate process to make different individuals or institutions work together for a goal or effect.

## Development

Long-term efforts aimed at bringing improvements in the economic, political, and social status, environmental stability, and the quality of life for all segments of the population. (DRAFT UK CAWG, Inter-Departmental Glossary of Planning Terminology.)

## Disarmament, Demobilization, and Reintegration (DDR)

A process that contributes to security and stability in a stabilization and reconstruction context by removing weapons from the hands of combatants, taking the combatants out of military structures, and helping them to integrate socially and economically into society by finding civilian livelihoods. (United Nations, Integrated DDR Standard.)

## Drivers of Conflict*

A source of instability pushing groups within a host nation toward open conflict.

## End State*

The ultimate goals of a society emerging from conflict.

## Humanitarian Assistance

Material or logistical assistance provided for humanitarian purposes, typically in response to humanitarian crises. The primary objective of humanitarian assistance is to save lives, alleviate suffering, and maintain human dignity. (United Nations Department of Peacekeeping Operations [UNDPKO], "Peacekeeping Operations Principles and Guidelines.")

## Human Capital

The stock of knowledge and skill embodied in the population of an economy. (Deardorff's Glossary of International Economics.)

## Humanity

The goal of alleviating human suffering in all circumstances, protecting life, and health and ensuring respect for the individual. (Derived from the International Committee of the Red Cross [ICRC], "The Fundamental Principles of the Red Cross.")

## Human Rights

A set of basic rights protected in international law that apply to all individuals regardless of gender, race, religion, ethnicity, and so on. In national constitutions, human rights are sometimes referred to as fundamental rights. (United Kingdom Department for International Development, "Safety, Security and Accessible Justice.")

### Human Security
Security that has two main aspects: (1) safety from such chronic threats as hunger, disease and repression; (2) protection from sudden and hurtful disruptions in the patterns of daily life—whether in homes, in jobs, or in communities. Such threats can exist at all levels of national income and development. (Derived from United Nations Development Programme, "1994 Human Development Report.")

### Independence
The autonomy of humanitarian actors from the actions or policies of any government, so that they are able to adhere to these principles. (Derived from the ICRC, "The Fundamental Principles of the Red Cross.")

### Impartiality
The principle that humanitarian assistance must be based on need alone, without regard to nationality, race, religion, class, or politics. (Derived from ICRC, "The Fundamental Principles of the Red Cross.")

### Informal*
For the purposes of this manual, refers to a system, process, or institution that is not officially controlled by the government.

### Internally Displaced Person (IDP)
Person, or groups of persons who have been forced or obliged to flee or to leave their homes or places of habitual residence, in particular as a result of or in order to avoid the effects of armed conflict, situations of generalized violence, violations of human rights or natural or human-made disasters, and who have not crossed an internationally recognized state border. (Derived from United Nations Office for the Coordination of Humanitarian Affairs, "Guiding Principles on Internal Displacement.")

### Integration*
The bringing together of capabilities in a coherent manner to achieve unity of effort.

### Legitimacy*
The degree to which the population accepts and supports the mission, its mandate and its behavior over time; the degree to which the local population accepts and supports the host nation government (which can include informal government structures as well); the manner in which the government attains power; and the extent to which regional neighbors and the international community accept the mission mandate and its actions and the host nation government.

### Marginalized Groups*
Marginalized groups suffer from a social, economic, or political process that renders an individual or an ethnic or national group powerless or to a lower social standing.

### Neutrality
A deliberate policy of not taking sides in hostilities or engaging in controversies involving politics, race, religion, or ideology. (Derived from ICRC, "The Fundamental Principles of the Red Cross.")

**Nongovernmental Organization (NGO)**
A private, self-governing, not-for-profit organization dedicated to alleviating human suffering; promoting education, health care, economic development, environmental protection, human rights, and conflict resolution; and/or encouraging the establishment of democratic institutions and civil society. (United States Institute of Peace, "The Guide for Participants in Peace, Stability, and Relief Operations.")

**Peacebuilding**
Measures aimed at reducing the risk of lapsing or relapsing into conflict, by strengthening national capacities for conflict management and laying the foundations for sustainable peace. (UN DPKO, "Peacekeeping Operations Principles and Guidelines.")

**Peace Enforcement**
Coercive action undertaken with the authorization of the United Nations Security Council to maintain or restore international peace and security in situations where the Security Council has determined the existence of a threat to the peace, breach of the peace, or act of aggression. (UN DPKO, "Peacekeeping Operations Principles and Guidelines.")

**Peacekeeping**
Action undertaken to preserve peace, however fragile, where fighting has been halted and to assist in implementing agreements achieved by the peacemakers. (UNDPKO, "Peacekeeping Operations Principles and Guidelines.")

**Predatory Economic Actors\***
Broadly refer to any group or individual who engages in or directly benefits from illegal economic activity that promotes violence and/or undermines efforts for good governance and economic development. These actors can exist inside or outside of government.

**Reconciliation\***
A process through which people move from a divided past to a shared future, the ultimate goal being the peaceful coexistence of all individuals in a society.

**Reconstruction**
The process of rebuilding degraded, damaged, or destroyed political, socioeconomic, and physical infrastructure of a country or territory to create the foundation for long-term development. (United States Army, *Field Manual 3-07: Stability Operations.*)

**Refugee(s)**
Individuals who are outside the country of their nationality due to well-founded fear of being persecuted for reasons of race, religion, nationality, or membership of a social group or political opinion. (Derived from United Nations, "1951 Convention Relating to the Status of Refugees.")

**Security Sector Reform (SSR)**
The set of policies, plans, programs, and activities that a government undertakes to improve the way it provides safety, security, and justice. (United States Department of State, United States Department of Defense, United States Agency for International Development, "Security Sector Reform.")

**Social capital\***
The resources that create a strong network of institutionalized relationships in society.

## Spoilers
Individuals or parties who believe that the peace process threatens their power and interests and will therefore work to undermine it. (United Nations Development Group and World Bank, "Draft Joint Guidance Note.")

## Stability
A characteristic of a state or a nation that determines its likelihood to continue or last. The tendency of such a state or a nation to recover from perturbations and resist sudden change or deterioration. (United States Department of State, Office of the Coordinator for Reconstruction and Stabilization, "DRAFT: U.S. Government Whole-of-Government Definitions.")

## Stabilization
Ending or preventing the recurrence of violent conflict and creating the conditions for normal economic activity and nonviolent politics. (UK Stabilisation Unit, "Helping Countries Recover From Violent Conflict.")

## Transparency
Connotes the conduct of public business in a manner that affords stakeholders wide accessibility to the decision-making process and the ability to effectively influence it. (Transparency International and UN Human Settlements Programme, "Tools to Support Transparency in Local Governance.")

## Unity of Effort*
The outcome of coordination and cooperation among all actors, even when the participants come from many different organizations with diverse operating cultures.

## Violent Conflict*
A clash of political interests between organized groups characterized by a sustained and large-scale use of force.

## Vulnerable Groups*
A group that is susceptible to attack, injury, discrimination, or other harm.

## Whole-of-Government
An approach that integrates the collaborative efforts of the departments and agencies of the U.S. government to achieve unity of effort toward a shared goal. (United States Army, *Field Manual 3-07: Stability Operations.*)

# U.S. Army Peacekeeping and Stability Operations Institute (PKSOI)

The U.S. Army Peacekeeping and Stability Operations Institute (PKSOI) was established by Headquarters, Department of the Army (HQDA) in 2003, as part of the U.S. Army War College (USAWC) at Carlisle Barracks, Pennsylvania. The organization is the successor to the Army Peacekeeping Institute (PKI), established in 1991 by General Gordon Sullivan, U.S. Army Chief of Staff. PKSOI is the Army's Center of Excellence for stability and peace operations at the strategic and operational levels. This includes support to HQDA for policy and strategy, the U.S. Army Combined Arms Center in its role as the Army's force modernization proponent for Stability Operations, and the USAWC for senior leader education. PKSOI accomplishes its mission by facilitating information sharing, project development, and integration of efforts among military and civilian government agencies, nongovernmental organizations, and international and multinational institutions in five broad areas associated with stability and peacekeeping: policy shaping, training and education, planning and execution, lessons learned, and doctrine and concepts.

# United States Institute of Peace

The United States Institute of Peace is an independent, nonpartisan, national institution established and funded by Congress. Its goals are to help prevent and resolve violent conflicts, promote post-conflict stability and development, and increase peacebuilding capacity, tools, and intellectual capital worldwide. The Institute does this by empowering others with knowledge, skills, and resources, as well as by directly engaging in peacebuilding efforts around the globe.

# Board of Directors